WILLIAM BLAKE
A new kind of man

WILLIAM BLAKE

A new kind of man

MICHAEL DAVIS

Again he speaks in thunder and in fire!
Thunder of Thought, & flames of fierce desire:
Even from the depths of Hell his voice I hear
Within the unfathom'd caverns of my Ear.
Therefore I print; nor vain my types shall be:
Heaven, Earth & Hell henceforth shall live in harmony.

(William Blake: *Jerusalem*, Plate 3, 'To the Public')

UNIVERSITY OF CALIFORNIA PRESS
Berkeley and Los Angeles

For Elaine

First published in 1977 in the United States by
UNIVERSITY OF CALIFORNIA PRESS
Berkeley and Los Angeles

Copyright © 1977 Michael Davis

Library of Congress Catalog Card Number: 77–71059

ISBN: 0-520-03443-0

Printed in Great Britain by
Latimer Trend & Company Ltd Plymouth

Contents

Illustrations

Dimensions given below (to the nearest eighth of an inch) are those of Blake's originals, here shown in reduced size except where otherwise stated. References in the text to colour plates are given in italic type; references to black and white plates in Roman. Illustrations not ascribed to other artists show Blake's work.

Black and White Plates

Between pages 64 and 65

34 'The Waters Prevailed upon the Earth', Genesis 7:24, sepia water-colour; $5\frac{3}{4} \times 4\frac{1}{4}$ in. (The Lake District Art Gallery Trust)

35 'The Magic Banquet', *Comus*, watercolour, 1805–10; $6 \times 4\frac{3}{4}$ in. (Museum of Fine Arts, Boston)

36 'A Vision', pencil and grey wash, $6\frac{3}{4} \times 7$ in. (Sotheby, Parke, Bernet & Co.)

37 'Angels Hovering over Jesus's Body in the Sepulchre', watercolour, c. 1800; $16\frac{1}{4} \times 11\frac{7}{8}$ in. (Victoria and Albert Museum, Crown copyright)

38 Anon.: 'Tottenham Court Road Turnpike and St James's Chapel' shortly after 1800 (Museum of London)

39 'Catherine Blake', pencil, c. 1802; $11\frac{1}{4} \times 8\frac{3}{4}$ in. (The Tate Gallery, London)

40 John Flaxman: likeness of the publisher Cromek (reproduced by permission of the Syndics of the Fitzwilliam Museum, Cambridge)

41 'Ezekiel's Vision of the Whirlwind', Ezekiel I, watercolour, c. 1805; $15\frac{5}{8} \times 11\frac{5}{8}$ in. (Museum of Fine Arts, Boston)

42 'Archangel Raphael with Adam and Eve', *Paradise Lost* 4:492–511, watercolour, 1808; $15\frac{1}{4} \times 9\frac{1}{4}$ in. (Museum of Fine Arts, Boston)

43 'The Last Judgment', watercolour, 1808; $19\frac{7}{8} \times 15\frac{3}{4}$ in. (Petworth House, The National Trust; photo Jeremy Whitaker)

44 'The Canterbury Pilgrims', engraving, 1810; $12 \times 36\frac{7}{8}$ in. (reproduced by permission of the Syndics of the Fitzwilliam Museum, Cambridge)

45 Stothard, engraved Schiavonetti and Heath: 'Chaucer's Procession to Canterbury' (reproduced by permission of the Syndics of the Fitz-william Museum, Cambridge)

46 Page from *Jerusalem*, relief-etching, 1804–20; $8\frac{5}{8} \times 6\frac{1}{4}$ in. (courtesy of the Trustees of the British Museum)

47 Visionary head: 'Caractacus', pencil, 1819; $7\frac{3}{4} \times 5\frac{7}{8}$ in. (private collection)

48 Frontispiece, *For the Sexes: The Gates of Paradise*, engraving, c. 1818; actual size (courtesy of the Trustees of the British Museum)

49 'Head of the Ghost of a Flea', pencil, c. 1819; $7\frac{1}{2} \times 6$ in. (The Tate Gallery, London)

50 A page from Thornton's *Virgil*; wood engravings, 1821; actual size (courtesy of the Trustees of the British Museum)

51 John Linnell, pencil, 1821: 'Blake and Varley' (reproduced by per-mission of the Syndics of the Fitzwilliam Museum, Cambridge)

52 Life mask of Blake aged 66 (reproduced by permission of the Syndics of the Fitzwilliam Museum, Cambridge)

53 Samuel Palmer: self-portrait, c. 1826 (Ashmolean Museum, Oxford)

54 'Geryon Conveying Dante and Virgil Downwards', Dante, *Inferno* 17, watercolour, c. 1826; $14\frac{5}{8} \times 20\frac{3}{4}$ in. (National Gallery of Victoria, Melbourne)

55 'The Whirlwind of Lovers', Dante, *Inferno* 5, unfinished engraving,

1827; engraved surface 9½ × 13½ in. (courtesy of the Trustees of the British Museum)

56 *Job*, plate 14, 1825; engraved surface 8¾ × 6¾ in. (courtesy of the Trustees of the British Museum)

57 Frederick Shields: 'The Blakes' Living-room, Fountain Court' (Central Library, City of Manchester)

58 Pencil, 1825: Linnell aged 33 (National Gallery of Art, Washington, Rosenwald Collection)

Author's Acknowledgements

This book could never have been written without the aid of many people. To them all I am deeply grateful and I wish to record here my thanks for the encouragement and help that they have given me. Sir Geoffrey Keynes, whose authoritative works on Blake have been my sure guide, has given his time to me with remarkable generosity and patience. To the learned enthusiasm of his conversation I am especially indebted, and I am particularly grateful to him. Mrs Joan Linnell Burton has been a most faithful friend and adviser: she has lent me books, introduced me to Blake scholars, read my manuscript very carefully and saved me from many errors. Mr Raymond Lister has given me generous encouragement, and he has studied my manuscript with a scholar's eye and made scrupulously detailed suggestions of great value. Mrs Marie Ingram and Miss Catriona A. Robertson kindly advised me about approaches to my work and about books to consult. Mr Roger Ellis, Master of Marlborough College, agreed to reduce my teaching load so that I could have time to write.

I hope that the many kind people who have helped me in a variety of ways but are not named here will accept my gratitude, and I wish to record my particular debts to the following: Mrs D. Howell for generously welcoming me to Blake's cottage; Mr Simon Brett for sensitively guiding me in some of my research, and Mr Robin Child and Mr Christopher Clarke for sharing with me their great knowledge of visual art; Mr David Whiting for making translations from a German catalogue; Dr and Mrs Charles McBurney and Mr Bill Hadman for their hospitality while I was working on this book; Miss Anne Kirkwood, Mr Stephen Bradley, Mr Nick Glazebrook, Dr Angus Harris and Mr Eric Phillips for their research on my behalf.

Mr Eric Chamberlain and Mr Duncan Robinson of the Fitzwilliam Museum, Mr James Holloway of the National Gallery of Scotland and Mr Richard Ormond of the National Portrait Gallery have given me especially valuable guidance. The staffs responsible for those collections have been unfailingly helpful, and so have the staffs of all the museums and libraries that I have visited, including the Department of Prints and Drawings of the British Museum; the Westminster and Lambeth Libraries; the London Museum; and the Libraries of the National Book League, the Royal Zoological Society of London, and the Wellcome Institute for the History of Medicine. I am also very grateful to Mr Gerald Murray and Mr William Latham, Librarians of the Memorial Library, Marlborough College; to the exceedingly patient staff of the Marlborough branch of the Wiltshire County Library; to the many librarians elsewhere who have helped to find books for me; and to Mr Bob Cooles at Battersea Parish Church, to Mr R. H. Hamlin at the College of Education, Bognor Regis, and to the staff of Chichester Record Office, for the trouble they took in showing documents to me.

With expert knowledge and sustained enthusiasm, Miss Margaret Willes and Mr Antony Wood, editors, and Miss Juliet Scott, picture researcher, have helped me enormously in the creation of this book, and Mr Andrew Best's advice has been a great support. I am very grateful to them and to Mrs Edna Halliday and Mrs Ivor Radford who typed my manuscript. Many relations and friends have stimulated my efforts by their interest, suggestions and the loan of books: I wish to thank them all, particularly my daughters, my son, and Dr Peter Carter, Mr Martin Evans, Mr E. G. H. Kempson, Dr Frank McKim, Mr Oliver Ramsbotham, Dr Andrew Reekie and Mr Martin Roberts.

I am very grateful to the owners of the pictures reproduced in this book for allowing them to be used as illustrations (they are acknowledged in the List of Illustrations), and to the authors and publishers who have let me quote from their works. The Oxford Standard Authors edition of *The Complete Writings of William Blake*, edited by Sir Geoffrey Keynes (Oxford University Press, second edition, 1966) is the source of all my quotations from Blake, and I thank Oxford University Press for their permission to quote from it.

I thank the Longman Group Limited for permission to quote (on page 79) the table from page 290 of *The Poems of William Blake* edited by W. H. Stevenson. The Trianon Press facsimiles of Blake's works, with commentaries and bibliographical histories by Sir Geoffrey Keynes, have been my constant aid. G. E. Bentley, Jr's *Blake Records* has proved invaluable: when quoting, I have modernized the spelling and punctuation of Blake's and Mrs Blake's contemporaries. I am very deeply indebted and grateful to the many excellent scholars and writers, past and present, who have helped to create a highway for all who wish to approach Blake. Some of their works which have particularly helped me are listed on pages 165–70.

To my wife I owe an incalculable debt of gratitude. She has created in our home a tranquil atmosphere appropriate to literary work; she has helped me with research, with typing and with proof-reading, and she has encouraged me in all aspects of the enterprise. Without her loyal, unselfish support I could not possibly have written this book: to her, my profoundest thanks.

M. D.

I

Boy and Apprentice

1757–79

'the Vigour I was in my Childhood famous for'

William Blake, looking back to his extreme youth at the age of about fifty, wrote: 'Inspiration & Vision was then, & now is, & I hope will always Remain, my Element, my Eternal Dwelling place. . . .' His bequest to us, the extraordinary pictures and poems which embody his ecstatic vision, are those of a man dedicated to giving bodily form to spiritual beings. His earthly life was significant not only because he saw and 'felt through all this fleshly dress Bright shoots of everlastingness', but because he also had the energy, courage, artistic skill and poetic power to reveal his vision.

He was born on 28 November 1757, and baptized in St James's Church, Piccadilly. He was the third son of a moderately prosperous hosier, at 28 Broad Street (1),* Carnaby Market, near trim little Golden Square, London, a highly respectable neighbourhood that had previously been fashionable. William's parents, James and Catherine Blake, had seven children, of whom five survived infancy. Their eldest son, also named James, was later to inherit the business in stockings, gloves and haberdashery from his father, who was an old-fashioned shopkeeper and a devout man: a dissenter, probably a Baptist attracted by the doctrines of Emanuel Swedenborg. Their second son died in infancy. Five years after his parents' marriage, William was born. His younger brother, the third surviving son and his parents' acknowledged favourite, John, earned his living as a baker; but he became dissolute and gave up this work. The next son, Richard, died in infancy; and Catherine, the only daughter, was born in 1764. Then, nearly ten years after William, in 1767, his favourite brother, Robert, was born.

Blake seems to have found his father lenient and affectionate and his mother tender and loving. Presumably it was she who taught the vigorous boy to read and write. He did not go to school: with his strong temper, he

---

* Numbers in brackets refer to the illustrations, those in italic type denoting illustrations in colour.

despised restraints and rules so intensely that his father dared not send him. Blake never regretted this. In his fifties he wrote:

> Thank God, I never was sent to school
> To be Flog'd into following the Style of a Fool.

He was always at heart a rebel. The boy was free to roam the fields, enjoy the woods and bathe naked in the ponds that London had not yet destroyed. Unspoilt country was not then beyond the reach of a lad of nine or ten from Golden Square. For Blake, the world was already a place of visions. When he was four, he saw God's head at the window; and the child—not surprisingly—screamed. At the age of eight or ten, on Peckham Rye, he saw a tree filled with angels. When he spoke of this at home, only his mother's plea prevented his honest father from thrashing him for telling a lie. She had beaten the child herself for saying he had seen the prophet Ezekiel under a tree in the fields. Many children see visions, but generally in youth the visionary eye begins to atrophy. In Blake, it never did.

To judge from his later physique, Blake must have been a thick-set, tough little boy with ruddy limbs, a broad face, snub nose and a shock of golden-red hair. The idyllic days of his childhood, when with his playmates he could throw off his clothes and rush into the stream, inspired the freshest lines in his earliest printed poems, the *Poetical Sketches*, which he had begun to write at the age of eleven. His own delight in the freedom he experienced shines afresh when he declares, in lines that make the senses tingle:

> The spirits of the air live on the smells
> Of fruit; and joy, with pinions light, roves round
> The gardens, or sits singing in the trees.

He grew up in a time of peace. In 1762, before he was five, the great war for the Empire ended. The British navy had driven the French from America and India, and hastened the Spanish Empire on its way to ruin. But this peace was fragile, 'modelled in gingerbread and ready to fall to pieces at the slightest touch', in the poet Chatterton's words of 1770. The young Blake's surroundings consisted not only of blissful fields and trees and streams, but also of grim places: a slaughterhouse, where some of the butchers were women, in Carnaby Market (3) round the corner from his home; a workhouse, in the Pawlett's Garden burial-ground nearby, where up to three hundred inmates were made to weave and spin; a neighbouring infirmary, to which they were moved when they were sick.

The boy's passion for drawing began as soon as he could hold a pencil, and he was always sketching. He drew men and animals, copied prints, and visited art-collections and sale-rooms to look at pictures. His parents were sufficiently perceptive and wise to encourage him. It is difficult to see his father—except through the distorting lenses of turbulent adolescence—as the harsh, forbidding father-figure against whom Blake rebelled in *Songs of*

Experience and later poems. The favouritism shown to his younger brother John by his mother and father may cast doubt upon their parental wisdom; but they were responsive enough to William's needs to send him, at the age of ten, to Pars's drawing school in the Strand. There the pupils copied plaster casts after the antique, but did not draw from the living figure. Blake's father also bought a few plaster casts for him and gave him enough money to buy prints—the basis of his collection, begun before he was fourteen. Referring to his earliest childhood, Blake later wrote: 'I Saw & I Knew immediately the difference between Rafael & Rubens.' Langford, the auctioneer, called Blake, 'his little connoisseur', and with friendly speed often knocked down a cheap lot to him. Blake disregarded those Italian paintings sought by popular taste, shrugged off the laughter of his young companions, and chose the works of Raphael, Michelangelo, Giulio Romano, and the two artists whom he idolized: Dürer and Martin Heemskirk. In art and in poetry, Blake instinctively preferred to take his own independent path. However, if he was to earn his living as a painter, he would need to be trained in the studio of a successful artist. The high premium needed for such an apprenticeship would, he insisted to his father, unjustly deprive his brothers and sister, and he suggested being trained as an engraver instead. The engraver's craft (4) was a menial one: by choosing it, Blake was confining himself to a humble, irksome life, virtually that of an artisan.

William Ryland, the eminent engraver, was suggested by Blake's father as a suitable master, but after they had visited his studio the fourteen-year-old boy objected: 'Father, I do not like the man's face: it looks as if he will live to be hanged.' Ryland then showed no prospect of the gallows. Twelve years later, however, he was hanged for forging a cheque.

Instead of him, James Basire (10), a member of a dynasty of engravers, was chosen to be Blake's master, for a premium of fifty guineas, half the price that Ryland would probably have charged. Basire, aged forty-one, was an engraver expert in conscientious drawing of a dry, hard, monotonous style which, though already becoming old-fashioned, was renowned for the firm and correct outline made by the burin or graver. He had engraved a few of Hogarth's designs, but his speciality was antiquarian work and he was official engraver to the Society of Antiquaries and to the Royal Society. He lived and worked at 31 Great Queen Street, where Blake presumably lodged during his seven-year apprenticeship from 1772 to 1779. Painstaking and industrious by nature, Blake was a good apprentice.

He would remain loyal to his master, as is shown in the pugnacious reminiscence comparing Basire to the engraver William Woollett. This was written when Blake was about fifty-three and Woollett was more fashionable than Basire: 'Woolett I know did not know how to Grind his Graver ... he has often proved his Ignorance before me at Basire's by laughing at Basire's knife tools & ridiculing the Forms of Basire's other Gravers till Basire was quite dash'd & out of Conceit with what he himself knew, but his

Impudence had a Contrary Effect on me.' As for Woollett's own work, he 'did not know how to put so much labour into a head or a foot as Basire did; he did not know how to draw the Leaf of a tree.'

Blake quickly learned his craft. Only a few months after beginning his apprenticeship, in 1773, when he was barely sixteen, he made his first known engraving, 'Joseph of Arimathea among the Rocks of Albion' (5), from a drawing by Salviati after Michelangelo. To the legendary figure of the bringer of the holy grail to Britain, Blake added a background of sea and rocks from his imagination. This plate, remarkable work for a beginner, is livelier in style than the engravings he made specifically for Basire and customers. Already Blake has incorporated the 'classical foot' of which the second toe is much longer than the big toe, a peculiarity that he always used in his drawing of feet. When he was over fifty he re-engraved this plate, and he wrote about his picture of the Last Judgment: 'I intreat, then, that the Spectator will attend to the Hands & Feet, to the Lineaments of the Countenances; they are all descriptive of Character, & not a line is drawn without intention. . . .'

Blake's first two years at Basire's passed smoothly enough, but then friction developed between the two or three boys working there. Blake was too simple and his fellow apprentices too cunning, according to Basire, who sent him out to Westminster Abbey and old London churches to make drawings to be engraved during the winter for the Antiquarian Society. Blake was always grateful to Basire for the opportunity this gave him to discover the beauty of Gothic monuments. In Westminster Abbey, drawing illustrations suitable for Richard Gough's *Sepulchral Monuments*, Blake perceived how to reach the style of art he was aiming at. He seized his chance to become an artistic draughtsman: the task of learning to engrave only other men's drawings could not so readily have offered him this.

Among his earliest subjects were the monuments of kings and queens surrounding the chapel of Edward the Confessor: Henry III, Eleanor of Castille, Philippa of Hainault, Edward III, Richard II and Anne of Bohemia. To get a better view of the figures, he often stood above them on the monuments. The heads he naturally considered to be portraits (some of them are, indeed, supposed to be 'from life') and all the Gothic ornaments delighted his imagination.

Boys from Westminster School were then allowed to roam about the Abbey in their free time. Instead of their usual games of football in the cloisters and hide-and-seek among the tombs, some of them had fun in mocking the absorbed young artist. One of the schoolboys, when Blake was poised aloft drawing, tormented him from below and then got up on a pinnacle, level with Blake's perch, to annoy him more. Blake, infuriated by these interruptions, lost his temper and flung him off.

During services and when visitors were not allowed to enter, Blake remained alone in the locked Abbey. Noise, bustle and worldly affairs were shut out, and the inward eye of the visionary artist in his late teens perceived, in his dim, vaulted solitude, a great procession of monks and priests, choristers and censer-bearers; entranced, he heard the chant of plain-song and chorale. Once he saw a vision of Christ and the Apostles. According to Blake's definition, written about thirty-five years later: 'A Spirit and a Vision are not, as the modern philosophy supposes, a cloudy vapour, or a nothing: they are organized and minutely articulated beyond all that the mortal and perishing nature can produce.' Blake asserted that 'all his imaginations' appeared to him 'infinitely more perfect and more minutely organized than any thing seen by his mortal eye. Spirits are organized men.' It is the artist's imagination that organizes them. In the last years of his life, Blake acknowledged that his earliest and most sacred recollections were from his days in Westminster Abbey.

Blake was there on a bright day in May 1774 when the Society of Antiquaries opened, for about an hour, the tomb of Edward I. The body had been embalmed on the King's own instructions when he was dying in 1307, and it had not been looked at since the reign of Edward III. Hundreds of years later, this next brief re-opening of the tomb in 1774 was considered a high treat by one of the antiquarians, who suggested that Basire should be present to record what might be seen. So unexpected, however, was the full splendour of the revelation that no eminent draughtsman came, and only young Blake himself was present as official artist: a swiftly-working figure, busily sketching among the absorbed group of select spectators. When the lid of the coffin was lifted, he drew the embalmed body of the King, perfectly preserved, crowned, and with a sceptre in each hand (6). The body was sumptuously robed in red damask, white tissue vividly jewelled, crimson satin and cloth of gold. The tomb was duly sealed again and Blake later made detailed sepia watercolour drawings from his sketches.

Blake is not known to have painted the spectacle in colour, although he would have been wonderfully equipped to do so. To his eyes the medieval world was visible not in monochrome, but in full rich colours, like the reds and gold in which he robed his kings when he painted the Adoration twenty-five years later. To him, Westminster Abbey was no bleached skeleton such as his contemporaries saw, but a brilliantly painted, gilded temple, made radiant again by the light of his imagination shining on faint traces of paint which he found as he climbed and sketched among the tombs. The style of his own original work shows the lasting impact of his apprenticeship in the Gothic world.

Aged sixteen and a half when he sketched the royal corpse and its regalia, Blake had already felt the heat of smouldering rebellious urges that were to excite and to inspire him all his life. As a man, he abhorred kings and all that they represented; and he drew, in the margin of Bacon's essays, a sketch of the devil defecating, from the top of a page, a chain of excrement that ends with the words: 'A King'. There is no evidence that Blake in adolescence rebelled against his tolerant parents or against his master, Basire: but when still a boy he was already expressing his intensely critical opinions in the margins of books generally revered.

Many years later, when annotating Sir Joshua Reynolds's *Discourses*, Blake wrote of the mature books he had read in his boyhood:

I read Burke's Treatise [*Of the Sublime and Beautiful*] when very Young; at the same time I read Locke on Human Understanding & Bacon's Advancement of Learning; on Every one of these Books I wrote my Opinions, & on looking them over find that my Notes on Reynolds in this Book are exactly Similar. I felt the Same Contempt & Abhorrence then that I do now.

Reverence and respect for the established authorities were sentiments alien to the independent, critical, intensely perceptive young artist who thought and felt for himself. He goes on to declare, with crushing simplicity, the cause of his scorn for Burke, Locke, Bacon and Reynolds: 'They mock Inspiration & Vision. Inspiration & Vision was then, & now is, & I hope will always Remain, my Element, my Eternal Dwelling place; how can I then hear it Contemned without returning Scorn for Scorn?'

Blake acquired great book-learning in his youth. He absorbed from the Bible, Shakespeare and Milton such a wealth of literature that his inspiration throughout his life naturally found expression in myths, images and phrases that he had discovered there. His immense knowledge was enriched from books which he possessed then or later in 'Latin, Greek, Hebrew, French, and Italian, besides a large collection of works of the mystical writers, Jacob Behmen, Swedenborg, and others', according to Frederick Tatham, and he was very widely read in English literature. Men of culture and learning came to Basire's, and the alert apprentice could have picked up from them much guidance, if he wanted it, in the world of books. At that time he owned the translation by Henry Fuseli of Winckelmann's *Reflections on the Painting and Sculpture of the Greeks*, a book which exalted the beauty of the naked human form, showed great admiration for the works of Michelangelo and Raphael, and so confirmed and strengthened Blake's own enthusiasms. 'I cannot paint Dirty rags & old shoes where I ought to place Naked Beauty or simple ornament,' he wrote in middle age. Even when the forms of men, women and children in his pictures are not nude, the clothes they wear serve rather to reveal their bodies than to hide them.

While living at Basire's, Blake probably managed to go home only on Sundays and for occasional evenings. In some of his spare time he wrote poetry, which he read aloud or sang to his friends. Most of his *Poetical Sketches*, written between his twelfth and his twentieth year, date from his time at Basire's. This little collection of lyric poetry, of fragments of blank-verse drama and of prose-poems, shows the young poet experimenting in a variety of forms and styles derived from many writers. Spenser, Shake-speare, Jonson, Milton, the Caroline poets, Akenside, Percy's *Reliques*, Macpherson's *Ossian* and Chatterton provide some of the influences on his early writing. Already, however, his own amazingly assured voice can be heard, when he is most successful in his phrasing and in his excitingly varied rhythms. Words from his ode 'To Summer' sing from the page, impart a vision and haunt the memory:

> curb thy fierce steeds, allay the heat
> That flames from their large nostrils!

Such vivid horses, and warm bodies like that of Summer himself with 'ruddy limbs and flourishing hair', would live again in Blake's visual art of later years. Other lines, such as these 'To the Evening Star', show a cool, delicate beauty:

> speak silence with thy glimmering eyes,
> And wash the dusk with silver.

Moreover, Blake is already sustaining excellence throughout whole poems, such as the song which begins 'My silks and fine array' and the ode 'To Autumn'. This, and the other masterly poems to the seasons, may have been written after the rest of the collection to serve as an introduction to it.

A dominant theme in some of the less memorable pieces is opposition to tyranny. Patriots are exhorted to rise against kings and tyrants, and the poet longs for power to restore peace:

> O for a voice like thunder, and a tongue
> To drown the throat of war!

Blake's horror of war was profound. While he was still writing his *Poetical Sketches*, he perceived terrifying portents of war: 'a mighty and awful change threatened the Earth.' Then, in 1775, as he was later to recall, 'The American War began. All its dark horrors passed before my face.' Such visions reduced young Blake to 'Nervous Fear'. In these early poems, he placed his feelings in historical settings and wrote about Gwin, King of Norway, King Edward IV and Samson. But the political and social themes, expressed through remote episodes, were to him living issues. Blake was acutely aware of what went on around him and he responded intensely to the events of his own time.

2

Young Artist, Poet and Husband
1779–87

'upon the ocean of business'

Blake left Basire in 1779, at the age of twenty-one, equipped to earn his living as a journeyman engraver. This meant that he was fully qualified to work for wages at the craft of incising, in metal plates, the figures, landscapes and all other designs that he had been given to be reproduced by printing. At this time most book-illustrations were engraved in copper, not wood. The designs were generally drawn by artists, and engraved by reproductive craftsmen who varied in quality from hacks to skilful experts. As Blake wrote twenty years later: 'To Engrave after another Painter is infinitely more laborious than to Engrave one's own Inventions.' Thanks to his thorough training and his hard work, Blake became one of the best engravers of his time. Before him, in England perhaps only William Hogarth had raised the craft of engraving to the height of art. Scrupulous craftsmanship was characteristic of Blake, whatever medium he used. Because engraving on copper was the work by which he earned his daily bread, and because all activities possessed for him symbolic importance, this craft—enriched by its spiritual and philosophic significance—played a vital part in his life.

But Blake's mastery of engraving did not suffice for him: he wanted to be a painter, not only an engraver with a flair for designing, and so he enrolled as one of the two dozen new students at the Royal Academy Schools in 1779. The Royal Academy had been founded in 1768, with the twofold purpose of training students free and holding yearly exhibitions at which any artists of distinguished merit could show their work. The first President was Sir Joshua Reynolds. Blake, after proving that he had talent and was prepared to use it, was entitled for six years as a student to draw plaster casts and nude models, and to attend exhibitions and lectures.

The Schools, ceremonially opened in 1771, were described as 'the most superb of any in the world and the best stocked with casts after the antique'.

To house them, King George III had allowed the disused royal apartments in a neglected palace, Old Somerset House in the Strand, to be repaired and altered. The Schools, set beside the Thames with a spacious tree-shaded garden, consisted of many rooms: the large ones were for drawing plaster figures; for the life class, where two men sat in turn for two hours each night (7); and for the Monday night lectures on anatomy, perspective, painting and architecture.

When Blake joined the Schools, eight years after they opened, the students were still supervised by the first Keeper, George Michael Moser, then over seventy. His pupils liked him for his ability and devotion. Swiss by birth, he had been the royal drawing-master during George III's boyhood, and he later engraved the King's first great seal. The Schools' librarian was Richard Wilson, the landscape painter. Anatomy lessons were given by Dr William Hunter (8), and the bodies of criminals who had been executed were sometimes allotted to the Royal Academy so that the art students could watch them being dissected. In 1776 two criminals were hanged and partly dissected by Hunter in Surgeon's Hall. The muscular development of the second criminal, a smuggler, was so remarkable that Hunter refused to dissect his body, but said it should be preserved. It was therefore moved to the Academy Schools, and placed in the attitude of the Dying Gladiator while the sculptor Carlini made a cast of it. Named Smugglerius by the students, it remained in the Schools for many years.

Blake declared that drawing from life was always hateful to him. He spoke of it as 'looking more like death, or smelling of mortality'. Perhaps the stillness of a model killed his vision. He was later seldom to use any models other than himself and his wife. Another instance of his independent approach to art is his sharp retort when Moser offered to guide his taste. Blake later recalled:

I was once looking over the Prints from Rafael & Michael Angelo in the Library of the Royal Academy. Moser came to me & said: 'You should not Study these old Hard, Stiff & Dry, Unfinish'd Works of Art—Stay a little & I will shew you what you should Study.' He then went & took down Le Brun's & Rubens's Galleries. How I did secretly Rage! I also spoke my Mind. . . . I said to Moser, 'These things that you call Finish'd are not Even Begun; how can they then be Finish'd? The Man who does not know The Beginning never can know the End of Art.'

Blake's preference was for a subject poetically treated in a sublime style and with a firm outline. Reynolds, President of the Royal Academy, to whom he showed some designs, recommended him to work with less extravagance and more simplicity and to correct his drawing. This Blake seemed to regard as an unforgettable affront.

By May 1780 he was a good enough painter to show a picture in the Royal Academy exhibition, the first to be held at the new Somerset House. His painting was of 'The Death of Earl Goodwin'. History paintings were often the occasion for artists, such as Benjamin West, to flatter the reigning monarch. Blake, however, used history painting to champion the republican cause, as did James Barry, 'the really Industrious, Virtuous & Independent Barry', as Blake later called him. Barry, an enthusiastic but embittered Irishman, described himself as 'a pock-pitted, hard-featured little fellow'. His temper was violent, his independence extreme and his work often vast in scale but generally feeble. He had passionate faith in history painting, and in his works he commented on contemporary events in America and in Europe, especially Ireland.

Blake, in 'The Death of Earl Goodwin', presents the sudden death of a strong hypocrite as a warning to tyrants. His other early history paintings, 'The Ordeal of Queen Emma' and 'The Penance of Jane Shore', show tyrants being moved to repentance and pity for their victims. History painting, for Blake, needed to present an allegorical meaning, the event being shown 'in its poetical vigour' to convey a prophetic message.

The 1780 Royal Academy exhibition of 489 works, with Reynolds, Gainsborough and Fuseli represented, attracted enormous crowds, though there were storms of prudish horror at the classical casts of undraped figures, 'the terror of every decent woman who enters the Antique Room'. The last section of a review of the exhibition in *The Morning Chronicle and London Advertiser*—a paper with the status of the modern *Times*—declared that 'though there is nothing to be said of the colouring' of 'The Death of Earl Goodwin', there 'may be discovered a good design, and much character.' This review was written under a pen-name by George Cumberland, who was to be a good friend to Blake for many years. Cumberland, an insurance clerk, wrote that he 'loved the fine arts from almost infancy and sought them out alone!' An amateur painter and etcher who fretted against his financial work at the Royal Exchange, he was one of a small, friendly group of young artists which included Blake. A man of high ideals and moral integrity, Cumberland lacked insight into Blake's extraordinary mind, yet he was one of the few men with whom Blake maintained a long friendship unclouded by quarrels. Blake's touchy, fiery, hypersensitive nature made unusual demands on others. In his last epic he wrote: 'I never made friends but by spiritual gifts, By severe contentions of friendship & the burning fire of thought.'

The young artists whose company Blake enjoyed at this time included the painter Thomas Stothard and the sculptor John Flaxman, both two years his senior. Flaxman (9) was attracted to Stothard by seeing some of his illustrations in a shop window, and the two became friends for life. In 1777 Stothard entered the Royal Academy Schools: he drew in pen and ink, used watercolours, and painted small family portraits. Two years later, he illustrated *Ossian* and a book on naval history, and his busy career as a book-illustrator began. A great reader and observer of nature, he was a copious and popular designer of all sorts of decorations for books. So industrious was he that even on his wedding day, in 1783, he worked at the Royal Academy Schools, where he casually invited a fellow-student to come home and celebrate the marriage by dining with him and his bride. From 1779 onwards, Blake was employed to engrave many of his drawings. This friendship was to last for more than twenty years.

Flaxman, the son of a plaster-cast maker, spent his childhood in his father's shop at the sign of the Golden Head in Covent Garden. The boy was delicate and weak, but when he entered his teens, his health began to improve. He was always busy behind his father's counter, drawing or modelling or trying to teach himself classics. Among the customers who noticed him was the Rev. A. S. Mathew, a benevolent clergyman in his thirties. Harriet, his cultured wife, welcomed the boy to their house in Rathbone Place, where she read aloud to him translations of Homer and Virgil, while he made sketches of those passages that took his fancy. His earliest commission was from a friend of the Mathews, for six drawings of classical subjects. From the age of twelve he exhibited his works; at fifteen he entered the Royal Academy Schools, and from the age of twenty he was regularly employed to design classical friezes and portrait medallions for Wedgwood ware. As time went on, Flaxman was increasingly liked and respected. His body had acquired a wiry tenacity and stamina, though he looked frail and hunched. His head was disproportionately big, and he walked with a sidelong gait. His jaw suggests stubbornness: and he was rigid in his religious beliefs, a personal mixture of puritan orthodoxy and mysticism derived from Swedenborg. Though later he made many drawings of the mystical *Book of Enoch*, he was not, like Blake, a visionary.

An intensely dramatic experience of deep concern to Blake occurred when he was twenty-two. The part of London in which he and many other artists lived and worked suffered days and nights of violence during a week of hot weather early in June 1780. The anti-Catholic petition sponsored by Lord George Gordon and approved at a meeting in Coachmakers' Hall, Great Queen Street, led to mob-rule on a terrifying scale. A crowd of fourteen thousand tried to break into the House of Lords. At night, a group of venomous-looking men, resolute, half-drunk but alarmingly quiet and in surprisingly good order, marched down Great Queen Street, about a mile east of Blake's home, towards Lincoln's Inn Fields, with lighted torches in their hands and spades, pickaxes, blacksmiths' hammers and crowbars on their shoulders. This was a prelude to destruction. That night in Great Queen Street (where nine houses were later gutted and their furniture burnt), ten fires blazed 'to burn those whom the mob called papishes'. In Warwick Street, only five minutes' walk from Blake's home, the chapel at the Bavarian Embassy was stripped, its windows were smashed and prayer-books, vestments and furniture were burned in the street. Broad Street, where Blake was born and brought up and lived with his parents after leaving Basire, was a place of violence, death and destruction (15). A volunteer in the London Military Association reported that a large mob ransacking a house there and burning the furniture in the street 'would not disperse and bid us fire and be damned. There was soon exhibited a scene of killed, wounded and dying.'

Blake, a revolutionary at heart, was in the front rank of the mob that surged down Holborn and stormed London's oldest and largest prison, Newgate. Perhaps he got caught up in the crowd and was carried unwillingly along, or perhaps he actively joined it on its way to free not only the four rioters arrested a few nights before but also about three hundred other prisoners. By now the riots had become an incoherent revolt against authority, an outburst by the frustrated poor egged on by fanatics and criminals. One spectator at Newgate, the poet George Crabbe,

... never saw anything so dreadful. The prison was ... a remarkably strong building; but, determined to force it, they broke the gates with crows and other instruments, and climbed up the outside.... They broke the roof, tore away the rafters, and having got ladders they descended ... flames all around them, and a body of soldiers expected. They defied all opposition. The prisoners escaped. I stood and saw about twelve women and eight men ascend from their confinement to the open air, and they were conducted through the streets in their chains. Three of them were to be hanged on Friday. You have no conception of the frenzy of the multitude.

The terrible flames and prisons, smoke and chains that appear in Blake's pictures and in his poetry owe some of their grim reality to this time of violence, during which 850 people were killed in London.

Blake's view of the responsibility of society for the quality of life in his time, and for such an eruption as the Gordon Riots, is tersely expressed in his proverb: 'Prisons are built with stones of Law, Brothels with bricks of Religion.' Perhaps on 6 June 1780 he did deliberately participate in the destruction of Newgate, a deed of symbolic power. His political ideas were radical. He shared and expressed in his work a sense of outrage at the war, already prolonged through five years, against the rebellious American colonists: exasperation with this war was indeed one of the many stimulants to the Gordon Riots. Blake also detested government. At Basire's he had engraved some of the many illustrations in a book of memoirs by Thomas Hollis, an ardent devotee of Milton's grand, ideal republicanism, and Blake found Milton's revolutionary fervour very congenial.

Blake lived his life on many levels, and some of them are apparent in his bold engraving, drawn in 1780, 'The Dance of Albion'. The assertive nude youth represents England's political awakening, but at a deeper level this engraving is linked with traditional wisdom. The position of the figure is based on a medieval book *Of Occult Philosophy*, by the German writer, soldier and physician Cornelius Agrippa, which caused a sensation in sixteenth-century Europe by its defence of oriental wisdom and which shows how man's body, 'the human form divine', expresses in its proportions the power of numbers. Man's body is the measure of the universe. Blake, self-taught and thirsty for all sorts of knowledge, read Agrippa's book and studied the illustrations. It expounds the esoteric idea, which Blake came to share, that pagan wisdom expressed Christian truths. The three main pagan sources of light were: the oriental wisdom of the Magi who came from the east to Christ; the ancient Jewish wisdom of the Rabbis, which was handed down orally from the time of Moses and has been preserved in the Hebrew tradition called Cabbala; and the classical wisdom that shone from Plato and Pythagoras. Blake's belief, that all religions are one, is in this occult tradition, the symbolism of which he absorbed and used to express his own ideas. His questing mind, stocked with self-acquired learning, found its natural expression in multiple meanings. His vision was complex. He came to think of it as fourfold, and more than twenty years after first designing 'The Dance of Albion', in 1802, he explained:

> Now I a fourfold vision see,
> And a fourfold vision is given to me;
> 'Tis fourfold in my supreme delight
> And threefold in soft Beulah's night
> And twofold Always. May God us keep
> From Single vision & Newton's sleep!

In Blake's mythology, Beulah represents the realm of the subconscious mind, source of inspiration and dreams, and Newton's sleep is unawareness of all spiritual values which make life worth living. Single vision is seen by the eye only; twofold vision sees *through* the eye and perceives the human values in all things; threefold vision reveals thought in emotional form and inspires creation; fourfold vision is mystical ecstasy. Blake's complexity of vision, which underlies his apparently simple pictures and poems, is embodied in numerous layers of meaning. His mind delighted in puns, in images that present a number of meanings at the same time. So it is that 'The Dance of Albion' (14) refers in the figure's pose not only to Agrippa's book *Of Occult Philosophy*, but also to a Roman diagram of human proportions; and the youth with hair like flame represents not only England, but also many individuals united, all members of one body, 'Multitudes of Men in Harmony'. This figure, a symbol of the people, dances to express independence and willingness for self-sacrifice.

Britain's war with France, which had broken out in 1778, aroused alarm about spies. On one occasion this involved Blake, possibly James Parker (who had been his fellow-apprentice at Basire's) and Stothard. Probably some months after the Gordon Riots, they went on a sailing and sketching trip for a few days up the Medway. While drawing on the shore, they were discovered by soldiers who suspected that they were spies surveying for the French government, and arrested them (13). Although the artists pleaded that they were only sketching for their own amusement, their provisions were brought ashore, a tent was improvised and a sentry was posted to guard them until their loyal, peaceful intentions could be vouched for by some Royal Academicians. Then the young men, released, spent a merry hour with the commanding officer.

Flaxman was so keen to have Blake's poems printed that he was willing to share the cost, but first he brought Blake into cultured society. Aspiring artists were welcome in the drawing-room of Mrs Mathew, which Flaxman had adorned with statuettes set in niches in the Gothic manner. Eminent middle-class people who patronized art, music and literature met in this room: and to Mrs Mathew, their hostess, Flaxman introduced Blake, now in his early twenties. The circle included Mrs Hester Chapone, who wrote *Letters on the Improvement of the Mind,* sang exquisitely, and drew with some skill, and Mrs Elizabeth Carter, of whom Dr Samuel Johnson said: 'My old friend Mrs Carter could make a pudding as well as translate Epictetus from the Greek.' Other visitors were the famous blue-stocking, Mrs Elizabeth Montagu—in the intellectual society of London she was for nearly fifty years the supreme hostess; Fanny Burney called her 'brilliant in diamonds, solid in judgment, and critical in talk'—and Mrs Hannah More, who was to become a close friend of William Wilberforce and to publish *Slavery, a Poem.*

To enlightened people such as these, Blake read his *Poetical Sketches* or sang them to his own tunes. Although he lacked the technical skill to write down his melodies, more knowledgeable musicians, charmed by their beauty, did so: but this music has not survived. Mrs Mathew enthusiastically persuaded her husband to join with Flaxman in sponsoring the printing, in 1783, of fifty copies of the *Poetical Sketches.* The Rev. A. S. Mathew also wrote a short, dry introduction, in which he apologized for the unrevised state of the sheets and explained that the author had not had leisure from his engraving to correct them. 'Conscious of the irregularities and defects to be found in almost every page, his friends have still believed that they possessed a poetic originality, which merited some respite from oblivion.' However, this introduction does not tell the whole story. If Blake had been interested in polishing his *Poetical Sketches* before publication, he would have made time to do so. Smooth rhythms conveyed the languid inertia that he despised in contemporary poems: he preferred to leave his works as they were, alive. He probably regarded these boyhood pieces as ephemeral exercises, but felt that he should not reject the kindness of his patrons by refusing to have the sheets printed.

A young man of Flaxman's talent and skill fitted happily into Mrs Mathew's encouraging circle, and flourished there. Blake, a young genius, strong in his opinions and unyielding in temper, with a spirit that would not be caged like a song-bird but free to soar like an eagle, felt the need to rebel and break away. His visits became less frequent.

At home, Blake's closest companion was his youngest brother, Robert, who was keen to become an artist. He was nearly ten years younger than William, his nature was amiable and affectionate, and William, who was devoted to him, taught him to draw. In Robert's sketch-book, William drew parts of the human body, such as lips, eyes, ears and legs, or a whole figure, for him to copy. In 1782, the year in which the American war ended, Robert probably entered the Royal Academy Schools to study as an engraver.

That summer, John Flaxman married Ann (known as Nancy) Denman, daughter of a gunstock-maker in Whitechapel. Reynolds, a sturdy bachelor, gloomily remarked: 'So, Flaxman, I am told you are married—if so, sir, I tell you you are ruined for an artist!' On the contrary, with the support of his devoted Nancy—an accomplished girl who had a taste for art and literature, a knowledge of French, Italian and some Greek, and skill and economy in running their home—Flaxman increasingly flourished in his work. First, the couple took the smallest house and studio in Wardour Street, near Blake who later called Nancy 'a good connoisseur in engraving'.

Shortly before Flaxman's marriage, Blake's developing interest in girls led to some disappointment, though by nature he was merry and convivial. (Alexander Gilchrist, Blake's Victorian biographer, recounts the story after Frederick Tatham.) Polly Wood, a 'lively little girl' whom Blake fancied, was pleased to go out with him, but not to marry him. His frustration led to jealousy and when he complained to Polly that she had been for a stroll with 'another admirer, "Are you a fool?" was the brusque reply—with a scornful glance. "That cured me of jealousy," Blake used to say'; but the affair upset him, and for a change of scene he went to stay on the river at Battersea, then a country village with good salmon-fishing. Market gardens flourished there, and the asparagus and cabbages were especially fine. The market-gardener in whose house Blake lodged was William Boucher. His daughter, Catherine, listened with deep sympathy to Blake's sad tale of Polly's disregard. Catherine's tender, affectionate manner immediately won Blake's love, so that he asked at once, 'with the suddenness peculiar to him, "Do you pity me?" "Yes indeed I do," answered she. "Then I love you," said he.' Before this, when her mother asked her which friend she 'could fancy for a husband, she replied that she had not yet seen the man'. On first coming into the room where Blake sat, however, Catherine instantly recognized him as her future husband, and nearly fainted from emotion.

The Bouchers were a respectable family, but humbler than the Blakes. Seven children, including two sets of twins in succession, preceded

Catherine. There is a dubious tradition that Blake's father was opposed to the marriage. However, when Blake was twenty-four and Catherine was twenty, about a year after they first met, they were married on Sunday 18 August 1782, in St Mary's, the parish church of Battersea. This had been recently rebuilt, and in later years Turner would sit in the bow window of its vestry to paint sunsets across the Thames. Catherine was—like most girls of her class—illiterate. Blake later taught her to read and write, as well as to draw and paint, but in the church register she duly made her mark, a cross, under William's signature. She was a vivacious, attractive girl, bright-eyed and dark-haired, and Blake would boast of her prettiness. His physical expectations are shown in the cryptic lines that he later jotted in his notebook:

> In a wife I would desire
> What in whores is always found—
> The lineaments of Gratified desire.

The newly-married couple made their first home in lodgings at 23 Green Street, a turning off Leicester Fields. This was still an open and peaceful place, where it was possible to hear the cock crow and to see a hen and chickens strut as calmly through the street as they would in a country town. Sir Joshua Reynolds lived in Leicester Fields. So did the surgeon and print-collector John Hunter and, next door to him, Hogarth's widow: while Blake, round the corner, toiled to earn his living as an engraver and to develop as an artist and poet.

In his labours, Blake was helped by his devoted wife who became perfectly attuned to him and his vision. 'Imagination is My World,' he wrote about eighteen years later. All human beings, he said, partake of the faculty of vision, but it is lost by not being cultivated: he cultivated his wife's and she came to share, in some measure, his power of seeing. On the practical level, she became highly accomplished in all the skills expected of her as his frugal housekeeper, his assistant printer and colourer of prints. She bore no children, but she helped him indirectly and sometimes directly to create his works, 'Infants emanating from him', winged thoughts expressed on pages that quiver with life. Blake spoke of his creations as his children who shake 'their bright fiery wings', and his wife shared humbly in their making. That it was indirectly a sexual fulfilment, evidence of 'Desire Gratified', the fruition of lovers united, is shown by much that Blake wrote, for instance the poem in his notebook:

> Abstinence sows sand all over
> The ruddy limbs & flaming hair,
> But Desire Gratified
> Plants fruits of life & beauty there.

The 'ruddy limbs' are Blake's; his hair, according to Tatham, 'stood up like a curling flame' in his youth, as can be seen in his wife's drawing of him as a young man. The most popular of their 'fruits of life & beauty', the *Songs of Innocence*, were created for children, and so were *The Gates of Paradise*, which Blake later adapted *For the Sexes*. He loved children and children loved him.

In the spring of 1784, Flaxman tried to arouse the interest of friends in Blake's poetry and in his 'historical drawings'. An attempt to raise a subscription to send Blake to Rome fizzled out: he was destined never to leave England or travel further from London than the Sussex Coast. For the sight of Michelangelo's and Raphael's greatest works of art he had to depend on engravings and on whatever copies his travelled friends brought home and showed him.

In the Royal Academy that May, Blake exhibited two watercolours influenced by the American War, 'A Breach in a City the Morning after the Battle' and 'War Unchained by an Angel—Fire, Pestilence, and Famine Following'. In July, his father died and was buried in Bunhill Fields, the burial ground of dissenters. Helped by a little money inherited from his father, Blake and his wife moved to 27 Broad Street (next door to the family home, number 28, where Blake was born). Here Blake set up shop as a printseller, in partnership with his old friend from apprentice days, James Parker, seven years older than himself, and married. Numbers 27 and 28 each consisted of four floors and a basement, sizeable homes. Next door to the Blakes and the Parkers lived James, William's eldest brother, hosier and haberdasher, who had taken over the family house and the family business after their father's death. Their widowed mother, their sister Catherine, and perhaps their younger brother—Blake's beloved pupil Robert—continued to live there too: though possibly Robert may have moved in to live with the Blakes at number 27. Blake had little in common with his pedestrian brother James and even less with their brother John, the dissolute baker, who had recently come to live just across Broad Street at number 29.

Looking back sixteen years later, when London had become 'a City of Elegance in some degree', with 'as many Booksellers as there are Butchers & as many Printshops as of any other trade', Blake remembered 'when a Printshop was a rare bird in London': its life was precarious. The partners' business in new and second-hand prints by other engravers did not thrive; and of their own publications no more than two are known, both engravings after Stothard by Blake, who had probably bought his own copperplate press by this time. Parker specialized in mezzotint, Blake in line-engraving, and Mrs Blake helped in the shop. Domestic harmony was occasionally disrupted by rows, such as one between Robert and Mrs Blake in Blake's presence. In the heat of discussion, she used words to Robert that William thought unwarrantable. Gilchrist writes of William: 'A silent witness thus far, he could now bear it no longer, but with characteristic impetuosity— when stirred—rose and said to her: "Kneel down and beg Robert's pardon directly, or you never see my face again!" ' He sounded as if he meant it. She ' "thought it very hard", as she would afterwards tell, to beg her brother-in-law's pardon when she was not in fault! But being a duteous, devoted wife, though by nature nowise tame or dull of spirit, she *did* kneel and meekly murmur: "Robert, I beg your pardon, I am in the wrong." "Young woman, you lie!" abruptly retorted he: "*I* am in the wrong!" ' So mutual confession restored harmony.

George Cumberland, the amateur artist and insurance clerk, came to Blake to learn engraving. Cumberland sought a method of printing poems cheaply and swiftly, and experimented with engraving them on copper. In January 1784, he sent his brother an engraved print of a poem and wrote of 'my new mode of printing—it is the amusement of an evening and is capable of printing 2000 . . . and the cost is trifling.' In a description published later in the year, Cumberland wrote that his method of printing 'cost very little more time than common writing'. Perhaps Blake was already considering how to combine the engraving of words and drawings on copper, as a means of creating coloured prints of poems which would resemble illuminated manuscripts.

He alluded to Cumberland's method in a rumbustious satire, *An Island in the Moon*, which he wrote probably in 1784 and left unpublished at the end of his life. In this burlesque the character Quid the Cynic, who is Blake's satirical presentation of himself in the lunatic England of his own day, reveals to a loyal admirer his plans for illuminating a manuscript: 'I would have all the writing Engraved instead of Printed, & at every other leaf a high finish't print—all in three Volumes folio—& sell them a hundred pounds apiece. They would print off two thousand.'

Blake, writing exuberantly at the age of twenty-six, has a high-spirited crack at the Antiquarian Society, the College of Surgeons and scientific lectures based on microscope slides. He satirizes John Hunter, younger and more celebrated brother of the Royal Academy's first Professor of Anatomy, William, as the surgeon Tearguts. Blake's friends might easily have seen who Jacko, Suction the Epicurean and Inflammable Gass the Windfinder represented, though time has made identification less certain now. Like all good satire, Blake's is of its own time but has a continuing impact.

The action of *An Island in the Moon* is principally at Quid's house, where the cynical artist is planning to make his fortune from the new Cumberland process as 'the Painter and the Poet'. He pursues money without neglecting art. Years later, Blake recalled his printshop venture as a mistake that tormented him and deprived him of vision: 'I thought my pursuits of Art a kind of criminal dissipation & neglect of the main chance, which I hid my face for not being able to abandon as a Passion which is forbidden by Law & Religion.' Quid, however, blithely created in the tradition of comedy, drinks rum and water and sings:

Honour & Genius is all I ask,
And I ask the Gods no more.

To him in his arrogant confidence 'Homer is bombast, & Shakespeare is too
wild, & Milton has no feelings: they might be easily outdone.' And as for
engraving their own poetry, even Milton and Shakespeare had not been
able to do that.

In contrast to Quid is Steelyard, a restrained and saintly man who bears
provocation 'more like a Saint than a Lawgiver'. A steelyard is a balance,
and the term is associated with merchants. Perhaps Blake, the instinctive
punster who makes another character refer to Locke's essay on human
understanding as 'An Easy of Huming Understanding, by John Lookye
Gent', summarizes in the name Steelyard the complexity of Flaxman.
Flaxman was kindly by nature, spiritually drawn to Swedenborg, and in
conduct precise and prim: when establishing himself as a sculptor in
Wardour Street he had held a job as a rate-collector, which needs steel
rather than sweetness.

Inflammable Gass, the enthusiastic scientist who has 'got a bottle of air
that would spread a Plague', is eager to show off 'a louse, or a flea' with his
apparatus of 'glasses, & brass tubes, & magic pictures'. He becomes so over-
excited that he breaks the bottles of wind that he 'took up in the boghouse'
and lets out the pestilence. When his show goes awry, he cries out, 'We are
putrified! We are corrupted! Our lungs are destroy'd with the Flogiston [a
hypothetical 'fire-stuff', phlogiston, believed to exist in all combustible
substances]. This will spread a plague all thro' the Island!' Beyond the enter-
taining caricatures in Blake's satire on philosophy, science, marriage and
religion, there looms the threat of fire and pestilence. Apocalypse, as always
in his vision of the world, is imminent.

Blake's burlesque includes many lyrics. These range from parody, dog-
gerel, a cricketing song and nonsense verses to stanzas of pastoral sentiment
which allude to Mrs Barbauld's *Hymns in Prose for Children*. Some of the
lyrics were to reappear in *Songs of Innocence*; and Blake was to develop
aspects of them further in *Songs of Experience*.

In the summer of 1785 Blake exhibited at the Royal Academy, for the last
time for many years. His works were three watercolours of Old Testament
episodes from Joseph's life, and one of 'The Bard, from Gray'. By now he
was experimenting with tempera—which he named 'fresco'—using diluted
carpenter's glue instead of the traditional egg-yolk as a medium. Always
questing after new techniques, he called oil paint 'a fetter to genius, and a
dungeon to art' because it lacked brilliance and blurred the 'wirey . . .
bounding line' which he thought essential to art as to life, a boundary
against chaos. Perhaps it was at the dinner to mark the opening of this
Royal Academy exhibition that the President, Reynolds, blandly remarked:
'Well, Mr Blake, I hear you despise our art of oil painting,' to which

Blake replied: 'No, Sir Joshua, I don't despise it; but I like fresco better.'

Despite support from Mrs Mathew, the partners Blake and Parker did not make a success of the printshop, although it had opened in a time of peace when prosperity was returning after the American war. Before Christmas 1785 the Blakes moved out, but the Parkers remained at 27 Broad Street for nine more years. Parker, although not very distinguished as an artist, was greatly respected for his amiable disposition, integrity, and good sense: he was to become a founder and a governor of the Society of Engravers. The Blakes settled round the corner to the north, about three streets away, at 28 Poland Street. For nearly five years, until 1790, they stayed in this house of three storeys and an attic. Only a few doors away, at number 22, stood a tavern which may already have been a cosmopolitan haunt of young artists. There Blake bought his porter and probably had a cheap meal sometimes. He may have celebrated his twenty-fourth birthday there when, as the inscription on the wall now says: 'In this Old King's Arms Tavern the Ancient Order of Druids was revived 28th November 1781.' Perhaps at that inn he met the Druid enthusiasts whose lore influenced his thought and found expression in his later mythology.

3

Revolutionary
1787–93

Blake's favourite brother, Robert, aged nineteen, fell seriously ill during the Blakes' second winter in Poland Street. Gilchrist writes: 'Blake affectionately tended him in his illness, and during the last fortnight of it watched continuously day and night by his bedside, without sleep.' The illness proved fatal, but the sick-room was to Blake, 'as to him most scenes were, a place of vision and of revelation.' In February 1787, Blake saw Robert die. 'At the last solemn moment, the visionary eyes beheld the released spirit ascend heavenward through the matter-of-fact ceiling, "clapping its hands for joy".' Exhausted by his devoted vigil, Blake fell into an unbroken sleep of three days and nights. Robert's body was buried in Bunhill Fields, but his spirit remained a living help and source of inspiration to Blake, who wrote in 1800 to console William Hayley, bereaved of a young son:

Thirteen years ago I lost a brother & with his spirit I converse daily & hourly in the Spirit & See him in my remembrance in the regions of my Imagination. I hear his advice & even now write from his Dictate. Forgive me for Expressing to you my Enthusiasm which I wish to partake of Since it is to me a Source of Immortal Joy: even in this world by it I am the companion of Angels. . . . The Ruins of Time builds Mansions in Eternity.

Blake writing from Robert's 'Dictate' is comparable with Milton composing *Paradise Lost* while the heavenly muse visits him in dream and dictates to him 'slumb'ring', or inspires 'Easy' his 'unpremeditated Verse'. In Blake's long poem entitled *Milton* which he engraved a few years after writing the letter of condolence to Hayley, he illustrates Robert's spiritual form (18).

Blake ascribed to Robert not only words to write but the technique of reproducing them with illustrations. During the 1780s there was much

C

33

interest in devising a method of printing from a solid plate of type, to be known as a stereotype, instead of traditionally from a body of type secured in a frame. After Cumberland's practical experiments came Robert's spiritual inspiration, when Blake had pondered on the problem of technique. 'In a vision of the night,' according to Gilchrist, 'the form of Robert stood before him, and revealed the wished-for secret, directing him to the technical mode by which could be produced a facsimile of song and design.' On his rising in the morning, Mrs Blake went out with half a crown, 'all the money they had in the world', and spent most of it 'on the simple materials necessary for setting in practice the new revelation.' Tatham says that the lack of cash was not, in fact, quite so complete, because 'Mrs Blake's frugality always kept a guinea or sovereign for any emergency, of which Blake never knew, even to the day of his death': but the technique made little money for him. In thirty-eight years' work it brought him no more that six years' income. He developed the technique, however, into a superb medium for his unique combination of gifts as poet and artist.

To print by the ordinary method—called intaglio—from a plate he had engraved or etched in the usual way, Blake would have first inked the plate's surface and then wiped it clean, so that ink remained only in his incised or etched lines. Paper was then pressed so hard against these lines that its surface was forced into them and took the imprint of the ink. Blake's new technique, however, produced a plate on which his words and designs stood out in relief: the background, not the lines, had been removed and printing needed only gentle pressure.

Experts are still not sure of the details of Blake's new method. It seems to have rid him of the need to write backwards onto a copper plate, although any trained engraver can easily write backwards and the need to do so would not have troubled Blake. Apparently he soaked a sheet of paper in a solution of gum arabic and soap, and let it dry. Then, with a quill or a reed pen, dipped in acid-resistant varnish such as etchers used for stopping-out, he wrote on the paper. This manuscript he placed face downwards on a heated copper plate. To transfer his lettering onto the plate he ran the paper and plate together through a press. The plate emerged with the paper sticking to it. When the plate had cooled he steeped it in water which dissolved the gum: the paper floated off in a few minutes and left the lettering, in reverse, sticking to the copper plate. He touched up the lettering as necessary with varnish and decorated it with designs around and in the text, using the same medium, varnish, on a brush. In this way, he illuminated his manuscript reversed. The plate was then ready to be steeped in a bath of diluted nitric acid for about six to eight hours. There the background was bitten down while the acid-resistant lettering and design remained unconsumed. To prevent erosion from below, the varnished surfaces had to be extended by laborious repainting two or three times.

When Blake finally removed the deeply etched plate from the acid bath, it emerged bearing his words and decoration in relief. He gouged out some of the larger spaces to prevent unwanted inking and with a graver added more detail to his designs, incising delicate lines in the unbitten surfaces. The plate was then ready to be inked and printed. By using a roller to ink it he risked spreading ink onto the bitten background, and so he usually inked an unused plate all over and pressed it onto the etched plate, perhaps by running both plates together through the press without applying much pressure. He then took a sheet of dry, moderately fine paper and printed his relief-etched plate onto it, lightly using an engraver's rolling press, a wooden machine with adjustable pressure. He could take proofs by simply laying paper on his inked plate and rubbing the back of the paper with a spoon.

Blake's early experiments in producing plates, by his difficult new method, yielded three series of tiny prints of terse, gnomic sayings with decorations. He printed them in various coloured inks, green, olive and brown, sometimes with two colours on one little plate, and occasionally he added watercolour washes. According to Gilchrist, Blake's economical, independent method relied on vision: loyally helped by Mrs Blake,

he ground and mixed his watercolours himself on a piece of statuary marble, after a method of his own, with common carpenter's glue diluted, which he had found out, as the early Italians had done before him, to be a good binder. Joseph, the sacred carpenter, had appeared in vision and revealed *that* secret to him. The colours he used were few and simple. . . . He taught Mrs Blake to take off the impressions with care and delicacy, which such plates signally needed; and also to help in tinting them from his drawings with right artistic feeling. . . .

Blake's words, in these little works of 1788, *There is no Natural Religion* (in two series) and *All Religions are One*, express some of his fundamental beliefs. Man is, by nature, 'only a natural organ subject to Sense', but his 'Poetic or Prophetic' power releases him from bondage to nature and he therefore apprehends more than his organs of perception, however acute, can discover. 'The desire of Man being Infinite, the possession is Infinite & himself Infinite.' To Blake, art and religion are the same thing. The poet is the prophet. God, 'the Poetic Genius', is 'the true Man', Christ. The application of Blake's religious philosophy is: 'He who sees the Infinite in all things, sees God. He who sees the Ratio only, sees himself only.' Blake concludes his denial of natural religion: 'Therefore God becomes as we are, that we may be as he is.' Already setting himself apart from popular belief, while asserting his role in Christian prophecy, Blake, at the age of thirty-one, subtitled *All Religions are One* 'The Voice of one crying in the Wilderness'. His argument is: 'As the true method of knowledge is experiment, the true faculty of knowing must be the faculty which experiences.' He believes that 'The Religions of all Nations are derived from each Nation's different reception of the Poetic Genius, which is every where call'd the Spirit of

Prophecy.' His final principle is: 'As all men are alike (tho' infinitely various), So all Religions &, as all similars, have one source.' He asserts: 'The true Man is the source, he being the Poetic Genius.' Blake was already deeply read in philosophy and symbolism, but the ideas that he accepted he wove into the fabric of his thought and made very much his own. The paradoxes and complexities of his later work are foreshadowed in these sinewy bold assertions, on the little pages that he did not issue but used as stepping-stones to greater works ahead.

His thought was much influenced by a friend of Cumberland and Flaxman, Thomas Taylor, the ardent Neoplatonist writer. Blake probably first met Taylor in the 1780s and heard him deliver a series of twelve lectures on Platonic philosophy to a distinguished audience at Flaxman's house, shortly before the Flaxmans left for Italy in 1787.

Seeking a metaphysic of mathematics, Taylor moved from Plato to Plotinus and the Neoplatonists. In them he found a blend of philosophy and religion which satisfied him and he eagerly set out, in quantities of rather stiff translations and commentaries, to interpret them to the modern world. With him, Blake explored mathematics, Greek ideas, and myths. Through Taylor, he absorbed ideas from Orphism and Neoplatonism which he made part of his own system of thought, and myths which he built into the structure of his works. Taylor openly accepted Greek polytheism. He was said to believe in reincarnation, and was whispered to revere his many pets at his small house in Walworth. Perhaps he is caricatured as Sipsop the Pythagorean in *An Island in the Moon*. Certainly he dismissed the visions of Swedenborg as delirious. Moreover, he scornfully rejected Christianity itself. In this, he crucially differed from Blake, who responded to the literatures of both Greece and Israel, while distinguishing clearly between the special values of Greek myth and of the Bible. Blake later repudiated 'The Greek Muses, which are not Inspiration as the Bible is', though he continued to use Platonic symbols. The 'Real Visions' of the Greeks had been absorbed into Blake's particular form of Christianity, and Taylor had helped him to see them.

Blake writes explicitly about other influences upon him, in a letter to Flaxman of 12 September 1800. He declares:

> Now my lot in the Heavens is this, Milton lov'd me in childhood & shew'd me his face.
> Ezra came with Isaiah the Prophet, but Shakespeare in riper years gave me his hand;
> Paracelsus & Behmen appear'd to me.

Paracelsus and Behmen (as Boehme was called in Blake's time) were transmitters and enrichers of the occult philosophy about which Cornelius Agrippa had written. Paracelsus, a sixteenth-century Swiss physician, lectured at Basle University discrediting traditional medicine. His own system was based on visionary Neoplatonic philosophy. The Cabbala, too, influenced Paracelsus who believed that true wisdom came from the East. He saw man's life as inseparable from that of the universe, and reality as fourfold in its nature. Alchemy, astronomy and theology were all essential to Paracelsus's medical practice. His insistence that 'imagination is creative power' chimed with Blake's belief in 'Imagination, The Divine Vision'. To Paracelsus, 'he who is born in imagination discovers the latent forces of nature', while Blake believed that 'to the Eyes of the Man of Imagination, Nature is Imagination itself'.

Paracelsus's Neoplatonic ideas and imagery influenced Jakob Boehme, a saintly shoemaker who was, Blake believed, divinely inspired. Boehme was an original German thinker deeply rooted in the occult tradition. In his mid-twenties—on Trinity Sunday, 1600—he received the illumination that 'in Yes and No all things consist'. This dialectical principle was to become the seed of his thought. He became a merchant and met travelled, learned men steeped in mysticism, the Cabbala and the doctrines of Paracelsus. He wrote many books, expressing his mystical thoughts in material symbols.

Blake was not only convinced, like Boehme, of the fourfold nature of existence and of the creative possibilities of conflict, but also haunted by Boehme's theory that man was originally a pure angel, containing the feminine spirit, balanced between dark and light worlds. Sexually undivided, man was the virgin image of God. Then man suffered a double Fall: firstly, into material form, the process condemned by Blake as 'vegetation', which includes division into two sexes, lustful and needing to reproduce; secondly, into sin and death, the fate of Adam and Eve. The first Fall occurred when Adam, tired of unity, fell asleep succumbing to the powers of the world, and gave form to Eve. The second Fall occurred in Eden. Not only were Blake's thought and imagery enriched by Boehme's ideas, he was also visually impressed by the illustrations to Boehme's works.

The influences that Blake acknowledged, in his letter to Flaxman, form an apocalyptic mixture of vast power. Milton and Shakespeare were the only two writers who, in Blake's opinion, mark 'the extent of the human mind'. Ezra was a visionary whose revelation, now known as the Second Book of Esdras (in the Apocrypha), much attracted students of the Cabbala. The contributions of the prophet Isaiah, of Paracelsus and Boehme were spiritually dynamic and cosmic in scope. Blake was great enough to make all these a part of himself.

In 1788, his commercial engraving included a frontispiece after the Swiss artist Henry Fuseli (26), who became a close and important friend, for John Caspar Lavater's *Aphorisms on Man*. The previous autumn, Flaxman and his wife had set out for Rome, with work to do for Josiah Wedgwood. They did not return for seven years. Meanwhile, as Blake wrote: 'When Flaxman was taken to Italy, Fuseli was given to me for a season.' Fuseli, a tiny man nearly seventeen years older than Blake, came from a family of painters in Zurich, where he was ordained a Zwinglian minister. After trying for over a year to undermine orthodoxy from within, he devoted himself to studying literature. With his fellow-student Lavater, of whom he was passionately fond, he exposed a corrupt magistrate and was advised to leave Switzerland. A fine classical scholar, a good linguist, and a devotee of Shakespeare and Milton, he came to London believing poetry to be his true vocation. There he wrote and translated, and his puritanism wore off in his indulgent pursuit of many interests. 'For anyone with a soul,' he declared, 'the London theatre alone is worth the journey.' After making his way to the studio of the President of the Royal Academy and showing him some of his drawings, at the age of twenty-seven he was able to write to Lavater who had become a pastor: 'Here is a bit of unadorned vanity for you: to be the greatest painter of my age, says Reynolds, I need only to go to Italy for a few years.' That spring he went to Italy, transferred his interest from literature to art and stayed eight years. In Rome, he lay on his back in the Sistine Chapel, day after day, enthralled by Michelangelo's paintings and (he sometimes added) recovering from the dissipations of the city. He was intoxicated by Michelangelo. He dressed like him, mimicked him and, when struck by a strange thought, would call out 'Michelangelo!'

At the age of thirty-eight Fuseli returned, in 1779, to London: for his whirlwind disagreements and his rages, he became known as 'the wild little hectoring Swiss-man' and, for his cultivation of terror in painting, as 'Painter in ordinary to the Devil', a nickname of which he was proud. London was his home for the rest of his long life. He first met Blake around 1782. Some five years later, after Flaxman went to Italy, the friendship of Fuseli and Blake was very close 'for a season' of about twelve years. During this time, Fuseli's reputation as an artist grew. His picture of 'The Nightmare'—a product of his insight that 'One of the most unexplored regions of art are dreams', as he wrote in his series of aphorisms—was a sensation in 1782. He was elected an Associate of the Royal Academy in 1788. As artists, Blake and he each influenced the other. Fuseli's dramatic drawings of soaring figures, with one leg foreshortened and the other outstretched, helped Blake to develop his free use of anatomy. Fuseli took back from Blake extensions of his own manner and acknowledged that 'Blake is damned good to steal from!' Fuseli, who objected on principle to mysticism in poetry, virtually ignored Blake as a poet, while accepting him as a painter and engraver.

Fuseli was a member of the radical circle of Godwin, Paine, Priestley and Mary Wollstonecraft (who pursued Fuseli for a while, although he had recently and happily married Sophia Rawlins, one of his models), and he drew Blake closer to Joseph Johnson, their publisher and Fuseli's intimate friend. In that era, when publishers were also booksellers, bookshops were meeting-places for writers. Gilchrist says that Johnson, who had employed

Blake as an engraver since 1780, gave 'plain but hospitable weekly dinners at his house, No. 72 St Paul's Churchyard, in a little quaintly shaped upstairs room.' Blake sometimes came to these Tuesday dinners.

He was stimulated by the intellectual ideas of Fuseli, who knew eight languages, owned a considerable library of ancient authors and wrote articles regularly for Joseph Johnson's literary magazine *The Analytical Review*. Fuseli probably did not regard Blake's ideas with absolute seriousness. On art, they agreed that outline is superior to colour, that portrait-painting is contemptible and that the truly great artist does not draw from nature. 'Damn Nature!' Fuseli exclaimed, 'she always puts me out'; and in the last year of his life Blake declared: 'Natural Objects always did & now do weaken, deaden & obliterate Imagination in Me.' Fuseli regarded himself as a visionary: 'I see the vision of all I paint—and I wish to Heaven I could paint up to what I see', but he thought that Blake let himself go too much in seeing visions. All the many disagreements of Fuseli and Blake about art sprang from their conflicting beliefs about its origins. Fuseli distinguished art from religion: Blake identified art with religion. Fuseli objected to mystical views of art—'You know I hate superstition'—whereas Blake believed that the artist's power is 'the gift of God'.

Johnson's publication in 1788 of Fuseli's very free adaptation of Lavater's *Aphorisms* was highly successful. Blake's excitement is clear from the notes and underlinings he made in his own copy with the declaration: 'I write from the warmth of my heart, & cannot resist the impulse I feel to rectify what I think false in a book I love so much & approve so generally.' Many of the aphorisms evoke his shining enthusiasm: 'Pure gold!', 'This was Christ', 'Bravo!', 'Sweet!', 'Noble!', 'This is heavenly', 'Most Excellent!' Lavater's 'Keep him at least three paces distant who hates bread, music, and the laugh of a child' is, to Blake, 'The best in the book!' Many aphorisms he marks 'Uneasy', sometimes with additions: for instance, after reading that a good man's 'enemies are characters decidedly bad', Blake notes, 'I fear I have not many enemies.' Other aphorisms move him to declare 'I hate scarce smiles: I love laughing' and 'Damn sneerers!' and, after reading about the worldly pietist who crawls, 'I hate crawlers.' He reveals his ardour in: 'Noble! But Mark! Active Evil is better than Passive Good', his frankness in: 'I know not what hiding love means', and his devotion to a woman whose ruling passion is not vanity in: 'Such a woman I adore.' One aphorism prompts him to show the contents of his pockets: 'I seldom carry money in my pockets; they are generally full of paper', and another to define hell as 'the being shut up in the possession of corporeal desires which shortly weary the man, *for* ALL LIFE IS HOLY.' Blake reveals himself in his notes on the *Aphorisms* as a spiritual, shrewd and practical man who responds warmly to love, hates hypocrisy, is passionate and direct in his opinions, but not naïve. Lavater disappoints him by failing to see that 'whatever is Negative is Vice' and that 'all Act is Virtue': 'the origin of this mistake in Lavater & his contemporaries is, They suppose that Woman's Love is Sin; in consequence all the Loves & Graces with them are Sin.'

Blake's reading, at this time, included theological books by Emanuel Swedenborg, the Swedish scientist and mystic to whose beliefs his father and elder brother James may have adhered. Unfortunately there is no evidence that Blake ever met Swedenborg, who died in London a few months before Blake's apprenticeship to Basire began in 1772. But certainly Blake was inspired by Swedenborg's works, describing them as 'well worthy the attention of Painters and Poets; they are foundations for grand things'; and for a short time Blake and his wife became members of the New Jerusalem Church, a sect inspired by Swedenborg's writings.

Swedenborg, who was born in 1688, was a most versatile and distinguished man. From 1734, he studied anatomy to discover the nature of the soul and spirit, and he travelled in Europe seeking anatomical knowledge. Enlightened by visions and dreams during these years, he was, so he later wrote, 'introduced by the Lord first into the natural sciences', and thus prepared for the opening of heaven to him in 1745. This revelation filled him with insight into the spiritual world, and he devoted the rest of his life to interpreting the scriptures, in many books. He was gifted with second sight and conversed with spirits of the dead. In London, 'the New Jerusalem gentleman', as he was called, was visited in 1769 by three enthusiasts who were then inspired to translate his voluminous works from Latin into English.

Many of Swedenborg's ideas are Neoplatonic, and the concept of a heavenly man, comparable with Boehme's heavenly Adam and the Cabbala's Adam Kadmon, appears in his work. He believed, like Boehme, that man was originally androgynous and that God maintains life's contraries in equilibrium. In Blake's copy of Swedenborg's *Wisdom of Angels Concerning Divine Love and Divine Wisdom*, Swedenborg's discussion of the reaction of man, the source of all evil, against God, the source of all good, prompts Blake to add: 'Good & Evil are here both Good & the two contraries Married.' Moved to greater eloquence by Swedenborg's reference to science as the source of understanding, Blake begins his longest note: 'Study Sciences till you are blind, Study intellectuals till you are cold, Yet science cannot teach intellect. Much less can intellect teach Affection.' He also reacts to Swedenborg's theory that two suns are necessary to creation: a spiritual, living sun, the source of love and intelligence, or life; and a natural, dead sun, the source of nature, or the receptacles of life. This, says Blake, is 'False philosophy according to the letter, but true according to the spirit'. 'The dead Sun,' he remarks, 'is only a phantasy of evil Man.' Swedenborg, like Lavater, moves Blake to assert the natural purity of love: 'it was not created impure & is not naturally so.' Finally Blake notes: 'Heaven & Hell are born together.'

Swedenborg believed that members of all the churches could share his beliefs; he never tried to found a sect. Nevertheless, in Easter week 1789 sixty or seventy believers met and signed a paper to declare their faith in the truths revealed to Swedenborg and to approve the establishment of the New Jerusalem Church. Among them were 'W. Blake' and 'C. Blake'. Thirty-two resolutions were unanimously adopted. They included assertions that the Old Church (which means *all* the other churches) is dead; any worship not addressed to the Divine Humanity, Jesus Christ, is lamentable; good conjugal love is better than any other; on the death of the material body (which will never be reassumed) man rises again in his spiritual body, the perfect human form.

After this conference, however, the Blakes withdrew from the new sect, and from this time onwards Blake did not worship in any church. Soon he was noting scornfully in the margin of Swedenborg's recent book, on *Divine Providence*: 'Lies & Priestcraft' and 'Predestination after this Life is more Abominable than Calvin's, & Swedenborg is Such a Spiritual Predestinarian. . . . Cursed Folly!' All Blake's notes on this book are critical, and soon he was exuberantly mocking Swedenborg and his followers in *The Marriage of Heaven and Hell*, a striking, paradoxical satire which exposes them as arrogant believers in predestination. Probably Blake had always been uneasy about some aspects of Swedenborg, in whom he found repugnant a streak of smugness and materialism. Copies of Swedenborg's works were sent to Joseph Johnson, in whose bookshop Blake would have discussed them with such critical writers as Fuseli, Godwin and the free-thinker Joseph Priestley. Within the sect itself, opinions clashed about how Swedenborg's writings on concubines should be interpreted. Some believers held that if a husband and wife did not agree, they might separate, and the man take a concubine. This sexual debate may have given rise to the gossip that Blake proposed to take a concubine, but that Mrs Blake cried and so he gave up the plan. Blake's theoretical approval of free love, revealed in his writing, is far more liberal than any Swedenborgian attitude: yet there is no evidence that, although childless, he ever planned to take a concubine, indulged in free love or was unfaithful to his wife. Blake was too independent to have stayed within any church, but he had absorbed much from Swedenborg. Years later, while still reacting against Swedenborg's belief in predestination and eternal death, he wrote admiringly: 'O Swedenborg! strongest of men, the Samson shorn by the Churches.' Blake's withdrawal from the congregation did not disturb his close friendship with two committed, devout Swedenborgians: Butts, who lived very close to him in a fine large house in Great Marlborough Street, and Flaxman.

Blake chose his spiritual teachers from the visionaries, artists and writers who burned with what he believed to be the true holy fire. Too constructive ever to learn uncritically, he took from them the inspiration that he wanted, but demanded his independence to make something new. Los, Blake's personification of the creative faculty in man, declares in *Jerusalem*:

I must Create a System or be enslav'd by another Man's.
I will not Reason & Compare: my business is to Create.

All sorts of slavery appalled Blake, and his works can be seen as variations on the theme of liberty and enslavement. The freedom that he considered most essential was spiritual freedom. His friend Samuel Palmer later recorded: 'He was fond of the works of St Theresa, and often quoted them with other writers on the interior life.' He owned, wrote Frederick Tatham, 'books well thumbed and dirtied by his graving hands in Latin, Greek, Hebrew, French, and Italian, besides a large collection of works of the mystical writers'. According to Palmer, 'The Bible, he said, was the book of liberty and Christianity the sole regenerator of nations'.

In the Europe of 1789, however, a political impulse like the American fervour inspired the people of France to seek life, liberty and happiness by revolution. Parisians seized the Bastille in July and peasants set fire to the archives: lies went up in smoke, for, as Blake wrote nine years later, 'Nothing can be more contemptible than to suppose Public RECORDS to be True.' In August the Assembly began to draft a Declaration of the Rights of Man and Citizen, incorporating the principles of Voltaire, Rousseau, Jefferson and Paine. The Declaration expressed a belief in freedom consistent with Blake's view that 'the Staminal Virtues of Humanity' should have liberty to act except when this involves 'the hindering of act in another'. Blake sympathized ardently with the revolution. He always, according to Gilchrist, claimed to be 'a faithful Son of Liberty; and would jokingly urge in self-defence that the shape of his forehead made him a republican. "I can't help being one," he would assure Tory friends, "any more than you can help being a Tory: your forehead is larger above; mine, on the contrary, over the eyes." ' The symbol of liberty was the red cap; in 1789, perhaps Blake wore one when he walked in the streets.

In that year he wrote *Tiriel*, his first attempt at myth-making and the first of his prophetic books—prophecy, in Blake's use of the word, being a revelation of eternal truths. This narrative poem is an attack on aged, hypocritical tyranny. Tiriel is the blind king of the material west. For the lamentable state of man, 'A worm of sixty winters creeping on the dusky ground', he blames the restrictive upbringing of children. He eventually curses his father and, still cursing, dies. Though the lines offer no hope, a glimmer of it is possible in the vines of ecstasy springing up round Tiriel's dead body in the last of Blake's twelve watercolour illustrations. As if intended for engraving, these illustrations are painted in tones.

The poem is written in septenaries, long lines of fourteen syllables with seven beats. In his later prophetic books, Blake would manage to fill such lines with baroque splendour and resonance. *Tiriel* lacks comparable richness. The arid violence and horror of the action; the ominous characters with strange names from such sources as Icelandic Eddas, Cornelius Agrippa, William Stukeley's *Abury, A Temple of the British Druids* and Swedenborg; the speeches which echo tones from the Bible, Shakespeare, Milton and Ossian; the dreamily epic landscape of melodrama and death— these formidable ingredients produce an atmosphere of sterile languor until (in lines written two or three years after the rest of the poem) vivid images, rhetorical questions and interesting rhythms give vitality to the final speech:

> Why is one law given to the lion & the patient Ox. . . .
> The child springs from the womb; the father ready stands to form
> The infant head, while the mother idle plays with her dog on her couch.

Blake was writing against slavery: spiritual, political, artistic and social. His layers of symbolism interact to produce a richness missing from the surface of the poem. Presumably dissatisfied with the work, he left it in manuscript, unengraved and unpublished.

In complete contrast to that unlovely attack on a world in which imagination has been murdered by repression, shines his exultant, endearing masterpiece of the same year, 1789, *Songs of Innocence*, surely a labour of love. In the 'Introduction', Blake shows himself inspired by the holy spirit of poetry first to pipe, then to sing and finally to write his songs with a reed pen dipped in watercolours. The poems that follow, perhaps owing some igniting sparks to such writers as Isaac Watts, Anna Barbauld and Mary Wollstonecraft, are radiant with ecstatic life. They need to be read in their illuminated form, each poem interacting and developing with Blake's coloured designs. The twenty-one songs in *An Island in the Moon* had shown him to be already at ease as a lyric writer, using a variety of forms to create many moods—satiric, pastoral, humorous—moving swiftly from the crude rumbustiousness of a drinking song to the child-like pathos of a street cry. Of the three songs from that work which reappear among the *Songs of Innocence*, only 'Holy Thursday' brings ironic undertones into the golden world of joy, fun, games and consolation.

His readers would be children, people of all ages whose hearts are innocent. He wrote, some years later: 'Innocence dwells with Wisdom, but never with Ignorance.' The knowledge possessed by the innocent child, as by the adult, arises from imagination, 'that is, God himself, The Divine Body . . . Jesus: we are his Members.' According to Blake's songs, 'Old John, with white hair', as well as 'Every child', has access to the world of holy, Arcadian Innocence, where the shepherd is identified with Christ, the good shepherd. This world of Innocence has its sorrows: the little black boy does not expect the little white boy to love him until their souls are freed from their bodies by death; another little boy is frightened and lonely; a motherless young chimney-sweep has to go out to work in the dark early morning; but there is sympathy for all in the full humanity of Jesus, who lives on in 'the human form divine'; there is consolation for all in the life of imagination; and there is joy for all in the chorus, shared by the whole of creation, in the youthful 'Laughing Song'. The innocent world is benevolently guarded. Sexual ecstasy has led to happy fruition. The young are tenderly cared for and the lost are found again.

However, shadows of Blake's London creep into his Arcadia. The children of 'Holy Thursday' and 'The Chimney Sweeper' in *Songs of Innocence* have been conditioned by their experiences in the city. Six thousand uniformed children, from all the London charity schools, would assemble for an annual service in St Paul's Cathedral, on specially erected stands, to hear a sermon and to sing hymns. To the public, this ritual seemed to be a sublime display of national munificence and charity. 'Holy Thursday' can, perhaps, be read without Blake's latent irony adding poignance to the glow of the children's radiant youth, or doubt as to the wisdom of the aged guardians. Similarly, his innocent sweep reveals little of the horror of working up the chimney, even though the boy has been sold to a life that feels like being locked in a black coffin. As an old shepherd sings in a poem Blake wrote around 1787:

> Innocence is a winter's gown;
> So clad, we'll abide life's pelting storm
> That makes our limbs quake, if our hearts be warm.

Flogged and half starved at charity boarding-schools, terrified and half stifled up soot-caked chimneys, many London children—girls as well as boys—suffered agonies. Blake knew this. The firm, intense joy of his songs rings out, beguiling the ear of Experience before any embittering visions of bruises on children's flesh, and of bleeding sores on callow knees and elbows, can intrude to spoil the music. Indeed, Blake may have intended his *Songs of Innocence* to provoke, satirically, the experienced readers who had lapsed into callousness and to reproach them 'with the errors of acquired folly'. Shortly before Blake's death, an anthology of protest at the lot of child sweeps, *The Chimney-Sweeper's Friend, and Climbing-Boy's Album* edited by James Montgomery, included 'The Chimney Sweeper', which was said to have been 'Communicated by Mr Charles Lamb, from a very rare and curious little work . . . Blake's *Songs of Innocence*'.

By presenting his *Songs* as he did, Blake enhanced them in a highly personal way (*2–5*). A medieval illuminated manuscript is not the product of a single mind that created words and decoration, but Blake's illuminated books are. He used visual symbols to add new dimensions to lyric symbols. For the *Songs of Innocence* he based his lettering on conventional Roman type, and applied superb artistry to integrating his decorations with his script. His visual symbols reward careful reading as richly as his words do. Every page is alive with trees, tendrils, flowers or thrusting forms which resemble flames and growing vegetation. Human life is engendered by flame-like forms such as illuminate the pages of 'The Blossom' and 'The Divine Image'. Birds and angels of joy fly ecstatically; and Blake himself, in his broad-brimmed hat, leans against the I of Innocence on the title-page and plays his pipe. The thirty-one plates that he etched for this work show mastery of the long, laborious technique already used for printing *There is no Natural Religion* and *All Religions are One*. For *Songs of Innocence*, Gilchrist says, 'the poet and his wife did everything in making the book— writing, designing, printing, engraving—everything except manufacturing the paper: the very ink, or colour rather, they did make.' The colouring in the early copies is very simple, in the later more elaborate. Mrs Blake stitched the loose leaves into paper covers, generally by lacing a cord through holes punctured an inch or two apart.

By the same process Blake completed the eight plates of *The Book of Thel*, and dated it 1789. This strong and delicate poem shows an innocent, unborn human soul, represented by the maiden, Thel, grieved by the transience of life, confronted by experience and recoiling in horror from the problems that await her on earth. During her contemplation of life she meets and speaks with symbolic beings, in this moist world of generation. They are spiritual forms of the virgin Lily of the Valley, the young Cloud, the infant Worm and its motherly Clod of Clay. All these, visualized as human shapes in the world of mutability, reveal to Thel the richness of their spiritual and physical lives: they give themselves to others. 'Every thing that lives Lives not alone nor for itself.' The Worm embodies Blake's belief that 'God is in the lowest effects as well as in the highest causes; for he is become a worm that he may nourish the weak.' The matron Clay, mother of the Worm, invites Thel to enter her house, the earth of Experience. The limpid pastoral world, which has been created in gently undulating verse, is instantly transformed with melodramatic violence: 'The eternal gates' terrific porter lifted the northern bar.' Through imagination, symbolized by the north, Thel enters the world of Experience. It is a visionary charnel house, a chamber of horrors. Here Thel finds her own grave. Like Plato's cave, it is a symbol for this world. She listens to the voice of sorrow: it breathes questions which probe the difficulties of life, its treacheries, appetites and restrictions. Appalled at the prospect of Experience, horrified by adolescent doubts which are already her own, Thel flees back to the spiritual world. She has chosen not to give herself as infant, child, bride, mother or corpse.

The apparently simple narrative of the poem can be read, on one level, as a distillation of myths and ideas given currency by Neoplatonists and alchemists. A source of inspiration is likely to have been Thomas Taylor's translation, in 1788, of Porphyry's treatise *On the Cave of the Nymphs*. In this, the soul descends from eternity for its brief existence in the temporal world and then returns to everlasting life. There is no evidence for the speculation that Mrs Blake ever suffered a miscarriage or a still-birth of a baby daughter, to whom *The Book of Thel* might be an elegy.

Blake sold more copies of *The Book of Thel* than of most of his prophetic books. Even so, the known copies made by him or Mrs Blake total less than twenty, at least twelve of them dating from the first five years after engraving. His method with such works was to keep the copper plates handy: he generally could not afford to advertise, but if and when a customer appeared Blake made the prints and coloured them. Though his later copies of this book are more richly coloured than his earlier copies, variations are less extreme than in some of his other works. In 1793 he asked three shillings for a copy; in 1818, two guineas; and in 1827, the year of his death, three guineas. His customers included Stothard, Cumberland and Butts.

While he was still living in Poland Street, Blake's awareness of the pain and complexity of life, his compassion for the plight of individuals whom he saw in the London streets, and his indignation against the smug callousness of society, moved him to write *Songs of Experience*. At the same time, his disillusionment with Swedenborg was finding vent in the satirical laughter of *The Marriage of Heaven and Hell*, another book that he would soon be producing in illuminated form. Meanwhile, his commercial work continued. In 1789 he made three of the eight hundred engravings for Lavater's *Essays on Physiognomy*. Fuseli supervised the publication of the English version of this vast and intriguing book.

In the autumn of 1790 the Blakes moved from Poland Street and its comparatively built-up neighbourhood to a much more open part of London: Lambeth, on the Surrey bank of the Thames, over the water from Westminster Abbey and the Houses of Parliament. About thirty-five minutes' walk from his old haunts near Golden Square and across Westminster Bridge stood the terrace house that Blake moved into, on the east side of Hercules Road. Lambeth was an area of fields, meadows and marshes, between Blackfriars Bridge to the north, and to the south, Lambeth Palace. Only beside the roads and lanes were there buildings, between was open space. Poplars and other ample trees provided 'Lambeth's shades', in which Blake delighted. His new neighbourhood, where he was to live for ten years, influenced his life and work profoundly.

Hercules Road runs from Westminster Bridge Road down to Lambeth Road: and Hercules Buildings (19), built since Blake's childhood, consisted of twenty-six attached houses. His, number thirteen, was one of the largest. He valued the space, 'a whole House to range in': four storeys counting the basement. The small, square rooms were light and well proportioned, with walls panelled to a height of three feet, marble mantelpieces and pleasant classic touches to the doors and windows. The many cupboards were useful for storing copper plates and engraver's tools, and in the small back-garden grew a vine and a fig tree. Down Hercules Road, after a turn to the right at the Charity School where children lived by sweated labour, beside the river rose Lambeth Palace, residence of the Archbishop of Canterbury. This should have been a source of spiritual light, 'Jerusalem's Inner Court'. At the top of Hercules Road the dome of St Paul's loomed up from over the Thames. On the right of the five-road junction, Asylum Cross, stood an institution which appalled Blake: the Royal Asylum for Female Orphans (21), a workhouse built on the site of the old Hercules Tavern. At the Asylum, girls between nine and twelve were supposed to be trained for domestic service, to be taught to read and write and to understand the four first rules of arithmetic. On the street corners bordering the north side of Asylum Cross were three rather seedy pleasure gardens, degenerating after their more palmy days: the Flora Tea Gardens, the Temple of Flora and the Apollo Gardens.

In *Milton*, a poem which was first inspired in Lambeth, Blake alludes to these places, his mundane but deeply significant surroundings. Using the name Tirzah to represent the mother of death, he surveys the harvest of human decadence, corruption and hardship:

> Beginning at Jerusalem's Inner Court, Lambeth, ruin'd and given
> To the detestable Gods of Priam, to Apollo, and at the Asylum
> Given to Hercules, who labour in Tirzah's Looms for bread.

In Lambeth creative poetic power, which he symbolized in the visionary form of Los, appeared to him (*10*). Blake stooped to fasten his shoe before walking out to seek inspiration for his poem *Milton* in the Vale of Lambeth:

> And Los behind me stood, a terrible flaming Sun, just close
> Behind my back. I turned round in terror, and behold!
> Los stood in that fierce glowing fire, & he also stoop'd down
> And bound my sandals on.

To Blake's ingenious mind, with its love of layers of meaning and its alertness to the spiritual essence of 'ordinary' life, the very name 'Lambeth' revealed its rich nature. *Beth* in Hebrew means 'house', so Lambeth is the house of the Lamb, to Christians a house of liberty. Therefore Blake closely identified Lambeth with his manifold symbol of liberty, of the divine vision in every individual, of the perfect society and of communion with God: Jerusalem, the bride of the Lamb. Blake spent a wonderfully productive decade in 'lovely Lambeth', where he stayed until 1800.

In its everyday cruelties, however, Lambeth was far from Jerusalem. A close neighbour of the Blakes was Philip Astley, rough-rider and breaker-in of horses, a sergeant-major turned circus-owner: energetic, rude and hot-tempered. Blake, looking out of his window one day, saw in Astley's garden a boy hobbling along with a log tied to his foot, as if he were a horse or an ass to be kept from straying. Blake called his wife and asked her about this.

The boy, she assumed, was being punished for some negligence. Blake was furious. Indignantly he strode out and demanded the boy's release from miseries unfit for a slave, let alone an Englishman. The boy was freed and Blake went home, to be followed by Astley, who had heard of Blake's interference and came to demand by what authority he had dared to intervene. Blake replied so warmly that he and Astley nearly came to blows: but eventually Astley, pacified, came to see that the boy's punishment was too degrading and to appreciate Blake's humaneness.

The plight of other children who lived close to him in the Lambeth Charity School and the Asylum continued to impassion Blake. They were slaves of sweated labour. The orphans in the Asylum sat at spinning wheel and loom, and in *Jerusalem* he wrote:

> Tho' hungry, they labour: they rouze themselves anxious
> Hour after hour labouring at the whirling Wheel.
>
> Their work is a drug, both stimulant and opiate. They weep . . .
>
> Yet they regard not pity & they expect no one to pity.

Blake pitied. He also, in his writings after the French Revolution, defied tyranny and fear. He was working among politically sympathetic friends, but there is no evidence that he was ever a close associate of Joseph Johnson's revolutionary writers: Priestley, Mary Wollstonecraft, Godwin, Tom Paine and Joel Barlow—the American who wrote an epic, *The Vision of Columbus*, before he came to Europe in 1788. Radical ferment in England, following the French Revolution, evoked repression and persecution by the government. Edmund Burke's attacks on the French Revolution prompted Paine to defend it in his political tract, *The Rights of Man*. This, one of the thirty-eight replies to Burke's *Reflections on the French Revolution*, appealed to the English to create a republic. In February 1791 Johnson printed the first volume of *The Rights of Man*, but he was so alarmed by Tory agitation and the risk of imprisonment (he was asthmatic) that he decided against publication. Another publisher produced the book and Johnson brought out an abridged version in August 1791. In that year he not only employed Blake as an engraver (two books by Mary Wollstonecraft, author of *A Vindication of the Rights of Man*, were among those then illustrated by Blake) but he also set up in type Blake's 'Book the First' of *The French Revolution*, 'A Poem in Seven Books'. Johnson got as far as printing the proofs of the first Book, but then abandoned the project. Perhaps Blake, a prey to 'Nervous Fear' of imprisonment, himself withdrew the poem, which he seems to have discontinued after the first Book.

It is an imaginative vision of historical events in Paris between 17 June and 15 July 1789. Blake gives epic diction to happenings described in newspapers; he moulds them to his prophetic pattern and adds apocalyptic overtones. He describes the defiance of the Third Estate which imposed its will on the King and eventually—after the fall of the Bastille—forced the with-drawal of troops from the region of Paris. Blake emphasizes the people's demand for peace: only when the 'war-breathing army' has been removed can liberty flourish.

The poem, intricately constructed on the pattern of the Book of Revela-tion, consists of a series of speeches and visions, some of them almost static tableaux like momentous historical and allegorical pictures. Passages of eloquent rhetoric spring out of the loose lines of eight or nine beats. The strength of the poem is in its ideas, dramatic structure and vivid word-pictures. Historical events and characters sometimes emerge in lurid and ironic outline. So the Archbishop of Paris, victim of Blake's hatred of repressive priests, is given a devilish role he did not play in history and rises from beneath 'In the rushing of scales and hissing of flames and rolling of sulphurous smoke'. 'Orleans, generous as mountains', passionately chal-lenges the Archbishop in terms which show the foundations of Blake's republican creed:

> go, merciless man! enter into the infinite labyrinth of another's brain
> Ere thou measure the circle that he shall run. Go, thou cold recluse, into the
> fires
> Of another's high flaming rich bosom, and return unconsum'd, and write
> laws.
> If thou canst not do this, doubt thy theories; learn to consider all men as
> thy equals,
> Thy brethren, and not as thy foot or thy hand, unless thou first fearest to
> hurt them.

American influence on the French Revolution is apparent to 'the ancientest Peer, Duke of Burgundy', himself representing the 'starry' forces which symbolize repressive power. Shall 'these mowers', he asks,

> From the Atlantic mountains mow down all this great starry harvest of six
> thousand years?

Burgundy, whose purple and crimson, colours of wine, are more ominously colours of blood, believes that 'the eagles of heaven must have their prey!' Against a vision of war and savagery, Blake sketches his ideal vision of universal peace and civilization. His spokesman is the messenger of the people, the Abbé de Sieyès, no repressive ecclesiastic but a wise priest of the future, who longs for the time when the millions of slaves to superstition, freed at last,

> May sing in the village, and shout in the harvest, and woo in pleasant gardens
> Their once savage loves, now beaming with knowledge, with gentle awe
> adorned;
> And the saw, and the hammer, the chisel, the pencil, the pen, and the
> instruments
> Of heavenly song sound in the wilds once forbidden.

D   49

This poem, clearer and more explicit than Blake's later prophetic books, is full of hope. Everybody is renewed. Even the King and his peers are reborn in the final sunrise, to join in the life of liberty and fraternity. The poem appears to be complete. Perhaps Johnson wanted an epic, which might prove less dangerous than a prophecy, and advertised a work that Blake would not agree to write. When blood began to flow in France and violence falsified Blake's prophecy, he spent no more time on the poem.

Dangerous days were to continue in England, while the French Assembly, in 1792, accorded French citizenship to Barlow and to Paine; but there seems to be no truth in the legend that Blake saved Paine's life by warning him to flee to France. In Leicester, a bookseller, described as a 'dirty little Jacobin', was sentenced to eighteen months imprisonment for selling *The Rights of Man*; but twenty thousand copies were estimated to have been sold in 1793 and Joseph Priestley helped the bookseller to edit a paper from jail. Nevertheless, Blake had cause to feel 'little blasts of fear' in an era when a revolutionary would, if discreet, avoid political subjects to keep himself out of Newgate.

Blake was always an adventurous, experimental craftsman, seeking new ways to give compelling visual form to his ideas. Soon after moving to Lambeth, he was evolving the method of colour-printing that was to yield a magnificent series of large prints in 1795. He drew a bold design in strong ink or colour on millboard, swiftly painted on it in colours mixed with a sticky medium (perhaps carpenter's glue diluted, instead of the egg yolk used in true tempera painting) and took an impression on paper. This blurred print, with its rough areas of colour, he then worked up with pen and ink, brush and watercolour. Subsequent prints from the millboard 'plate' were weaker in intensity and needed more work with pen and brush. Blake used this technique, Gilchrist says, 'because he could vary slightly each impression; and each having a sort of accidental look, he could branch out so as to make each one different. The accidental look they had was very enticing.'

Blake experimented with this 'monotype' technique in illuminating the prints of his *Songs of Innocence*. He used opaque, sticky paints on the relief-etched plates and achieved a rich, granulated quality. After making a few sets of prints in this way, he reverted to transparent washes of water-colour when illuminating his songs, but he sometimes used colour-printing and washes on the same plate.

His engraving for Johnson in the early 1790s included important commissions. Blake was extremely busy during these years with his own creations in words and designs, but his burin earned his daily bread. According to Frederick Tatham, the Blakes could afford not only necessities but comforts at that time, and they lived in a 'pretty clean house of eight or ten rooms and at first kept a servant.' After experiencing the inconvenience of employ-ing a servant, Mrs Blake managed without. She 'did all the work herself, kept the house clean, and herself tidy, besides printing all Blake's numerous engravings, which was a task alone sufficient for any industrious woman.' From Johnson came work for *The Botanic Garden*, a poem by Erasmus Darwin, which includes an engraving of 'The Fertilization of Egypt' by Blake, after a drawing by Fuseli (20). Engravings of the Portland Vase (the celebrated funeral vessel of blue and white glass) were made for this book by Blake, from drawings he did either of the vase itself or of a Wedgwood replica. The vase shows symbols of the Eleusinian mysteries, in which Thomas Taylor and Blake were particularly interested.

Blake was named among the 'eminent engravers' who, according to the publishers, Johnson and Edwards, 'promised their assistance' in making plates for a superlative edition of Milton, to be edited by William Cowper, the poet who had written *The Task*, and illustrated by Fuseli. Cowper's mental illness caused the project to be abandoned. In October 1791, the editor of the third volume of Stuart and Revett's *Antiquities of Athens*, one of the most eminent scholarly works of the time, and already thirty years in the making, wrote—at Cumberland's suggestion—to invite Blake to engrave William Pars's drawings for it. (As a boy, Blake had spent five years at the drawing school in the Strand run by William Pars's elder brother, Henry.) Blake replied later in October: 'tho' full of work he is glad to embrace the offer of engraving such beautiful things. . . .' He engraved four plates, from drawings which William Pars had made in Athens on a trip financed by the Dilettanti Society, and dated them 3 April 1792—some months later than he had hoped.

The letters that Blake wrote he composed with great care, but from time to time he was a reluctant correspondent. He neglected even so close a friend as Flaxman, neither did he answer letters from Captain John Sted-man, an adventurous character who had written and illustrated a book for which Blake was making engravings. Through this work, Blake and Stedman became friends.

Stedman, thirteen years older than Blake, had been an officer in the Scots Brigade, a regiment of mercenary troops in Holland. While he was indulging in riotous living in Holland, the cruelty of European planters in Surinam (Dutch Guiana), on the north-east coast of South America, pro-voked their Negro slaves to rebel. Stedman took part in an expedition to protect the planters. In Surinam, he fell in love with Joanna, a beautiful mulatto slave girl, aged fifteen, natural daughter of a Dutch planter. When Stedman became dangerously ill, she nursed him. He married her and she bore him a son, Johnny. On the return of the Dutch Scots Brigade to Europe in 1777, Stedman could not afford to buy Joanna's freedom from slavery: though they were both grief-stricken, he left her behind. In Holland, he remarried and retired from the army because of ill-health. With his

Dutch wife, and Johnny who had joined him from Surinam, he came to England and settled at Tiverton in Devon. There he raised a family and in 1790 completed his *Narrative of a Five Years' Expedition against the Revolted Negroes of Surinam from the year 1772 to 1777*. Johnson published it in two volumes in 1796, and at least sixteen of the eighty-six plates, after Stedman's own drawings, were engraved by Blake, who undertook nearly all those which show how the slaves were treated (23).

In Surinam Stedman was revolted by the brutal treatment of the Negroes. His *Narrative* records that his 'ears were stunned with the clang of the whip and the dismal yells.' As an army officer, whose task was to subdue the slaves, he could do little to reduec the horrible punishments that he saw: but he could—and did—write a book to reveal the abuse of power. The drawings that he made in Surinam of people, animals and plants were distributed among eight engravers, including Francesco Bartolozzi, RA, engraver to the King.

On 1 December 1791, Stedman noted in his *Journal*: 'About this time I received above forty engravings from London, some very well, some very ill. . . . Now the use of sugar is laid aside in Great Britain, in order to enforce the abolition of the Slave Trade. [A bill to abolish it had been rejected by the Commons in April, but the abolitionist movement continued to gather impetus.] I wrote to the engraver, Blake, to thank him twice for his excellent work, but never received any answer.'

Stedman had become a friend of the Blakes by 1794, when he gave a blue sugar cruse to Mrs Blake and was with Blake at a dinner party which included Johnson and Bartolozzi whose engravings Blake found soft and monotonous. Stedman painted portraits—he gave an oil portrait to Blake— and wrote verses. Because he wrote, drew, and opposed slavery he was redeemed, in Blake's mind, from the taint of soldiering, and he was an acceptable visitor to 13 Hercules Buildings.

Blake saw many Negroes in the London streets: runaway slaves, their flesh indelibly branded with their owners' marks; paid servants, apprentices, vagrants. Many of the Negroes who had served with the British forces in America were sent to London at the end of the war and became beggars. Although over four hundred were shipped off to Sierra Leone, many stayed in London and continued to be a social problem for years as 'vagrant blacks'. Conversation with Stedman filled in the background of such poor outcasts. Blake's passionate *Visions of the Daughters of Albion*, which he was writing and engraving in 1792, was affected in its attitude to slavery by the cruel subjects of his illustrations for Stedman's book, and in its narrative by Stedman's marriage to Joanna. Blake's poem is a protest against various restrictions besides the slavery of Negroes, and a plea for liberty in religion, morality and sex. It shows deep sympathy towards women, and attacks their oppressors. Life's cruelties and restrictions, which Blake sees to be all interrelated, prompt his challenging motto on the title page: 'The Eye sees more than the Heart knows.' Only when human hearts experience true feeling will there be freedom from the tyrannies we see every day.

Using names derived from Macpherson's *Ossian* and African words in Stedman's *Narrative*, Blake tells in stirring poetry, with a biblical ring, how the maiden Oothoon, 'the soft soul of America', uncertain whether to give herself in love, accepts the persuasion of a golden flower and delightedly offers herself to her lover, Theotormon. America, land of freedom as well as of slavery, is an example in its liberty to the oppressed womanhood of England, 'the Daughters of Albion'. Oothoon's brief joy is shattered by Bromion, a figure of violent sea-storm: at sea, many slaves died on their passage from Africa. Bromion, tyrannous enslaver of 'the swarthy children of the sun', rapes her and scornfully offers her as a pregnant harlot for Theotormon to marry. Theotormon is jealous, but he rejects Oothoon as defiled. He ties her and Bromion back to back in the cave of mortal life and then, her accepted but wronged lover, he sits despairingly on guard at its entrance beside the sea of time and space:

> beneath him sound like waves on a desart shore
> The voice of slaves beneath the sun, and children bought with money,
> That shiver in religious caves beneath the burning fires
> Of lust, that belch incessant from the summits of the earth.

Stedman's Joanna enslaved in Surinam and the child bound to sweated labour in Lambeth are alike: victims of society's greed and of its loveless, lustful repression. Oothoon calls for Theotormon's eagles to rend away her defiled flesh so that she may reflect his image on her 'pure transparent breast'. They rend her body and 'her soul reflects' his puritanical smile (22).

Oothoon tries to give Theotormon the insight into love that the golden flower gave her; but he is too dejected and timid to trust himself to the experience of living. His will is tormented and paralysed by the white man's Christian theology which tells him that his love is impure. Bromion doubts whether there is any aspect of life beyond the senses, any pleasure that is not material, any freedom from rigid laws.

Finally, Oothoon appeals to Urizen, symbol of reason, the law-giving restrainer of impulse, the avenging conscience:

> O Urizen! Creator of men! mistaken Demon of heaven!
> Thy joys are tears, thy labour vain to form men to thine image.

Blake may have derived Urizen's name from 'your reason', or from the Greek word (root of the English 'horizon') which means 'to limit'. Urizen, in Blake's thought, is the limiter of eternal delight: he created this world, using the limiting compasses. He cut man off from a life completely spiritual and imprisoned him in flesh. As the jealous God of the Old Testament he was the author of the Ten Commandments. Oothoon's plea to him, much of it magnificent rhetorical poetry, is addressed to the despot tyrannizing over love in the name of religious restraint. Loveless marriages, which Mary Wollstonecraft inveighed against as 'legal prostitution', cause Oothoon to lament with the bride who, burning with youth,

> is bound
> In spells of law to one she loathes . . .
> . . . & all the night
> To turn the wheel of false desire, and longings that wake her womb
> To the abhorred birth.

In contrast to this hell is the heaven of life freely lived and of love freely given in 'virgin bliss': that is, pure enjoyment. Virginity is not abstinence but innocence, the state of childhood and youth which frankly accept sensuality.

> Infancy! fearless, lustful, happy, nestling for delight
> In laps of pleasure: Innocence! honest, open, seeking
> The vigorous joys of morning light; open to virgin bliss.

The apparently respectable person teaches the innocent to fear and despise 'virgin bliss'.

Oothoon, though she has been raped, is still a virgin, 'Open to joy and to delight where ever beauty appears'. She tells Urizen, Father of Jealousy, that the places of religion and self-denial are the secret chambers where the virgin pines and the youth creates 'an amorous image In the shadows of his curtains and in the folds of his silent pillow'. Against such horrible darkness, 'impressed with reflections of desire', Oothoon cries: 'Love! Love! Love! happy happy Love! free as the mountain wind!' With this she contrasts the loveless marriage 'that drinks another as a sponge drinks water', a manifestation of

> self-love that envies all, a creeping skeleton
> With lamplike eyes watching around the frozen marriage bed.

Blake's mind was occupied at this time by the twin themes of freedom in love and freedom from jealousy. A number of the lyrics in his notebook show this. There is no external evidence to prove them autobiographical.

Oothoon's awareness of the undefilable nature of the soul is so complete that she will even provide girls for Theotormon to wanton with 'In lovely copulation': and she will watch without jealousy. In freedom, all living things 'behold their eternal joy'. Every morning she wails to him to join in life's happiness: 'Arise, and drink your bliss, for every thing that lives is holy!' He remains unmoved, 'conversing with shadows dire', and for the third and last time comes the poem's refrain: 'The Daughters of Albion hear her woes, & eccho back her sighs.'

In Blake's illustrations, Oothoon is white, as befits the soul of slavery, whether its fleshly 'cloud' is the body of a European, an African or an

American slave. She could say, with the little black boy in *Songs of Innocence*, 'I am black, but O! my soul is white.' Blake was familiar with arguments presented in parliamentary debates on the slave trade. In April 1792, the Commons passed a motion calling for the end of it. Blake expressed hope by painting a rainbow on his title-page.

He continued to work on his illuminated *Songs of Experience*, a task of perhaps five years, ending in 1794. In these songs he explores the problems of good and evil. He balances individual poems and the whole series against *Songs of Innocence*, so 'Shewing the Two Contrary States of the Human Soul.' He combined both series of songs in one volume, moving a few poems from *Innocence* to *Experience* and varying the order of the fifty-four plates in different copies of the book, which he continued to print and colour, when commissioned by customers, until the end of his life. The essence of his thought on life before and after the Fall is condensed into the complete *Songs*. The Fall is experienced by every person. It occurs in each individual's life at adolescence and changes Innocence into Experience. So Blake's frontispiece to the whole book, which shows Adam and Eve against flames expelling them from Eden, tells the story of everyone. The frontispiece to *Songs of Experience* shows a youth advancing. In Blake's symbolism, the right hand and foot usually act spiritually, the left materialistically: this youth's right foot is forward because his journey into Experience is spiritual. On his head he balances the Covering Cherub of corrupt selfhood. Beside him, baleful ivy climbs up a tree. The title-page shows two young people mourning beside the corpses of their parents, while loving figures above are parted by spiky leaves.

Blake introduces the songs with 'the voice of the Bard', the prophet. God called to Adam in Eden: the Bard calls to fallen man in the modern world to awake from materialism and, in the free life of imagination, forsake the 'starry floor' of reason and the 'wat'ry shore' of time and space. Then day will break. Earth answers despairingly, imprisoned by reason and by restrictions on free love. The jealous creator of the material world, who brutally separated man from the divine unity and marked him for death, freezes the bones of earth in a heavy chain.

The paradox of love, in its selfless Innocence and selfish Experience, is condensed into the dozen lines of 'The Clod & the Pebble' in *Songs of Experience*. Blake expressed his theory of contraries, about the same time, in the sharp prose of *The Marriage of Heaven and Hell*: 'Without Contraries is no progression. Attraction and Repulsion, Reason and Energy, Love and Hate, are necessary to Human existence.' Some of the *Songs of Experience* are brilliantly condensed and show Blake as a master of lyric poetry. 'The Sick Rose' conveys, in eight short lines, the agony and ecstasy of love in a material world. The other flower lyrics are comparably disquieting. They sum up the frustrations of love beset by envy and hypocrisy. In 'My Pretty Rose Tree' the poet tells how he was offered the flowers of extra-marital love: he refused them, but nevertheless his wife—his pretty rose-tree—was jealous and reproachful. 'The Lilly' shows a more perfect love than 'The modest Rose'. These symbols, and the stories of discord that they imply, provide no adequate basis for believing that the childless married love of the Blakes was beset by any unusual torments, complexities or frustrations.

It is tempting, however, to read 'A Poison Tree' as a fragment of Blake's mental autobiography. A man ill-suited to repress anger, he contrasts in this poem the curative relief of wrath expressed, with the fatal hypocrisy of wrath concealed. The manuscript of this poem is ironically entitled 'Christian Forbearance'. Blake's Christ was a man like himself, passionate and open, made in the image of the poet. As he wrote more than twenty years later:

> The Vision of Christ that thou dost see
> Is my Vision's Greatest Enemy:
> Thine has a great hook nose like thine,
> Mine has a snub nose like to mine.

The design on the plate of 'A Poison Tree', which shows the poet's dead victim stretched out on the ground under the barren, weeping branches, is one of the most lurid in the book. The corpse lies as if crucified, like 'A Negro on the Rack' engraved by Blake for Stedman's *Narrative*. Illustrations to *Songs of Experience* are harsher than those to *Songs of Innocence*, and the lettering slopes rather more.

Blake's sense of social outrage is allied to his scorn of priest and king in 'The Chimney Sweeper'. This little child, unlike his counterpart in *Songs of Innocence*, though still happy at times, knows that he is the victim of hypocritical parents. They are smugly in church, praising the Establishment which approves of clothing him 'in the clothes of death'—rags and soot—and of sending him out to cry ' 'weep, 'weep!' in the snow. Among the most wretched children in London were those whose parents (perhaps gin-sodden) sold them to chimney-sweeps. A movement to protect such children had begun in 1760; but as late as 1824 the poet James Montgomery protested at the 'personal slavery' of the little sweeps, many of them no older than seven, a few as young as five when they were first made to climb up chimneys. Blake did not exaggerate the plight of the child-sweep, who, according to Montgomery, 'partakes in some degree of the fate of the negro.' One boy apprenticed to a Lambeth sweep was sent out at three a.m. in deep snow and harsh cold to sweep some chimneys at Norwood. He managed to sweep two chimneys, but on his way home he died of cold, as recorded in Montgomery's anthology of protest.

The plight of all poor children in a city of cold charity moved Blake to write 'Holy Thursday' in *Songs of Experience*. This poem is a stark attack on the wealthy country that allowed such wretchedness. To house the many unwanted children abandoned in the streets, and illegitimate children handed over to parish officers, charity-schools were crammed. In some of these unhappy boarding-schools, six or eight children had to share a bed. In all charity-schools there was pressure to keep the children subservient to those who were not the objects of charity. School uniform was constantly worn. At church twice on Sundays and at the Holy Thursday service the children sang hymns from their special books.

In 'London' (4), Blake expressed his concern for every Londoner, condemned to the 'charter'd' city where all life is ruled by business, itself the product of crippled minds. Blake looked below the surface of life to the essential miseries of mankind and he condensed them into horrifying images that should destroy complacency in Church and State. While 'the hapless Soldier's sigh Runs in blood down Palace walls' and pleads for an end of war, 'the youthful Harlot'—blasting the 'Infant's tear' and blighting 'the Marriage hearse'—invokes a purer social order in which marriage gives fulfilment and prostitution has no place. 'The Human Abstract' shows how fear of life's uninhibited richness breeds 'religious' approval of pity and mercy. These depend on keeping others unhappy. Hypocrisy of this sort was shown in the training of children from the workhouse for services of the lowest kind. The callous apprenticeship of some parish children was as inhumane as allowing others to die in infancy. Little girls, especially vulnerable, were often sent in their early teens as drudges, or domestic slaves, to the worst families. For instance, at the age of twelve a certain Anne Barnard was bound apprentice to a woman who cried old clothes in the street while her husband worked in a Lambeth pothouse. They lived in a garret in Westminster. Anne, left alone there to mind the baby, was raped by an inmate of the house.

In 'The Tyger' (5), Blake moves entirely into the visionary world. By superb artistry, he takes his readers with him to question the source of good and evil, and of their possible reconciliation. The enigmatic picture of the tiger below the poem is ferocious in some copies, tame in others, realistic in none—though Blake could have seen a live tiger had he wished, for animal shows were popular in London. In his youth, three tigers were on view in the Tower of London, and the entrance fee was threepence or a dog or cat as food for the lions and tigers. The roar of the tiger in Pidcock's menagerie could be heard in the Strand, and Stubbs's celebrated painting, 'The Tiger', was on view when Blake was a twelve-year-old pupil at Pars's. However Blake's Tyger came into his vision, he saw it 'Within the dark horrors of the Abysses': but he chose to depict the beast without the ravenous appetite that makes his later picture of the Ghost of a Flea, for example, a frightening creation.

In other *Songs of Experience*, Blake contrasts exultant freedom with repression by priest, father, nurse and schoolmaster. He considers how body is related to soul, and life to death. 'The Voice of the Ancient Bard', a poem which Blake moved from *Songs of Innocence*, concludes the sequence with a harp-song of affirmation calling to 'Youth of delight'. The new age is dawning. Doubt and 'clouds of reason' are dispelled, conflict is ended. Although many casualties have fallen by the way, the 'Image of Truth' is 'new born', and all survivors can exult in its nativity.

In a supplementary, abandoned plate, 'A Divine Image', Blake expresses utter disillusionment with humanity: there is nothing in man except cruelty, jealousy, terror and secrecy. Perhaps Blake made this uncoloured plate in a mood of despair at the war with France, which broke out in February 1793, less than a fortnight after the execution of Louis XVI. For Blake, despair had followed hope and joy. In September 1792, the anti-revolutionary armies of the European powers, commanded by the Duke of Brunswick in their attempt to invade France, had been routed at Valmy, while in Paris, France was proclaimed a republic. Blake celebrated this as a victory for the powers of truth, a dawn of enlightenment. He triumphantly wrote, in biblical poetic prose, 'A Song of Liberty', with joyful verses of stirring rhetoric. Orc, the fiery youth who embodies revolution, destroys the tablets of Urizen's law that upheld kings. He frees the horses of intellect and proclaims the defeat of the Austrian lion and the Prussian wolf:

> the son of fire in his eastern cloud, while the morning
> plumes her golden breast,
> Spurning the clouds written with curses, stamps the stony law to
> dust, loosing the eternal horses from the dens of night, crying:
> EMPIRE IS NO MORE! AND NOW THE LION & WOLF SHALL CEASE.

Blake included this song in *The Marriage of Heaven and Hell*, as a rousing finale to the work which consists of an introductory poem ('The Argument') and six sections of satirical prose. He probably began to write this highly original, provocative and assured presentation of his philosophy in 1789 and finished etching the twenty-seven illuminated plates around 1794. In this book, Blake in his early thirties reveals much of himself. Swedenborg's *Heaven and Hell and their Wonders as heard and seen by the Author* provided the title for his boisterous mockery of the Swede's doctrines. Blake did not attack any wildness in the 'Wonders' of Swedenborg, but the narrowness of his conventional, curbing mind. With impudent relish, Blake inverts established attitudes towards 'what the religious call Good & Evil. Good is the passive that obeys Reason. Evil is the active springing from Energy. Good is Heaven. Evil is Hell.' For Blake, obedience to reason is worship of heaven's restraining father, the 'good' God who binds man in materialism and hypocrisy: but obedience to imagination is enjoyment of hell's liberating son, the 'evil' devil who inspires art and energy.

On the basis of this creed, the satiric Blake of *An Island in the Moon* builds a dizzying structure of paradoxes. He shocks, amuses, and provokes thought. The title-page shows the infernal regions where a devil and an angel embrace against clouds and flames, while other figures soar into space and above them all, on earth, a couple walks. To Blake, as to the alchemists, in the words of Paracelsus: 'that which is above is like that which is beneath, and that which is beneath is like that which is above.' 'The Argument' declares that the paths of truth have been corrupted by false religion and the just man has been provoked to wrathful revolt. Then, below a picture of a nude woman bathing in flames of energy and above a picture of an infant's birth, Blake declares: 'As a new heaven is begun, and it is now thirty-three years since its advent, the Eternal Hell revives. And lo! Swedenborg is the Angel sitting at the tomb: his writings are the linen clothes folded up.' Swedenborg claimed that in 1757, the year of Blake's birth, he had been granted a revelation of the birth of a new age. That was thirty-three years previously: thirty-three, the age of Christ at his death and resurrection, and the age of Blake now, when he greets 'the return of Adam into Paradise' and the revival of hell's imaginative energies in himself. He casts aside the outworn creed of Swedenborg with its passive morality, shows that contraries inspire progression and proclaims the gospel of the new Messiah, the devil, whose voice declares these contraries to traditional religion:

1. Man has no Body distinct from his Soul; for that call'd Body is a portion of Soul discern'd by the five Senses, the chief inlets of Soul in this age.
2. Energy is the only life, and is from the Body; and Reason is the bound or outward circumference of Energy.
3. Energy is Eternal Delight.

Blake asserts: 'Those who restrain desire, do so because theirs is weak enough to be restrained; and the restrainer or reason usurps its place & governs the unwilling. And being restrain'd, it by degrees becomes passive, till it is only the shadow of desire. The history of this is written in Paradise Lost.' This section ends: 'Note: the reason Milton wrote in fetters when he wrote of Angels & God, and at liberty when of Devils & Hell, is because he was a true Poet and of the Devil's party without knowing it.'

There follows the first of five Memorable Fancies. These parody Swedenborg's Memorable Relations, narratives of what he saw and said when he was carried up to heaven. Swedenborg's snobbish angels and his prosaic hell provoked Blake to write with satiric zest: 'As I was walking among the fires of hell, delighted with the enjoyments of Genius, which to Angels look like torment and insanity, I collected some of their Proverbs. . . .' These Proverbs of Hell, aphorisms far more memorable than those by Lavater on man and by Fuseli on art, include:

Drive your cart and your plow over the bones of the dead.

The road of excess leads to the palace of wisdom.

The cistern contains: the fountain overflows.

The tygers of wrath are wiser than the horses of instruction.

The head Sublime, the heart Pathos, the genitals Beauty, the hands & feet Proportion.

Exuberance is Beauty.

Sooner murder an infant in its cradle than nurse unacted desires.

Truth can never be told so as to be understood, and not be believ'd.

No bird soars too high, if he soars with his own wings.

What is now proved was once only imagin'd.

Always be ready to speak your mind, and a base man will avoid you.

Damn braces: Bless relaxes.

Blake then describes how religious systems and priests came into being. He gives depth to his proverb: 'As the catterpiller chooses the fairest leaves to lay her eggs on, so the priest lays his curse on the fairest joys.' Eventually 'men forgot that All deities reside in the human breast', as imaginative ideals.

In the next Memorable Fancy, a dinner-party conversation with the prophets Isaiah and Ezekiel, Blake defines his own true function as prophet, poet, artist and craftsman. He looks forward to the impending apocalypse, when

the whole creation will be consumed and appear infinite and holy, whereas it now appears finite & corrupt.

This will come to pass by an improvement of sensual enjoyment.

But first the notion that man has a body distinct from his soul is to be expunged; this I shall do by printing in the infernal method, by corrosives, which in Hell are salutary and medicinal, melting apparent surfaces away, and displaying the infinite which was hid.

If the doors of perception were cleansed every thing would appear to man as it is, infinite.

For man has closed himself up, till he sees all things thro' narrow chinks of his cavern.

So Blake the poet, artist and craftsman aims to open man's perceptive organs and reveal infinity. He asserts that 'God only Acts and Is, in existing beings or Men.'

In another dramatic and vivid Memorable Fancy, Blake travels through rational Christianity with a Tory angel to the edge of a boundless void, the traditional hell. When the Leviathan of revolution swims towards them, the angel escapes by climbing up into the mill of rationalism, while Blake—the creative, open-minded, radical artist—remains alone and is rewarded by a vision. 'I found myself sitting on a pleasant bank beside a river by moonlight, hearing a harper, who sung to the harp; & his theme was: "The man who never alters his opinion is like standing water, & breeds reptiles of the mind." ' Blake joins the angel in the mill and after spectacular flights and revelations they quarrel briefly and part. 'Opposition is true Friendship,' Blake comments.

Blake next openly declares his attitude to Swedenborg:

Now hear a plain fact: Swedenborg has not written one new truth. Now hear another: he has written all the old falsehoods.

And now hear the reason. He conversed with Angels who are all religious, & conversed not with Devils who all hate religion, for he was incapable thro' his conceited notions.

. . . Any man of mechanical talents may, from the writings of Paracelsus or Jacob Behmen, produce ten thousand volumes of equal value with Swedenborg's, and from those of Dante or Shakespear an infinite number.

But when he has done this, let him not say that he knows better than his master, for he only holds a candle in sunshine.

A devil in the final Memorable Fancy expounds to an angel. The devil analyses the attitudes of Jesus and concludes: 'Jesus was all virtue, and acted from impulse, not from rules.' The angel is converted, embraces 'the flame of fire', becomes a devil and is now Blake's

particular friend; we often read the Bible together in its infernal or diabolical sense, which the world shall have if they behave well. I have also The Bible of Hell, which the world shall have [presumably from Blake's pen and copper plates] whether they will or no.

One Law for the Lion & Ox is Oppression.

After this assertion of the needs of individuals, Blake celebrates the triumph of political radicals everywhere with 'A Song of Liberty'. So ends the book whose sharp ambiguities, versatility and irreverent humour bubble with imaginative energy, the power that Blake hoped would be generated by this *Marriage*.

4

Passionate Workman
1793–1800

'I have labour'd hard indeed, & have been borne on angel's wings'

Blake's independence of thought may have led him to behave eccentrically, but not in the whimsical way that some stories about him suggest. Gilchrist writes that Thomas Butts, Blake's patron, called one day and found the Blakes sitting naked in the summer-house at the end of their garden. ' "Come in!" cried Blake; "it's only Adam and Eve, you know!" Husband and wife had been reciting passages from *Paradise Lost*, in character.' If there is truth in Gilchrist's dubious story, then the pair may have been testing, with their nude bodies, postures for use in Blake's designs. There is less warrant for the apocryphal story that the vine growing in the garden was deliberately left unpruned because Blake objected to interfering with nature. A more likely account, consistent with Blake's Proverb of Hell 'Where man is not, nature is barren', is that Mrs Blake trained the vine very carefully, and with her husband and the Flaxmans—who returned from Italy after seven years in 1794—sat under its branches from which hung clusters of ripe fruit for her wine-making. The fondness of the Blakes for the natural pleasures of the country is certainly shown by their long walks. After an early-morning start, they would walk far out, dine at an inn and return home the same evening after covering forty miles. A favourite route was through Croydon (still a compact, clean and cheerful Surrey town) to the fertile meadows of Walton-on-Thames, much of the way along lanes and footpaths.

Blake's speech was blunt and his manner open. According to George Richmond, the pious Flaxman asked Blake: 'How do you get on with Fuseli? I can't stand his foul-mouthed swearing. Does he swear at you?' 'He does,' Blake replied. 'And what do you do?' 'What do I do?' echoed Blake, 'why—I swear again! and he says astonished: "Vy, Blake, you are svaring!" but he leaves off himself!' Blake spoke openly of his visions, and naturally surprised his more prosaic listeners. His relief-etching (now usually known as 'Urizen Creating the Universe') of the bearded creator leaning out of the sun to strike the first circle of the earth with his golden compasses, was inspired by the vision which—according to Gilchrist—Blake declared 'hovered over his head at the top of his staircase' in 13 Hercules Buildings, where there was a large blank area of wall above a small window. He often said that this vision 'made a more powerful impression upon his mind than all he had ever been visited by.' Ghosts, Blake said, did not appear much to imaginative men. The only one he ever saw came stalking down the stairs one evening in Lambeth. Blake, Gilchrist wrote, was standing at the garden door, when he looked up and saw a horrible, grim figure descending, 'scaly, speckled, very awful'. Blake ran out of his house in terror. It is not surprising that tales about the oddities of this visionary artist, daring thinker, honest and outspoken man, should have been distorted and multiplied. Blake, the whimsical lunatic, never existed.

But Blake, the genius who ranks in stature as a writer with Chaucer, Spenser, Shakespeare and Milton, and as an English romantic artist stands supreme, was naturally beyond the full comprehension of even his closest friends.

One of these was Thomas Butts, a clerk in the office of the Commissary General of Musters (later called the War Office) whom Blake had come to know before leaving Poland Street. Butts (27) was a devoted buyer of his works. For many years he was to go on faithfully buying Blake's books and pictures, even when nobody else would, so building up a splendid collection and giving Blake encouragement and friendship. By the late 1790s, the Blakes and Buttses were meeting regularly on Tuesday evenings.

To show how it is possible to travel through life and through death in eternal happiness, Blake in 1793 engraved *For Children: The Gates of Paradise*, a tiny book comprising seventeen deceptively simple emblem pictures, briefly titled or captioned. They form a witty, provocative series, in the Renaissance tradition of emblem books. This book of visual riddles is for readers uncorrupted by materialism, and therefore childlike in their wisdom. Blake first drew his little designs in pencil in the sketch-book that he had inherited from his brother. By 1793 he had drawn something on almost every page left blank by Robert. He then turned the book round and, starting at the back, wrote in it the first drafts of *Songs of Experience* and other lyrics. The first words he wrote among Robert's drawings were dated June 1793, a time of war, economic disaster, bread riots, repression and general fear: 'I say I shan't live five years and if I live one it will be a Wonder.' His mood of despair was transient: in his line engraving 'War' or 'The Three Accusers', inscribed in the second state 'Our End is Come', dated the same month, it is his enemies, the rulers of Britain, who are enveloped in flames and agonized by fear. Blake himself, subversive but neglected, was alarmed by the persecution of Paine and of Joseph Priestley (the discoverer of oxygen and a Unitarian Minister): but despite his personal fears, he worked boldly on to open man's immortal eyes.

His hope that Joseph Johnson would publish *For Children: The Gates of Paradise* was unfulfilled. Only one of the five known surviving copies of the engraved book was certainly given to a child. Fuseli gave it to her, but not until thirteen years after the book's creation. Perhaps he had bought it partly to encourage his friend Blake, when it first came out, priced at three shillings. This, according to Blake's *Prospectus* of 10 October 1793, was the same price as *The Book of Thel* and *The History of England*, 'a small book of Engravings', no copy of which is now known. The costliest item, at twelve shillings, was 'Job, a Historical Engraving', in which the figure of Job's wife is very expressive. This large engraving shows Blake's early interest in the story of Job's sufferings.

Because *For Children: The Gates of Paradise* was not in demand, Blake carefully wrapped up his engraved plates and stored them safely, as was his custom. Many years later he revised and reprinted these enigmatic emblems.

Early in this decade, Blake's prophetic books achieved a new height of visual richness and power when he illuminated his relief etchings of *America: A Prophecy*. Joel Barlow's epic poem, *The Vision of Columbus*, in which Columbus prophetically visualizes the American war, may have contributed to Blake's symbolic account of the American revolution. Blake's text, written in a script of flowing beauty, is integrated into cloud-shapes which are part of the boldly dramatic pictures. In this book, which Blake may have been writing for some years before he dated his title-page 1793, the rebellious figure Orc develops in conflict with Albion's Angel, the spirit of England. Blake writes in fervour and confidence. Orc (*1*), imprisoned during the fourteen years between the publication of Rousseau's *Social Contract* in 1762 and the American Declaration of Independence, has been physically chained, though his spirit has soared and taken the forms (significant in alchemy) of eagle, lion, whale and serpent. Now he has reached puberty. He breaks free. 'The hairy shoulders rend the links; free are the wrists of fire.' He seizes the nameless daughter of his jailer, Urthona ('Earth Owner', the creative imagination, the Holy Spirit), impregnates her womb and engenders rebellious life on the American plains and throughout the world: 'In Mexico an Eagle, and a Lion in Peru.' The etched plate of the 'Preludium' shows Orc pushing himself out of a furrow in the ground, thrusting up wherever man struggles to be free, even if rebellion proves abortive as in Mexico and Peru.

The visionary figures that enact Blake's drama of Armageddon and apocalypse include Washington, Franklin, Paine, the American warriors Allen, Gates and Lee, and 'the thirteen Angels' of the American colonies. They are shadowy, but Orc, risen from the Atlantic, is

> Intense! naked! a Human fire, fierce glowing, as the wedge
> Of iron heated in the furnace: his terrible limbs were fire.

1   Site of Blake's birthplace and family home, 28 Broad Street, Westminster (now
re-named 74 Broadwick Street)

2   Anon.: Jew's Harp Tea Gardens, Marylebone, a scene of Blake's golden boyhood memories

3 (*Opposite top*) Carnaby Market, near Golden Square, Soho, by Cornelius Varley, c. 1805, when the neighbourhood was decaying

4 (*Opposite below*) Anon.: 'The Art of Etching and Engraving', 1748, showing tools and techniques familiar to Blake. *a* Muse; *b* draughtsman; *c* engraver; *d* blackening plate with a taper so that etcher can see what he is doing; *e* removing bubbles from plate in acid bath; *f* muslin screen to diffuse light; *h, i, k* how to engrave, hold burin, sharpen it; *l* how to clean off burr from edge of burin; *m, n* how to hold etching needle; *o* jug for stopping-out varnish; *p* funnel, filter and bottle for etching ground; *q* acid bath; *r* eraser; *s* etching needles; *t* brush for stopping out varnish; *u* file for smoothing plate's edge; *w* plate

5 (*Right*) 'Joseph of Arimathea among the Rocks of Albion', 1773: Blake's engraving shows a spurned Christian prophet, builder of Glastonbury Cathedral

6 (*Below*) Sepia drawing by Blake, 1774: 'King Edward I in his coffin'

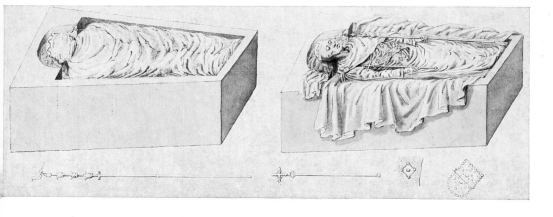

7   Pugin and Rowlandson: 'Drawing from Life, Royal Academy'

8   Johann Zoffany: 'Dr William Hunter Lecturing'; Reynolds with ear trumpet; the bald muscle-man was cast from a flayed Tyburn corpse

9   John Flaxman, aged 24, self-portrait; pencil; no longer with the veneer of a 'complete coxcomb'

10   Anon.: James Basire, engraver. Blake's master

11   Catherine Blake: portrait of Blake in late twenties, probably an 'ideal design' drawn after his death

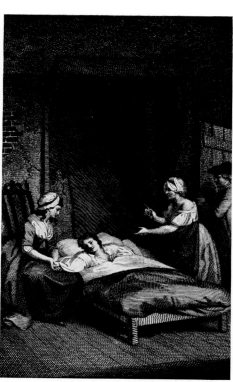

12 (*Left*) Stothard, engraved Blake: illustration to Sarah Fielding's romance *David Simple*; David pities the sick young man and pays his rent

13 (*Below*) Stothard, Blake and perhaps Parker, prisoners when boating: drawn by Stothard under detention; etched

14 (*Opposite*) 'The Dance of Albion', 1780, engraved c. 1800. Blake's inscription calls American colonies 'Nations' and quotes from Milton's Samson, heroic, self-sacrificing

'Albion rose from where he labour'd at the Mill with Slaves
Giving himself for the Nations he danc'd the dance of Eternal Death'

15 (*Opposite top*) Francis Wheatley: 'Riots in Broad Street', 1780; engraved for Boydell by James Heath, whose 'lame imitation' of draughtsmanship Blake derided

16 (*Opposite below*) Collings, engraved Blake, 1784: 'May-Day in London'; wigged sweeps and milkmaids dancing

17 (*Right*) Ink and wash, Blake's notebook, attributed to Robert: 'Oberon and Titania', fairies dancing above. Blake based a beautiful plate on this drawing

18 (*Right below*) Relief etching finished in watercolour, 1808–15: Blake's brother Robert, from *Milton*. Some pages before, a similar star fell to the left foot of William, Robert's mirror image

19 Frederick Adcock: 13 Hercules Buildings, now demolished; it faced houses, fields, the Thames and Westminster

20 Fuseli, engraved Blake, 1791: 'Fertilization of Egypt'. Blake developed the bearded rain-god from Fuseli's sketch of Anubis and the star

22 A page from Blake's Notebook; verses surround a sketch for *Visions of the Daughters of Albion*; Theotormon's eagle rends Oothoon's bosom

21 (*Left*) Pugin and Rowlandson: 'Dining Room, Royal Asylum', 1808. The chaplain was a Swedenborgian; perhaps this connection attracted the Blakes to Lambeth

23 (*Left*) Stedman, engraved Blake, 1796: 'A Negro on the Rack', a horrifying episode in the *Narrative*; Blake preferred not to sign this plate

24 (*Below*) Colour print: 'Newton', 1795; scientific compasses rigidly mark the scroll, emblem of imaginative creation; left, a polypus, symbol of materialistic society, vegetates

25 (*Opposite*) Pencil drawing, *Vala* manuscript, c. 1797: 'Enitharmon', Los's lovely Emanation

Say me & thou annihilate evaporate & be no more
For thou art but a form & organ of life & of thyself
Art nothing being Created Continually by Mercy & Love divine

Los furious answerd. Spectre horrible thy words astound my Ear
With irresistible conviction I feel I am not one of those
Who when convinced can still persist. tho furious. controllable
By Reasons power. Even I already feel a World within
Opening its gates & in it all the real substances

Of which these in the outward World are shadows which pass away
Come then into my Bosom & in thy shadowy arms bring with thee
My lovely Enitharmon. I will quell my fury & teach
Peace to the soul of dark revenge & repentance to cruelty

So Spoke Los & Embracing Enitharmon & the Spectre
Clouds would have folded round in Extacy & Love uniting

26 Fuseli: self-portrait, aged 40 to 50; black chalk heightened with white. Lavater saw ambition in Fuseli's physiognomy: 'his own merit escapes him not'

27 Blake's miniature of Thomas Butts, c. 1804

28 Hull: William Hayley, 1800; Blake's possessive patron

29 Henry Edridge: Thomas Stothard, RA, 1795

Vala

Night the Seventh

This Night begins at line 153 the following comes in at the End

Now in the Caverns of the Grave & Places of human seed
The namcless Shadowy Vortex stood before the face of Orc
The Shadow reard her dismal head over the flaming youth
With sighs & howling & deep sobs that he might lose his rage
And with it lose himself in meekness she embracd his fire
As when the Earthquake rouzes from his den his shoulders huge
Appear above the crumbling Mountain. Silence waits around him
A moment then astounding horror belches from the Center
The fiery dogs arise the shoulders huge appear
So Orc rolld round his clouds upon the deeps of dark Urthona
...
Silent as despairing love & strong as jealousy
The hairy shoulders rend the links free are the wrists of fire
Red rage redounds he roams his human form from his forests black
They howl around the flaming youth rending the namcless Shadow
And running they flew immortal upon these solid darkning borne
Ielous that She was Vala now become Urizens harlot
Long sought she war song rouzd red Orc in his ... fury
And round the namcless shadowy Female in her howling terror
When all the Elemental Gods join in the wondrous Song
Sound the War trumpet terrific Souls clad in attractive Steel
Sound the Shrill fife Serpents of war. I hear the northern drum
Awake, I hear the flapping of the folding banners
The Dragons of the North put on their armour
Upon the Eastern sea direct they take their course
The glittering of their horses trappings stains the vault of night
Stop we the rising of the glorious king. spur spur your clouds

30   Manuscript page: *Vala*; on a proof for Young's *Night Thoughts*; engraving of
the poet, pierced by grief's thorns; nightingale and lark sing

31   T. M. Barnes, lithograph, 1800: 'View from the Slopes of Highgate Archway', looking towards St Paul's

32   Miss M. G. Evans: 'Blake's Cottage', watercolour, c. 1925. Cottage right, Fox Inn left: both remain

His thundering voice shakes the Druid temple, which Blake associates with the vast stones of Stonehenge and Avebury, symbols of Natural Religion and of human sacrifice. Challenged by Albion's Angel and reviled as Antichrist, Orc claims 'To make the desarts blossom, & the deeps shrink to their fountains'. He will

> renew the fiery joy . . .
> That pale religious letchery, seeking Virginity,
> May find it in a harlot . . .
> Because the soul of sweet delight can never be defil'd.

Blake describes the plagues of war 'Falling upon America' but recoiling 'On Albion's Angels' and smiting Bristol and London. These cities were most involved in American trade and therefore supremely opposed to the war, but England was generally sickened and mass desertions weakened the army. Although the traditional Bard of Albion 'Hid in his caves', he 'felt the enormous plagues' and, symbol of degenerate poetry, became deformed: 'a cowl of flesh grew o'er his head, & scales on his back & ribs.' Then 'The doors of marriage are open,' the priests who shackled people in the marriage bond now flee and regeneration begins. The revolutionary flames of Orc melt the heavens, so that Urizen emerges howling from above to pour forth his snows—

> Leprous his limbs, all over white, and hoary was his visage,
> Weeping in dismal howlings before the stern Americans

—until France, twelve years after the battle of Yorktown, has guillotined Louis XVI and 'reciev'd the Demon's light.' The European countries, shocked by Albion's plague-stricken plight, desperately try to shut the five gates of repression (the senses that limit man's apprehension of infinity) against Orc's advancing fires.

> But the five gates were consum'd, & their bolts and hinges melted;
> And the fierce flames burnt round the heavens, & round the abodes of men.

Closely linked in substance with *America*, and written and illuminated soon after it, is another poem about recent historical events, *Europe: A Prophecy*. This presents an earlier part of Blake's myth of mankind. The frontispiece is 'Urizen Creating the Universe': Blake delighted in colouring separate prints of this for the rest of his life. Later copies of *Europe* contain a poetic preface in which he records a lute-song about the five senses, sung by 'a Fairy, mocking, as he sat on a streak'd Tulip'. The fairy sits on Blake's parlour table and dictates *Europe* to him.

After this account of inspiration as a product of the senses, comes the deeply disturbing 'Preludium', a development of the 'Preludium' to *America*, and the Prophecy itself begins. At the birth of Christ, peace comes to earth, but already the repressive sons of Urizen call for a crucifixion.

E   65

Enitharmon, the luxurious subtle queen, seductress of man whom she seeks to dominate and bind, calls her family round her. Orc, her firstborn son, is in her power. She contemplates her night of bliss and plans to enhance it by beguiling mankind, so 'That Woman, lovely Woman, may have dominion'. Enitharmon, whose name may be derived from *'zenith'* and *'harmony'* contracted and fused, is the 'Eternal Female', embodiment of spiritual beauty. She subtly perverts religion to enhance her power, telling 'the Human race that Woman's love is Sin'.

Enitharmon sleeps. Her 'female dream' is of the world as Blake sees it, dominated by a false official religion of chastity, repression and revenge, a world in which sexual energy is perverted into war. The disastrous fortunes of 'Albion's Angel', recounted in *America*, are here resumed. After the defeat of British arms in the American colonies, Parliament collapses. Blake, who could gaze across the Thames to Westminster from his home near Lambeth Palace, visualizes the roof, smitten by wind-driven clouds of plague, collapsing on the heads of the rulers, who silently follow Albion's Angel to 'his ancient temple, serpent-form'd, That stretches out its shady length along the Island white.' This Druid temple casts a shade across the country. Blake believed that the Druids, though they were at first inspired prophets, had later degenerated to a cult which sacrificed human lives in the stone temple at Avebury, on the slaughter-stone at Stonehenge, and at other haunts.

William Stukeley, the seventeenth-century antiquary and friend of Sir Isaac Newton, had depicted the great stones of Avebury in the form of a serpent stretching across the Wiltshire downs, and interpreted this as an emblem of Christ's divinity. His ideas were known to Blake, who was familiar with Druid lore from various sources. Blake developed, over the years, the varied Druidic lore he had absorbed, and it became part of his intricate mythology. Druidism symbolized, to him, the religion of the savage, natural man: deism. The deists' claim that reason could comprehend religion made revelation redundant: but to Blake, revelation meant life. He always fought the deists because they denied the spirit and fettered imagination.

In *Europe*, Albion's Angel stands on the Stone of Night, which is the Druids' altar and authority's pulpit-stone, and sees Urizen on the Atlantic. Enitharmon dreams them in her long sleep, while 'Albion's cliffs & London's walls', where the rulers live, are enveloped in mists. 'The youth of England', under compulsion, listen—as they had to the Royal Proclamation of 1792 against 'divers wicked and seditious writings'—to Albion's Angel, 'aged ignorance' who 'preaches, canting'. His voice (that of William Pitt mustering England's youth against the Jacobins) howls in the revolutionary flames of Orc. From Westminster, the howling 'Guardian of the secret codes' (the bewigged Lord Chancellor, Thurlow, dismissed in 1792) has been driven out:

> his furr'd robes & false locks
> Adhered and grew one with his flesh, and nerves & veins shot thro' them.

He flees grovelling, and 'he drag'd his torments to the wilderness. Thus was the howl thro' Europe!'

Sleeping, oblivious to the downfall of authority, Enitharmon laughs in triumph to see mankind repressed by 'morality' and government: 'Every house a den, every man bound.' On an illuminated page corrupt with insects and webbed by spiders who have enmeshed a human being, Blake describes the people chained, their bones soft and bent. His bold, full-page illustrations show dramatically the results of war. Women prepare to boil a child for food. A sombre bell-man walks past a plague-stricken family. A powerful youth, fettered to a prison floor, crouches appalled: his jailer strides up the stone steps and leaves him there.

Enitharmon's dream reaches its climax when Albion's Angel, his flesh consumed by Orc's flames, 'siez'd in horror and torment The Trump of the last doom; but he could not blow the iron tube!' His three futile attempts to blow it are followed by the efforts of 'A mighty Spirit' from Albion, 'Nam'd Newton: he siez'd the trump & blow'd the enormous blast!' The angels fall through the wintry skies, howling as they seek their graves. So the creator of the rational, materialist, anti-Jacobin universe, Newton, evokes not a resurrection but the Armageddon which ends the eighteenth century.

Enitharmon awakes from her dream of domination, unaware that she has slept for eighteen hundred years, from Christ's birth until his revolutionary second coming when Blake writes *Europe*. Orc shoots away from her. The golden chariot-wheels are red with blood. Lions rage, tigers devour, 'And Enitharmon groans & cries in anguish and dismay' when the counter-revolutionary war against France breaks out in 1793. Above the picture of a naked young man, heroic like Aeneas, rescuing his wife and daughter from the flames of war and ascending the classical ruins of reason and materialism, the poem ends: Los, the creative imagination, arises,

> And with a cry that shook all nature to the utmost pole,
> Call'd all his sons to the strife of blood.

The avenging Christ has come.

The spiritual world-history continues in *Africa* and *Asia*, two short poems perhaps written at different times but etched and colour-printed as separate parts of *The Song of Los* and dated 1795. They complete the story of Orc's fiery revolt against Urizen's world-domination. At the feast of Eternity, Los sings the story in this cycle of narrative poems, *Africa*, *America*, *Europe*, *Asia*. The sequence of repression, which provokes revolt, starts in *Africa*. Adam and Noah see Urizen give laws to the nations. Abstract philosophy is spread through Brahma, Hermes Trismegistus (mythical source of the alchemists' wisdom), Pythagoras, Socrates and Plato. Orc is chained to Mount Atlas, as Prometheus was to the Caucasus.

Jesus sorrowfully hears the voice of slavery, but accepts the rule of law. The human race begins to wither, 'fearing the joys of Love', and only the diseased propagate. Mahomet and the Norse gods also contribute to the obliteration of eternity. A philosophy of the five senses is complete and Urizen, hypocritically weeping, gives it into the hands of Newton and Locke. 'Clouds roll heavy upon the Alps round Rousseau & Voltaire', disseminators of natural religion which spreads over the whole earth. The last line of this poem, 'The Guardian Prince of Albion burns in his nightly tent', is also the first line of *America*, in which the defeat of Albion's Angel begins, to be continued in *Europe* on British and, later, French soil.

Asia tells how the 'thought-creating fires of Orc' spread to eastern lands whose spider-like kings, in counter-revolution, restrain their people by famine, pestilence and poverty,

> And the privy admonishers of men
> Call for fire in the City,
> For heaps of smoking ruins

such as Blake had seen in the Gordon Riots. Urizen, in retreat from Europe, hears the cry of Asia's kings. He retires to Judea, 'his ancient place' of the Mosaic Law. Orc, a serpentine pillar of flame, rages from Europe. The dust of the dead becomes living flesh and the Grave in delight 'shakes Her hollow womb & clasps the solid stem.' Rivers of 'milk & blood & glandous wine . . . rush & shout & dance' over the land. *The Song of Los* ends: 'Urizen wept.' The millennium, it is implied, will surely follow after this ecstatic resurrection.

The colour-printed illustrations, sombre and mottled, have probably darkened with age: indeed, Blake's colouring in general, when it was first seen, must have been far more brilliant than it is now. He was continuing to experiment with methods of colour-printing. On the coal-burning kitchen range he warmed his copper plate and his colours mixed with glue-tempera, and then he painted this heavy pigment onto the plate with a brush of ox or squirrel hair, known as camel (sable brushes he disliked). He pressed his paper lightly onto the plate by hand, and peeled it off enriched by an opaque image of subtly varied texture which he then touched up and finished with delicate brush-strokes.

In 1795, he used his developed techniques to create a superb series of twelve large colour prints from thick colours painted on millboard, subtly worked up with watercolour and ink. No more than three copies are known of any one design, all taken from a single application of paint to millboard; and each copy, bearing less paint than its predecessor, is unique. His varied subjects include 'Elohim Creating Adam', 'Nebuchadnezzar', 'Newton' (24), 'Pity', 'Hecate' and 'The House of Death'. Although no single theme seems to run through the series, each print reveals a different part of his profound philosophy. His Newton is a nude youth, perhaps submerged in the sea of the material world. Blake respected Newton, as he did Bacon and Locke: all three, despite their errors, were seekers after truth and he later placed them, in his epic *Jerusalem*, among 'The innumerable Chariots of the Almighty'. A scientific trinity who gave form to error, they are counterparts of 'Milton & Shakspear & Chaucer', who expressed truth. The form of Newton is related to one of Michelangelo's figures on the ceiling of the Sistine chapel. Blake's pictures, like his writings, are often deeply derived from other artists' works, but his genius makes them into fresh creations of new richness. These magnificent prints remained unsold for years. Even his loyal patron, Butts, did not buy a set until it was ten years old.

Less elaborate than the complex, lavish *Europe*, but created at about the same time and dated 1794, *The Book of Urizen* is a more condensed, subtly structured work. In it, Blake uses simple 'swift winged' words in lines of four beats to present a part of his expanding myth. This poem is virtually bare of topical allusions. Its effect, as Blake's contemporary Allan Cunningham wrote, is 'powerful, dark, terrible'. Blake intended this work to begin a series of 'Books of Urizen', but changed his mind and the sequel to this volume he called *The Book of Ahania*. He had promised to issue the Bible of Hell, 'which the world shall have whether they will or no': *The Book of Urizen* is the Genesis of such a scripture, written as chapters and verses and illuminated with dramatic designs. These look vast, although they are only pocket-sized (6). Blake was a master of scale. He could conjure up a giant, a rose or an ant so that each seemed to be its true size, perfectly proportioned to the page.

The Book of Urizen can be read as a satire on genesis stories in the Bible, Plato and Milton. In Blake's myth, the Eternals, in infinite life, see with horror an 'Unknown, unprolific, Self-clos'd, all-repelling' void, a 'soul-shudd'ring vacuum'. It is Urizen who, like the creator in Boehme, creates by introspection, 'Brooding shut in the deep'. Because creation is separation from eternity, it is also a fall, the work of one who opposes the unquenchable burnings of a limitless life of impulse shared by Eternals. Labouring alone in 'Nature's wide womb', Urizen writes the secrets of his wisdom on eternal brass. They are his laws, which create 'All the seven deadly sins of the soul': this orthodox God is Satan too. Eternity, furious, rolls wide apart. Urizen both creates, and is, a world: 'vast, petrific . . . like a womb . . . like a black globe . . . Like a human heart'. He is rent from Los, imagination: but reason cannot exist without imagination. Los, as a watchman and a blacksmith, tries to limit the formlessness of Urizen's 'Unorganiz'd' state, which he imagines is a temporary madness. (Organized form was always prized by Blake the designer.) Los rivets every change and imposes time on introverted Urizen. In an agonized parody of God's day-by-day creation of the world, Los, shrinking from his terrible task, forges the body which encloses Urizen from eternal life.

A vast Spine writh'd in torment
Upon the winds, shooting pain'd
Ribs, like a bending cavern;
And bones of solidness Froze
Over all his nerves of joy.

Los completes the trembling, howling form, its limbs outstretched, crucified across the world: Urizen's 'eternal life Like a dream was obliterated.'
Sharing Urizen's fall, Los, the eternal prophet, is now sundered from
eternity by the abyss. In anguished self-pity he himself divides, 'For pity
divides the soul'. Life in cataracts pours from him. It shrinks into 'a round
globe of blood Trembling upon the Void' and he becomes the tearful
female, Enitharmon, besides being the active male, Los. This double fall of
Los, first out of eternity, second out of sexual unity, resembles the double
fall of Adam in Boehme.

Now, instead of the male and female principles within Los uniting to
create, they are divided. The wondering Eternals shudder, call the first
female Pity, and flee from her. Then, to hide the pair, they 'Spread a Tent
with strong curtains around them' and name it Science, knowledge limited
by our restricted senses. Impelled by self-love, man begets his likeness. An
act, not of new creation but of repetition, engenders the 'Worm', embryo of
Orc. At his revolutionary birth, fierce flames issue from Enitharmon. A
chain girdle of jealousy inevitably grows round the bosom of Los the father.
He and Enitharmon bind Orc to a rock 'Beneath Urizen's deathful shadow'.
Urizen awakes to life; hungry and 'Stung with the odours of Nature' he
begins to explore and to measure, using a brazen quadrant and golden compasses. He is sickened because he sees 'That no flesh nor spirit could keep
His iron laws one moment', laws which inevitably result in his curse.
Urizen wanders over the cities of Egypt, land of slavery. Drawn out from
his sickened soul is a cold shadow, like a spider's web, which he leaves behind him wherever he goes. Its twisted cords and knotted meshes form The
Net of Religion—not true religion, which is inspiration, but the control of
men's beliefs and lives. In cities, the senses contract 'Beneath the dark net
of infection', 'woven hipocrisy'. Laws of prudence, which limit imaginative
living are called 'The eternal laws of God'. Finally, as a pillar of fire, Fuzon
—the Orc-like rebel who represents Passion—leads an exodus of those
children of Urizen who are not yet enmeshed: they call 'the pendulous
earth' Egypt (bondage), and leave it, as Blake wanted men to leave deism.

Individual twists of meaning are given to each of the seven known copies
of *The Book of Urizen*, as to copies of other illuminated books, by Blake's
significantly different ordering of his plates. The visual splendour of this
book is not found in its sequels, *The Book of Ahania* and *The Book of Los*.
These shorter books, dated 1795, he etched on copper—not in relief, but in
the conventional, less laborious way—and printed by the intaglio process.
He added colour-printed illustrations to some of the pages, but made only

one copy of each book, which suggests that he was dissatisfied with the works and laid them aside. Parts of the poems he would develop in his later, more expansive writing.

The Book of Ahania tells how Fuzon, a figure of flames and sparkling hair, moulds 'into a vast Globe his wrath, As the thunder-stone is moulded'. This circular form, self-containing and therefore hated by Blake, is Fuzon's missile against Urizen. 'Roaring with fury he threw The howling Globe' which, in flight, lengthens into 'a hungry beam', a fiery arrow or spear. Against this, Urizen upheaves the broad disc of his cold, dead sun, 'forg'd in mills where the winter Beats incessant.' The 'laughing', phallic beam tears through the beaten mass of the shield and divides the cold loins of Urizen, stimulating his lust which is parted from him as a female, Ahania, symbol of Pleasure. At the same time as his lust takes this separate form, his jealousy is aroused. He calls Ahania 'Sin'. He kisses her, weeps over her and hides her in darkness. She becomes a faint shadow in chaos, 'circling dark Urizen, As the moon anguish'd circles the earth.'

The poem ends with a beautiful, evocative lament of Ahania. Lacking the form of a living creature, she weeps 'on the verge Of Non-entity' for Urizen, who has cast her from his bright presence and her golden palace, where she used to find 'babes of bliss' on her beds 'And bosoms of milk' in her chambers 'Fill'd with eternal seed'. Urizen she describes as a farmer, his lap full of seed, his hand full of generous fire as he 'Walked forth from the clouds of morning . . . to cast The seed of eternal science' on the human soul. From this first indication that Urizen is a farmer, his 'eternal' agricultural nature will develop in *The Four Zoas*. Blake's mythical figures are not fixed and limited. Their organic natures and relationships grow and change as the shimmering relief-map of Blake's expanding, undulating, burrowing mind is revealed piece by piece, layer after layer, in his writings and pictures. This map is of a living world. Its landscape is ever developing, not arbitrarily, nor for the sake of artistic neatness, but always according to Blake's passionately held beliefs. Urizen, a most complex figure, architect and builder of this world is, in his eternal vocation, the ploughman and sower.

The Book of Los retells with variations the story, already told in *The Book of Urizen*, of Los forging Urizen's body. Los, not law-giving Urizen, is the creator in this version of Genesis, a dream-like evolution (nightmarish, surrealist), which culminates when Los sees the backbone of Urizen writhing, 'Hurtling upon the wind . . . like an iron chain Whirling about in the Deep.' The body of Urizen, cursorily described with four rivers flowing from its heart, becomes our world, 'a Human Illusion', and the fragmentary poem abruptly ends.

Perhaps Blake was too busy with other work, an immense project of illustrating Edward Young's *Night Thoughts*, to present these Lambeth books as sumptuously as their predecessors, but his interest in technique never flagged. About 1794, he recorded in his notebook how 'To Woodcut on Pewter', a method he used for engraving 'The Man Sweeping the Interpreter's Parlour'. In 1795, he was developing his watercolour technique. Rather than lay a monochrome wash over a drawing to tint it, he now chose to apply colour direct to white paper.

During these busy years, Blake's contacts with Stedman were particularly close. Stedman was now having much trouble with the printing of his Surinam *Narrative*. He relied on Blake as his most trusted friend in London, and perhaps as his intermediary with the publisher Johnson, whose proofs disappointed him deeply. Stedman's *Journal* gives glimpses of these unquiet days in London. Astley's Amphitheatre, scene of equestrian feats, conjuring and fireworks, was only a few minutes' walk from Blake's house. In the small hours of Sunday, 17 July 1794, it caught fire and 'London was nearly burnt' by the accident, Stedman notes.

A month later Astley's house, 'Hercules Hall', which stood in a yard almost directly behind 13 Hercules Buildings, was 'burnt down tonight by accident.' This eventful night continued with a riot, incited by the suicide of a press-ganged man from an attic window in Charing Cross. In July 1795, Stedman recorded: 'Many riots in England etc. Dreadful thunder and lightning. Bread very dear and scarce.' In August he was again in London. 'The Bill passes against seditious meetings. . . . Plague and famine is expected. . . . Twelve people were hanged in six months in London. . . . I visit Mr Blake for three days, who undertakes to do business for me when I am not in London. I leave him all my papers. . . . Damn Bartolozzi [the engraver]. He goes away. . . . Johnson [the publisher] uncivil all along. . . . Abershaw etc. hanged [on Kennington Common, within walking distance of Blake's house].'

Next month he noted: 'London—everything made up. All knaves and fools, and cruel to excess. Blake was mobbed and robbed.' These misfortunes of Blake, so laconically mentioned, seem less startling against their background of a seething city depicted in Stedman's *Journal*. Perhaps this was the robbery which occurred one day when the Blakes went out to visit friends, leaving no-one in their house: thieves carried away plate worth £60 and clothes worth £40. (Blake's chief source of income, commercial engraving, generally brought him £5 to £25 for an engraved plate.) That he was not, at this time, too poor to be worth stealing from, is supported by Tatham's story that Blake lent £40—nearly all his available money—to a free-thinking writer on philosophy who pleaded that his children had nothing to eat. Blake called on him the next Sunday, and was mortified to discover that much of the money had been immediately squandered by the philosopher's extravagant wife on new clothes for herself. She even had the audacity to ask Mrs Blake's opinion of a very gorgeous dress, bought the day after Blake's compassionate loan.

A week before Christmas 1795, Stedman, back home at Tiverton, sent 'a goose to Johnson, and one to Blake'. In the next months he wrote many letters to Blake and, at last, after 'no less than seven or eight long years' of hard work, he eventually saw his moving Surinam *Narrative* handsomely published in 1796. One reviewer mentioned the 'neatly engraved' plates; another the 'uncommon elegance' of their style. Stedman died eight months later.

Warmly optimistic by nature, Blake had hoped to sell many copies of his illuminated books. As his *Prospectus* of 1793 shows, he felt sure of success as painter and poet. His works, presented in his own style of book-production—'more ornamental, uniform, and grand, than any before discovered, while it produces works at less than one fourth of the expense'—would prove 'worthy of public attention': and then 'the Author is sure of his reward.' Readers were not, however, prepared to strive for vision by grappling with Blake's poetry. It was too tough, too strange, too exacting in its private myths. He sold so few copies that in 1794 he reluctantly issued two books of designs shorn of text, a magnificent selection of relief etchings and coloured prints which he made for his friend and admirer Ozias Humphry, a successful miniature painter whose eyes were failing. Blake disappointedly 'Printed without the Writing, tho' to the Loss of some of the best things. For they when Printed perfect accompany Poetical Personifications & Acts, without which Poems they never could have been Executed.' Blake decided to seek public favour by other means.

It was time he did so. Offers, available to lesser but established men were not being made to him. Barry, Fuseli, Reynolds, Romney, Smirke, Stothard, West and a host of other eminent artists were commissioned to paint pictures based on Shakespeare, for Alderman John Boydell's new, specially built gallery in Pall Mall. Crowds flocked to the exhibition. Boydell, himself a trained engraver who had done much to raise the status of engraving in England, was elected Lord Mayor of London in 1790. He hoped to bequeath his Shakespeare Gallery paintings to the nation. Engraved and published in a sumptuous edition, they were a great success. Blake's haunting colour prints of 'Pity' and 'Hecate', made about 1795, show his amazing power to conjure up Shakespeare's imagery. But Boydell, when commissioning work from painters and engravers for his Shakespeare Gallery, passed Blake by until 1799: as an artist, Blake was not established. By 1795, his artist-friends Stothard, Cosway and Humphry had all been elected Royal Academicians, and Fuseli—despite temporary friction with Reynolds, who supported a rival candidate—had been elected too. Blake, aged thirty-eight, journeyman engraver, with a pile of his own superb prophetic books ignored, had as yet made original engravings on copper for works by only two other writers. Now, abounding in creative exuberance, he was commissioned to illustrate, on a vastly lavish scale, a very popular, established work by a writer dead ten years: the *Night Thoughts* of Edward Young, rector of Welwyn, in Hertfordshire.

This graveyard poem in blank verse, written by Young in his early sixties after the death of his wife, was published in 1742–5 and achieved enormous success. Its nine parts or 'Nights', comprising 9,761 lines of vaguely Miltonic, Augustan meditations on life, death and immortality (all composed either at night or when Young was on horseback) were dismissed by Fuseli in 1775 as 'pyramids of dough'. But Dr Samuel Johnson could ask 'who has not read them?' and confidently expect the answer 'nobody'. Robespierre kept them under his pillow throughout the raging of the Terror. And Blake found them stimulating and challenging enough to inspire him to paint no less than 537 watercolour illustrations—uneven in quality, as such a quantity was bound to be, but many of them exciting and some of them superb—between 1795 and 1797 (7).

Richard Edwards, a prosperous publisher who specialized in books of prints, thought that a costly illustrated edition of Young's living classic would sell like Boydell's *Shakespeare Gallery*. Blake had not worked for Edwards before, so Fuseli may have acted as intermediary and helped to get Blake talked about. Artists certainly discussed the *Night Thoughts* project. Joseph Farington, RA, landscape painter and diarist, noted on 19 February 1796: 'West, Cosway and Humphry spoke warmly in favour of the designs of Blake, the engraver, as works of extraordinary genius and imagination. Smirke [an illustrator] differed in opinion, from what he had seen; so do I.' A few months later, on 24 June, Farington wrote: 'Fuseli . . . mentioned Blake . . . whose genius and invention have been much spoken of. Fuseli has known him several years, and thinks he has a great deal of invention, but that . . . the whole of his aim is to produce singular shapes and odd combinations. . . . Blake has undertaken to make designs to encircle the letter-press of each page of Young's *Night Thoughts*.' Blake drew illustrations round the inlaid text, using Indian ink on a brush; then he added watercolour. Undemanding as ever about money, he was to be grossly underpaid. He must have undertaken the vast work because it stirred him and he hoped it would, at last, win him public esteem. The entry in Farington's diary continues: 'Blake asked 100 guineas for the whole. Edwards said he could not afford to give more than 20 guineas, for which Blake agreed. Fuseli understands that Edwards proposes to select about 200 from the whole and to have that number engraved as decorations for a new edition.' Blake's despicably low rate of pay was therefore to be less than, in today's terms, four pence a watercolour, each page measuring about 17 by 13 inches. For engraving his designs he was probably paid a guinea a plate.

Farington continues: 'Fuseli says, Blake has something of madness about him. He acknowledges the superiority of Fuseli, but thinks himself more able than Stothard.' In January 1797, various artists including Stothard and Farington 'supped together and had laughable conversation. Blake's eccentric designs were mentioned. Stothard supported his claims to genius, but allowed he had been misled to extravagance in his art, and he knew by whom'—presumably Fuseli. John Hoppner, the portrait painter, ridiculed Blake's designs, likening them to 'the conceits of a drunken fellow or a madman. "Represent a man sitting on the moon, and pissing the sun out: that would be a whim of as much merit." Stothard was angry, mistaking the laughter caused by Hoppner's description.'

While Blake was working on *Night Thoughts*, some designs which he had made for a translation of Bürger's *Leonora* were decried. Another craftsman, Perry, had engraved Blake's three designs. Blake's frontispiece, a scene of spectral horror, was said by an anonymous critic in *The Analytical Review* 'to produce an effect perfectly ludicrous, instead of terrific.' However, in the autumn of 1796 Blake received a tribute from an appreciative friend. Cumberland, who had given up insurance work more than ten years before and was now living at modest leisure in Windsor Great Park, published *Thoughts on Outline*, a small book in which he discusses the importance of outline, particularly to the Greeks, Michelangelo and Raphael. Cumberland himself had drawn the twenty-four illustrations, and in an appendix he paid tribute to Blake for condescending to engrave eight of them ('a compliment, from a man of his extraordinary genius and abilities, the highest, I believe, I shall ever receive') and further for teaching him to engrave the rest of the plates himself, so enabling him to reduce the price of the book.

Blake's earliest extant letter to Cumberland, of 6 December 1795, tells him precisely how to wax a plate for etching. Cumberland also learnt from Blake to value outline. Blake's own attitude, a legacy from Basire, was that

The great and golden rule of art, as well as of life, is this: That the more distinct, sharp, and wirey the bounding line, the more perfect the work of art; and the less keen and sharp, the greater is the evidence of weak imitation, plagiarism, and bungling. Great inventors, in all ages, knew this. . . . Rafael and Michael Angelo and Albert Dürer are known by this and this alone.

Some months after receiving *Thoughts on Outline*, Blake, with 'pricks of conscience', wrote to thank Cumberland tardily for his 'beautiful book'. The letter glows with encouragement.

Blake worked amazingly fast on *Night Thoughts*. Before the summer of 1797 ended, not only were the 537 watercolours finished, but forty-three of the first 156 had been selected, engraved and published in an atlas-sized volume which contained the first four Nights of the poem on thick paper with ample margins, and at the end, an explanation of the engravings, perhaps by Fuseli. Blake much enriched one copy by splendidly watercolouring the engravings. Some other copies were coloured from this pattern, but most were expected to be sold unpainted. Edwards's advertisement announced a 'Magnificent Edition', intended to comprise four volumes. Using colossal figures, austerely large spaces and masses, and spurning charm, Blake went far beyond elucidating a text already clear. He comments on themes or images that he has found in the poem, and presents his own philosophy and criticism of life in symbolic designs, many of them intricately linked. Working through monumental engravings which tend—despite their beauty of line—to appear very dry and too gigantic in scale, he creates his own emotionally strong world of wide vision, precise physical detail and provocative thought far beyond the pedestrian realms of Young's poem.

The impact of Blake's designs for *Night Thoughts* is profound: but the public in 1797 did not feel it. A banking crash had devastated the market and a cloud of economic gloom hung over all the arts. The public ignored the book. Edwards abandoned publication after the first volume.

Blake must have been very depressed, but now he began to make a fair copy, in a beautiful copperplate hand on large sheets of paper, of a prophetic book that he had been writing for about two years. He intended this song of Eno, the mother of all poetry, to be about the death and judgment of the Ancient or Universal Man, the giant who is all the universe. At first Blake called the long poem *Vala*, the name of his goddess of nature, veil of the spirit. His sub-title, 'A Dream of Nine Nights', suggests the poem's development while he was illustrating *Night Thoughts*, which was a vision of nine midnights. Blake intended to illuminate and relief-etch *Vala*, but in 1797, when he is likely to have finished his first version of all nine Nights, he probably could not afford the copper plates for yet another work unlikely to sell. However, he continued to revise this two-thousand-line poem repeatedly. Abandoning his copperplate script as the third Night developed, he moved—in swifter handwriting—onto the large, left-over page-proofs of his engravings for *Night Thoughts*. He had printed these on his own press, to see at every stage how his engravings were developing. The blank text-spaces provided good manuscript paper for *Vala*, the first of Blake's three poems on an epic scale (30). Over the years Blake doubled its length to four thousand lines. It is his only prophetic book which still exists in manuscript.

This vast, magnificent and haunting poem tells, as if in dream, the terrible story of the conflict between the four basic aspects of man: reason (Urizen), imagination (Urthona, in his degenerate form named Los), passion (Luvah, in his degenerate form named Orc) and body (Tharmas). Only when these four are in universal brotherhood in man can a perfect unity, a state of Eden, exist. Over a period of perhaps as much as fifteen years, Blake changed, complicated and added to his manuscript as his ideas proliferated. Events occur in the poem with the unexplained inevitability of dreams. There is no clear narrative line, no controlled dramatic structure: but total conviction. Blake was enthralled by his visions and ideas. His concern for poetic form and his mastery of it are less apparent. However, his finest passages, rhythmically compelling, rise above rhetoric to splendid poetry in the form of septenary lines, such as he had used in five previous books.

Continuing work on the conflicts and ecstasies, agonies and desires of his 'Four Mighty Ones' and their feminine counterparts or Emanations (25), Blake eventually—some ten years or more after he had begun his first draft —re-named this developing poem *The Four Zoas*, from the Greek *zoa*. Perhaps by mistake, he added a plural to *zoa*, already a plural form. He found the four Zoas called, in translation, 'living creatures' in Ezekiel 1.4–24 (an elaborate description of their visionary appearance to the prophet Ezekiel) and 'beasts' in Revelation 4.6–8. In a new sub-title, Blake named the Ancient Man, who is asleep for most of the poem, Albion. Blake's Zoas and Emanations are in torment because of the selfish aggressiveness which pervades most of the poem. Until they are all unselfishly in balance, harmony, peace and happiness cannot prevail in the many-layered, seemingly endless void which Blake's passionate dream-figures animate and which represents both man and the universe.

Vala is Blake's personification of disruptive female power, which is able, in mother and seductress, to dominate the male. The lovely form of Vala 'drew the body of Man from heaven' into the 'dark Abyss'. At that time Luvah, the Prince of Love, was bereft of his Emanation, Vala. He seized the chariot of light from the naked 'bright beaming' youth, Urizen as yet unfallen, who resembled Apollo. When Urizen fell into the state of Satan, or error, because of his desire for dominion, he aged and became the repressive, jealous, white-bearded hypocrite already depicted in Blake's earlier work. In the material world, Urizen is the son of Albion and Vala, and the charioteer of the material sun. In heaven, after Luvah had seized Urizen's chariot of light, drawn by the horses of instruction, 'How rag'd the golden horses of Urizen, bound to the chariot of Love.' Not until Urizen resumed control in his rightful place could reason and love fulfil their creative functions and the discords of *Vala* end.

The degenerate birth of Luvah, as Orc, followed his embryonic development in Enitharmon's womb from reptile to fish, bird, beast and, eventually, infant as already described in *Urizen*. Blake's idea of the development of the human embryo prefigures Haeckel's nineteenth-century theory, which has since been discredited. In *Vala*, when the 'Enormous Demons' first saw the terrible child, Orc, they cried: 'Luvah, King of Love, thou art the King of rage & death.' Love suppressed had turned to hate. The revolutionary Orc, fettered, escaped by reverting to the form of a worm. He grew again to a serpent. Urizen compelled him to 'stretch out & up the mysterious tree' in Eden. Orc, corruption of the revolutionary ideal, became the tempter. Eventually, burning himself out, 'Orc began to Consume in fierce raving fire' and 'The tree of Mystery went up in folding flames.' Purged of his degenerate form, Luvah is reunited with Vala, first through a wonderfully idyllic dream.

Urthona, the dark, mysterious Zoa, fell as a raging serpent, a 'Glitt'ring monster', into 'a cavern'd rock' in the world of Tharmas, who represents the senses and the body. Only at the end of *Vala*'s long sequence of events, in which Los has been the active part of him, does Urthona reappear briefly in his regenerate form to provide true knowledge. He

> rises from the ruinous Walls
> In all his ancient strength to form the golden armour of science
> For intellectual War.

Tharmas, the last Zoa to be named, was once the mildest son of heaven, wandering as a shepherd with his Emanation, Enion. In Blake's few pencil sketches of him, he is a youth. When the war of Luvah and Urizen divided the Zoas, Tharmas, the mighty father, fled howling. He quarrelled with his Emanation, Enion. Separated from him, she reduced him to a Spectre. 'The Spectre is in every man insane & most Deform'd': Blake gave the name 'Spectre' to that selfish, rational part of a divided personality which seeks to dominate the whole. Each of the four Zoas has his unnamed male Spectre besides his named female Emanation. Blake recognized these in his own mind. They prefigure the 'animus' and 'anima' of Jung's psychology. Blake wrote in his notebook:

> My Spectre around me night & day
> Like a Wild beast guards my way.
> My Emanation far within
> Weeps incessantly for my Sin.

The Spectre of Tharmas 'is Eternal Death.' In a brutal mating with Enion, it begets the twin infants, Los and Enitharmon (her name combines her parents' names). Involutions of relationship condemn the Zoas, Spectres and Emanations to a nightmarish labyrinth of desires. Tharmas, parted from Enion, seeks her in vain. He becomes, because of his sexual frustration, 'a Rage, A terror to all living things', although the emotion inherent in him is pity. Urizen tries to curb Tharmas's rage, and only when he gives up this attempt does Urizen shake off the snows of age and resume his glorious brightness. In restored harmony, Tharmas and Enion are reunited and eventually Tharmas feeds his flocks again upon the hills.

Blake left his manuscript of *Vala, or the Four Zoas* unfinished when he died. It is highly complicated by many large and small changes and illustrated with pencil sketches, most of them undeveloped, but a very few enriched with a light wash of watercolour. Rubbing out has reduced the sketches, some of which are of great beauty and interest. The erotic element, dominant in a few, is not obsessive or anguished.

In this complex poem Blake tried to build all his myths together. He fitted sections, lines and phrases from his earlier prophecies into the massive, ever-expanding fabric of this one, an epic on the scale of Homer, Dante and Milton, but without the architectural discipline that makes a vast work seem logical. His allegorical Zoas and their Emanations have characteristics but not personalities. The Zoas' few physical details recur as if in a dream: blue watery eyes of Tharmas the Neptune-figure, sparks that issue from the hair of Los. For Blake 'Fable or Allegory is seldom without some Vision.' His allegorical scheme shows astonishingly advanced insight into human urges, conflicts, repressions, tensions and eruptions. More than a century before Freud and Jung, Blake found the mind of Universal Man not only in the Bible, the alchemists and Neoplatonists, but in himself, and recreated it in poetic allegory. The various aspects of the Zoas, when tabulated, show the elaborate map of correspondences which Blake developed to convey his vision of four-fold truth. When any figure takes on a characteristic of another, the natural order is disturbed.

	URTHONA/LOS	LUVAH/ORC	URIZEN	THARMAS
emanation	Enitharmon	Vala	Ahania	Enion
nature	imaginative, wrathful	passionate, desiring	rational, controlling	compassionate
occupation and status	blacksmith, eternal prophet	wine-grower, prince of love	farmer, prince of light	shepherd, mariner
element	earth	fire	air	water
place in the body	heart/ear	loins/nose	brain/eyes	bowels/tongue
compass-point	north	east	south	west

In *Vala* Blake builds no framework out of contemporary affairs, but the background of his London, with its polluting smoke and open drains down the middle of the street, is apparent in

> cities, turrets & towers & domes
> Whose smoke destroy'd the pleasant gardens, & whose running kennels
> Chok'd the bright rivers.

And Blake, as always, is outraged by the plight of children 'sold to trades Of dire necessity, still laboring day & night' in despair, and by the degradation of 'slaves in myriads, in ship loads'. He is appalled that the simple workmanship of craftsmen is being replaced by factory jobs in which workers 'file And polish brass & iron hour after hour, laborious workmanship' for 'a scanty pittance of bread, In ignorance to view a small portion & think that All', because each worker is bound to a single process only. Christ was eventually to save humanity in *Vala, or the Four Zoas*: but although the Bible inspired, from the start of the poem, some aspects of theme, imagery, diction and narrative, the work was not, in its early drafts, overtly Christian.

Around 1797, besides beginning to write out a fair copy of *Vala*, Blake started a series of designs which resembles in form his watercolours for *Night Thoughts*. Paintings on large paper were to surround the printed, inset text of poems by the poet Thomas Gray, author of 'Elegy Written in a Country Churchyard', who had died in 1771. Blake had known his work since boyhood and acknowledged it as a source of inspiration by exhibiting in the Royal Academy in 1785 a watercolour entitled 'The Bard, from Gray'. This larger project of illustrating the 1790 edition of Gray's poems is announced in a letter to a friend in Italy from Mrs Flaxman, an ardent admirer of the illustrations for *Night Thoughts* by Blake: 'Flaxman has employed him to illuminate the works of Gray for my library.' It is conceivable that this new series of illustrations had originally been planned for publication by Edwards. Then *Night Thoughts* failed and publication was abandoned, so Flaxman—elected Associate of the Royal Academy in 1797—as usual tried in a practical way to help his friend who lacked public recognition: stepping in as prospective buyer of the single painted copy, Flaxman personally commissioned the work. Blake illuminated 116 pages with watercolour and Indian ink, using up large sheets of fresh paper left over from *Night Thoughts*. To introduce his own work, he wrote before the first poem, 'Ode on the Spring':

> Around the Springs of Gray my wild root weaves.
> Traveller repose & Dream among my leaves.

Blake puns on 'Springs' and 'leaves'. His injunction to dream shows that he wants to free the subconscious mind of the traveller seeking the gates of paradise. Gray's poems, despite their charm and learning, seldom by themselves release the mind from pessimism and prudence.

'The Bard' is the poem by Gray to which Blake responded most wholeheartedly as illustrator. Mythical bards, singing poetic prophecies and smiting their harp-strings to accompany visionary messages of revolution, had a political as well as a personal appeal to Blake, himself an ignored prophetic bard in a stricken country. Blake may have intended a pacifist's message in 'A Battle', the last of his designs for 'The Fatal Sisters', a picture of battle-slaughter somewhat similar to two of the most violent of Flaxman's drawings for the *Iliad*—Flaxman won fame throughout Europe for his seventy-three Homeric drawings, which had been commissioned in Rome.

The tepidity of most of Blake's paintings for 'Elegy Written in a Country Churchyard' implies a criticism of Gray's despondent attitude to death. As an illustrator of poets, Blake's roles extend from faithful, approving interpreter with a piercing eye for verbal detail to pugnacious warrior-artist. When poetry has erred, he leads it on into the paths of truth for which the poet has striven but failed. Blake's opposition is true friendship:

> For the Soldier who fights for Truth calls his enemy his brother:
> They fight & contend for life & not for eternal death.

Blake's most brilliant treatment is of the playfully moral, mock-solemn 'Ode on the Death of a Favourite Cat'. This urbane poem Blake wittily developed and seriously enriched. In his six sharp, deft pictures, the poem appears as an allegory of human and animal nature, and as a comment on the transforming power of sex and jealousy. Gray's drowning cat emerges eight times from the water, but Blake entitles his last picture for this poem 'Nine times emerging from the flood' and shows a completely human woman, developed from a cat, now resurrecting in prayer to a fuller, tenth life outside the sea of time and space. On the book's last page, Blake inscribed his own charming poem 'To Mrs Ann Flaxman', who prized the book highly and kept it for the rest of her life.

Blake exhibited 'The Last Supper', painted in tempera on canvas, in the Royal Academy exhibition of May 1799. That summer, Cumberland introduced him to the Rev. Dr John Trusler, a friend and neighbour from Englefield Green, near Egham. Trusler was the author of *The Way to be Rich and Respectable*. He made money himself from farming, astrology, and—ingeniously—from the sale of sermons printed to look as if they had been handwritten. These printed sheets saved worldly parsons the chore of composition, gave them extra leisure for fox-hunting, cock-fighting and backgammon, and brought Trusler £150 a year.

Trusler commissioned Blake to paint 'Malevolence': paintings of 'Benevolence', 'Pride' and 'Humility' were intended to follow. However, the materialistic priest and the unworldly artist soon disagreed. Blake found himself compelled by his own 'Genius or Angel to follow where he led', and this was not in the direction that Trusler had hoped. Blake resented interference and demanded freedom 'for fear I should Evaporate the Spirit of my Invention' who, Blake wrote, visited his slumbers, as the Muse used to visit Milton and as the commandment of the Lord used to visit the prophet Balaam. Trusler did not like Blake's watercolour of 'Malevolence' which shows two 'Fiends Incarnate' planning murder, as they lurk enviously at the mouth of a cave. Trusler found it too obscure and fanciful: it lacked the realistic life and manners of Rowlandson's caricatures, so he sent it back to Blake with a letter full of criticisms. '*Your fancy*,' he wrote, 'from what I have seen of it, and I have seen variety at Mr Cumberland's, seems to be in the other world, or the world of spirits, which accords not with my intentions, which, whilst living in this world, wish to follow *the nature of it*.' On this, Blake commented to Cumberland: 'I could not help Smiling at the difference between the doctrines of Dr Trusler & those of Christ.' To Trusler, Blake had written on 23 August 1799:

I really am sorry that you are fall'n out with the Spiritual World, Especially if I should have to answer for it. . . . You say that I want somebody to Elucidate my Ideas. But you ought to know that What is Grand is necessarily obscure to

F   81

Weak men. That which can be made Explicit to the Idiot is not worth my care. . . .

I percieve that your Eye is perverted by Caricature Prints, which ought not to abound so much as they do. Fun I love, but too much Fun is of all things the most loathsom. Mirth is better than Fun, & Happiness is better than Mirth. I feel that a Man may be happy in This World. And I know that This World Is a World of Imagination & Vision. I see Every thing I paint In This World, but Every body does not see alike. To the Eyes of a Miser a Guinea is more beautiful than the Sun, & a bag worn with the use of Money has more beautiful proportions than a Vine filled with Grapes. The tree which moves some to tears of joy is in the Eyes of others only a Green thing that stands in the way. . . . As a man is, So he Sees. . . .

But I am happy to find a Great Majority of Fellow Mortals who can Elucidate My Visions, & Particularly they have been Elucidated by Children, who have taken a greater delight in contemplating my Pictures than I even hoped. Neither Youth nor Childhood is Folly or Incapacity. Some Children are Fools & so are some Old Men. But There is a vast Majority on the side of Imagination or Spiritual Sensation.

Cumberland, who regarded Blake as a genius with some odd religious views, wrote on this letter, which Trusler—closing the episode—gave him: 'Blake, dimmed with superstition.'

However unconventional—even dangerous—Blake's ideas were, he expressed some of them ardently in notes on the pages of books that he was reading. *An Apology for The Bible*, by Robert Watson, Bishop of Llandaff, 'in a Series of Letters addressed to Thomas Paine', who had criticized one of the bishop's sermons, was annotated by Blake in 1798. That November, Johnson entered the King's Bench prison to serve a nine months' sentence for publishing the mildly radical works of the Rev. Gilbert Wakefield, which included the pamphlet *Reply to the Bishop of Llandaff's Address*. Johnson continued to run his publishing business from prison, and to hold his weekly dinners, but Blake seems not to have attended them there. His fear of being hanged for sedition drove him to darken the allegory cloaking his radical ideas, which he believed to be the gospel of Jesus, and to write on the back of Watson's title-page: 'To defend the Bible in this year 1798 would cost a man his life. The Beast & the Whore rule without control.' In the safe privacy of his own copy of Watson, Blake could dare to write openly what he believed. He ends his introductory notes: 'I have been commanded from Hell not to print this, as it is what our Enemies wish.' Here, as in *The Marriage of Heaven and Hell*, Blake uses Hell to mean inspired impulse, arising from the subconscious mind and leading to salvation.

Watson says in his preface that he is trying to defend revealed religion against 'the deistical writing of Mr Paine'. Blake, avowed enemy of deism, declares of his fellow-radical: 'Paine has not attacked Christianity. Watson has defended Antichrist', for instance in a book on 'The Wisdom and Goodness of God, in having made both *Rich and Poor*.' Blake's creed is that 'God made Man happy & Rich, but the Subtil made the innocent, Poor. This must be a most wicked & blasphemous book.'

When Watson accuses Paine of railing and sarcasm, Blake counter-accuses: 'Can any man who writes so pretend that he is in a good humour? Is not this the Bishop's cloven foot? Has he not spoil'd the hasty pudding?' Paine, according to Watson, believes that all prophets are lying rascals. Blake notes: 'Every honest man is a Prophet; he utters his opinion both of private & public matters. Thus: If you go on So, the result is So. He never says, such a thing shall happen let you do what you will. A Prophet is a Seer, not an Arbitrary Dictator.' Later, Blake notes: 'The Gospel is Forgiveness of Sins & has No Moral Precepts; these belong to Plato & Seneca & Nero' . . . 'Well done, Paine!' and finally 'It appears to me Now that Tom Paine is a better Christian than the Bishop. I have read this Book with attention & find that the Bishop has only hurt Paine's heel while Paine has broken his head. The Bishop has not answer'd one of Paine's grand objections.'

These notes suggest that Blake enjoyed the cut-and-thrust of verbal argument. No record remains of his conversations with the most argumentative of his friends, Fuseli. Blake—attentive, shrewd, outspoken—would have been a match for the loud-voiced, witty and sarcastic little Swiss. Blake, also very short in height, was the more robustly built, with eyes prominent, bright and visionary; Fuseli's eyes were piercing and brilliant, and a fever caught when he was thirty-one had left him with prematurely white hair and trembling hands. Both men enjoyed being provocative, and neither suffered fools gladly. The style of their aphorisms shows Blake to have been the more absolute and devastating in presenting opinions; but he did not speak violently and, unlike Fuseli, he acquired no reputation for invective. The minds of both men were eager and wide-ranging. Fuseli was prone to long, melancholy moods. Usually, Blake was not, although his nervous temperament exaggerated the punishment he risked for sedition (not hanging, but imprisonment might have been his fate) and he suffered from intense fears. He was, however, optimistic by nature, and unlike Fuseli he was supported by an all-embracing religious faith, though not by membership of any church or sect.

Blake relied much on individual friends to give him confidence and fellowship, although he was fiercely independent in money-matters and would not accept charity. The unfailing, careful, loving devotion given to him by Mrs Blake, whose handsome looks had soon become worn by her hard-working married life, could not fully compensate for Blake's lack of a supporting, cohesive circle of friends and patrons, such as would probably surround a successful artist, engraver or poet. Fuseli relied on the wealthiest banker in England, Thomas Coutts, to support him financially and socially. Blake, unsuccessful and absorbed in his visionary work, was an outsider. Despite all his contacts with artists and engravers, he did not fit into any group or even into any class. Warm-hearted, he loved Fuseli, whose own need for love was probably less intense because of his worldly success, and whose liking for Blake was strong but less warm than Blake's for him.

Blake's fervent, exasperated tones when he talked politics can be heard in the notes which he wrote in his copy of Bacon's *Essays* around 1798. Francis Bacon, who aspired to high office under Elizabeth I and became the Lord Chancellor of James I, aroused in Blake a passionate contempt. On the title-page of Bacon's *Essays* Blake wrote: 'Good Advice for Satan's Kingdom.' Blake despised the book because of its 'Contemptible Knavery & Folly'. That ministers arouse more public envy than kings is 'A Lie! Every Body hates a King.' As for a king being a mortal god on earth—'O Contemptible & Abject Slave!' cries Blake, and later 'Blasphemy!' Bacon on the subject of health prompts Blake to declare 'Excess in Youth is Necessary to Life.' As for taking medicine merely to accustom the body to it, Blake finds this 'Very Pernicious Advice . . . The work of a Fool to use Physic but for necessity'. Blake was blessed with health. 'I believe my Constitution to be a good one,' he wrote at the age of sixty-eight,

but it has many peculiarities that no one but myself can know. When I was young, Hampstead, Highgate [31], Hornsea, Muswell Hill, & even Islington & all places North of London, always laid me up the day after, & sometimes two or three days, with precisely the same Complaint & the same torment of [a cold in] the Stomach, Easily removed, but excruciating while it lasts & enfeebling for some time after. Sr Francis Bacon would say, it is want of discipline in Mountainous Places. Sr Francis Bacon is a Liar. No discipline will turn one Man into another, even in the least particle, & such discipline I call Presumption & Folly.

In almost three years, between the failure of *Night Thoughts* and the summer of 1800, Blake was employed to engrave designs for only six or seven books, including some plates after Fuseli in 1797 and the re-engraving, on a smaller scale, of the plates for Darwin's *Botanic Garden*. In 1799 Flaxman designed a vast 'Naval Pillar or Monument', including a colossal statue of Britannia triumphant 230 feet high, to celebrate Nelson's victorious battle of the Nile. Flaxman commissioned Blake to engrave the prospectus. Blake made three engravings of the monument, which was never built.

In these difficult times, while the war against France dragged on and the Netherlands campaign proved disastrous, Fuseli suffered disappointment with his Milton Gallery. This cherished project had developed from his paintings that were to have been engraved and published in Cowper's edition of Milton, since abandoned because of Cowper's mental illness. The popular success of Boydell's Shakespeare Gallery spurred Fuseli on to exhibit, in May 1799, his forty paintings illustrating Milton. A variety of the most fashionable artists had contributed to the Shakespeare Gallery: only Fuseli exhibited in the Milton Gallery. It failed and closed. However, he had the consolation of being elected Professor of Painting in succession to Barry at the Royal Academy.

While cash continued to be scarce, Fuseli and Johnson understandably tried to discourage Blake from creating more of his prophetic books. Although these were the works in which he felt best equipped and most truly commanded to embody his vision, hardly anybody wanted to buy them. Blake, driven in on himself and sapped of confidence, felt hounded away from his true vocation by Johnson and Fuseli; and even 'the meer drudgery of business', engraver's work, was not coming his way. However, in August 1799 he wrote to Cumberland about a regular commission from Butts for Biblical paintings. Blake had gratefully accepted Butts's kind gesture to a friend in need:

As to Myself, about whom you are so kindly Interested, I live by Miracle. I am Painting small Pictures from the Bible. For as to Engraving . . . I am laid by in a corner as if I did not Exist, & . . . Even Johnson & Fuseli have discarded my Graver. But as I know that He who Works & has his health cannot starve, I laugh at Fortune & Go on & on. I think I foresee better Things than I have ever seen. My Work pleases my employer [Butts], & I have an order for Fifty small Pictures at One Guinea each, which is Something better than mere copying after another artist. But above all, I feel myself happy & contented let what will come; having passed now near twenty years in ups & downs, I am used to them. . . . Fortune . . . Alone is the Governor of Worldly Riches, & when it is Fit She will call on me; till then I wait with Patience, in hopes that She is busied among my Friends.

5

At Felpham

1800–04

'this valley of misery & happiness mixed'

By 1800, when Blake was forty-three, his most lucrative years as an engraver had passed and so had his most intensely prolific years as a poet and artist, although he was yet to produce masterpieces of superb visual and poetic splendour. The new century was to bring a dramatic change in his life and to entwine his fortunes intimately with those of William Hayley: he was a patron of Flaxman and the artist George Romney, and a friend of the poet William Cowper and the historian Edward Gibbon.

Hayley (28), twelve years Blake's senior, was born in 1745 in Chichester. A fever in boyhood left him with a defective hip and a life-long limp. At Cambridge he painted and he continued to do so until 1772, when a cold in his eyes which were, he wrote, 'drowned in blood', permanently weakened them. In 1767, determined to write for the stage, he came to London, and settled at 5 Great Queen Street. However, his plays were rejected by theatre managers, so he began an epic poem. He was fascinated by books and pictures, and as he collected prints he presumably went to look at those that Basire had for sale at nearby 31 Great Queen Street. Hayley, the tall lame poet, and Blake, the stocky red-haired apprentice, living in the same street between 1772 and 1774, must often have seen each other and may well have conversed at Basire's.

In 1774 William Hayley and his wife Eliza moved from London to Eartham, their small family estate about eight miles north-east of Chichester. Hayley loved having friends to stay, including the Flaxmans and the neurotic portrait-painter Romney, to whom he addressed *The Epistle on Painting*. This successful poem launched Hayley on an astonishing career as a popular poet, whose best-seller, *Triumphs of Temper*, written in 1780, established him—Ozias Humphry said—as 'the *work-basket poet* of that day: his verses were upon every girl's sopha.' Samuel Johnson could not get beyond the first two pages of *Triumphs of Temper*. The poem's simple theme is that if a girl wants a good husband she needs a good temper. The autumn of 1780 brought proof that the poet was not finding in his frigid, childless Eliza all that he desired in a wife. On 5 October Miss Betts, housemaid at Eartham, gave birth to Hayley's illegitimate son, Thomas Alphonso. Eliza, on medical advice, went to stay at Bath and then her marriage crumbled. But Hayley, 'The Hermit of Eartham' as he liked to call himself, continued to enjoy his home. There he entertained his friends, acted as amateur doctor to his tenants and poured out a prodigious flow of tepid verses at amazing speed. 'Everything about that man,' Southey wrote, 'is good except his poetry.'

Hayley inspired respect and affection among artists. At a select dinner in Hampstead in 1786 to launch Boydell's Shakespeare Gallery, he was acceptable as a man of learning and taste. Young Tom, his intelligent, high-spirited and charming son, who was learning Latin at the age of four from the delighted Hayley, and Greek before the age of six, was destined for a medical career: but in 1794 Romney wrote that 'dear Tom' was discovering 'a growing passion for the noble art of sculpture'. Flaxman, four days after returning to London from seven years in Rome, made a handsome offer to Hayley: 'Send him to me! I will instruct him in all the little I know, and it shall not cost you a farthing. . . . In your absence I will be his father, and my dear Nancy promises to look to his morals.'

Tom, aged fourteen, was apprenticed on 15 February 1795. He loved his work. 'The vigour with which I attack the clay,' he wrote, 'makes me eat a great deal.' On 6 July, Flaxman's birthday, they visited the Shakespeare Gallery in the evening and drank tea somewhere on the other side of the river—perhaps at 13 Hercules Buildings, for Blake was one of Flaxman's oldest friends.

Tom studied extremely hard, reading history, Greek and Latin besides learning to sculpt. Heavily overworked, at the age of fifteen and a half he fell ill. Flaxman sent him to Eartham to recover. During Tom's few weeks at home, Hayley discussed with him a plan to build a smaller house, a Marine Turret, nine or ten miles from Eartham in the little seaside village of Felpham, to the east of Bognor. Tom soon returned to work at the Flaxmans'. By March 1797, he was making a Druid's head out of a fragment of a Stonehenge monolith and in April, at Felpham, he laid the first stone of the Marine Turret.

However, he was far from well, though doctors could find nothing wrong with him. On 5 March 1798, Hayley, now seriously alarmed, himself discovered that Tom's malady was curvature of the spine. Paralysis followed: before Tom was eighteen, he lost the use of his legs. Very bravely he endured great pain. Knowing that Tom was dying, Hayley hurried to finish the *Essay on Sculpture*, a series of verse epistles addressed to Flaxman, for which Tom had drawn 'The Death of Demosthenes'. To engrave this and a vignette of Tom's head as decorations for the printed poem, Flaxman recommended his needy friend, Blake.

Hayley expressed delight at 'that worthy, ingenious' engraver's 'outline of dear Tom's Demosthenes', but Blake's engraving of Tom at the age of sixteen, from a medallion by Flaxman, deeply disappointed Hayley: 'the dear, juvenile, pleasant face' looked heavy, sullen, sulky. Tom, wrote Hayley, agreed with him that the drawing was all wrong. Blake improved his first plate, but Hayley deferentially suggested further touches to 'add a little gay juvenility'. Hayley appreciated Blake as 'a *kind-hearted Brother of Parnassus*' and confided in him 'the heart-rending affliction of seeing a child so justly beloved *perishing by slow tortures*'. Tom lived long enough to help correct the proofs of the *Essay on Sculpture* and to enjoy seeing his drawing of Demosthenes engraved by Blake; he died on 2 May 1800 at the age of nineteen years, five months.

Four days later Blake wrote to Hayley, with the engraved vignette of Tom: 'I am very sorry for your immense loss, which is a repetition of what all feel in this valley of misery & happiness mixed. I send the Shadow of the departed Angel: hope the likeness is improved. . . . I know that our deceased friends are more really with us than when they were apparent to our mortal part.' This letter goes on joyfully to affirm Blake's spiritual companionship with his brother Robert.

In May, Blake exhibited his tempera 'The Loaves and Fishes' at the Royal Academy and twelve-year-old Tommy Butts, son of Thomas Butts for whom Blake was painting Biblical pictures, noted in his diary on Tuesday 13 May: 'Mr and Mrs Blake and Mr T. Jones drank tea with mama.' As the summer wore on, Blake, sapped of confidence by his sense of failure and depressed by what he called his 'stupid Melancholy', shrank from burdening others and dared to visit few friends. On 2 July he wrote to Cumberland:

I begin to Emerge from a Deep pit of Melancholy, Melancholy without any real reason for it, a Disease which God keep you from & all good men. Our artists of all ranks praise your outlines & wish for more. I have been too little among friends which I fear they will not Excuse & I know not how to apologize for.

In July, Hayley sent Blake Tom's copy of *Triumphs of Temper*, and invited him down to the Turret for a few days to work on a new picture of Tom from the boy's self-portrait in crayons, and to engrave a portrait of Tom by Romney.

Blake had never before travelled so far from London, or lived so close to the open sea. The Turret was a mere ten-minute walk from the wide, sandy beach where village boys played cricket and a few enthusiasts, including Hayley, stepped out to bathe in the English Channel. One or two bathing machines had recently arrived, to protect the modesty of swimmers, but nudity was acceptable early in the morning. Bognor, a country walk away from Felpham, was only then being developed as a watering place, with new Georgian squares, terraces and crescents. Felpham was unspoilt, a tiny village set in fields that stretched to the shore: Blake found it beautiful and he stayed on to perfect his work.

Hayley warmed to his 'good, enthusiastic friend' Blake, and Blake warmed to him. The bereaved father's inflamed love for his son probably moved Hayley to exaggerate, in his own mind, the strength of Blake's feeling for Tom, whom Blake must often have met at the Flaxmans': but Blake's sympathy and liking for Hayley were obvious. Hayley was an exceptionally kind-hearted patron of the arts, a scholarly enthusiast whose help had been sought and gladly received by men of distinction. In 1790 he had been offered the poet laureateship at the death of Thomas Warton but, as a Whig whose beliefs might prove incompatible with the post, he had refused it. He was well known, and he might be able to do much for an engraver and painter who wanted to work locally. Blake, seeking a change of fortune, decided to move to Felpham. He rented from the land-lord of the Fox Inn, for £20 a year, the thatched cottage nearest to the sea (32). About two hundred yards seawards of the Turret garden, sixty yards from the Fox Inn and a quarter of a mile from the shore, the sturdy cottage still remains.

Only a few days before Tom died, Hayley had suffered the grievous blow of the death of a dearly loved friend, the poet William Cowper. To the memory of these two people for whom his heart ached, Hayley deter-mined to dedicate his abundant literary energies and his time. He would write his *Memoirs* of Tom and the *Life of Cowper*. In biography, Hayley was not a novice. He had written a life of Milton (which had at first proved too radical for publication), but, because of Cowper's insanity and the deter-mination of his formidable cousin, Lady Hesketh, to keep family secrets unbroken, the first biographer of Cowper was to have an unusually exacting task. As a preliminary, Hayley assured her on 22 July that Cowper's portrait by Romney could be engraved without even being moved from the library of the Turret:

for a most worthy, enthusiastic engraver, who has within these few days finished for me a small drawing . . . has attached himself so much to me, that he has taken a cottage in this little marine village to pursue his art in its various branches under my auspices; and as he has infinite genius with a most engaging simplicity of character, I hope he will execute many admirable things . . . with the aid of an excellent wife, to whom he has been married seventeen years, and who shares his labours and his talents.

Butts, delighted, thought that the intended move to Felpham would lead Blake to fortune. Flaxman, more cautiously optimistic, wrote to Hayley:

I see no reason why he should not make as good a livelihood there as in London, if he engraves and teaches drawing, by which he may gain considerably, as also by making neat drawings of different kinds: but if he places any dependence on painting large pictures, for which he is not qualified, either by habit or study, he will be miserably deceived.

Meanwhile, Blake prepared to move from London. On Friday 12 September he wrote joyfully to Flaxman, who by introducing Blake to Hayley had made Felpham possible: 'It is to you I owe All my present Happiness. It is to you I owe perhaps the Principal Happiness of my life.' Blake hopes that his 'Dearest Friend . . . will forgive the Poetry', and then writes:

> I bless thee, O Father of Heaven & Earth, that ever I saw Flaxman's face.
> Angels stand round my Spirit in Heaven, the blessed of Heaven are my
> friends upon Earth . . .
> And now Flaxman hath given me Hayley his friend to be mine, such my lot
> upon Earth.

Mrs Blake, equally happy and grateful, wrote to Mrs Flaxman:

it is only Sixty Miles, & Lambeth was One Hundred [from Hampstead], for the terrible desart of London was between. My husband has been obliged to finish several things . . . before our migration; the Swallows call us, fleeting past our window at this moment. O how we delight in talking of the pleasure we shall have in preparing you a summer bower at Felpham, & we not only talk, but behold! the Angels of our journey have inspired a song to you.

Mrs Blake's letter continues with a poem of unalloyed delight by Blake, asking Mrs Flaxman to entice her husband to Blake's cottage:

> Away to Sweet Felpham, for Heaven is there;
> The Ladder of Angels descends thro' the air;
> On the Turret its spiral does softly descend,
> Thro' the village then winds, at My Cot it does end.

Instead of the Blakes setting out on Tuesday 16 September as arranged, their journey had to be postponed, as Blake told Hayley: 'My Dear & too careful & over joyous Woman has Exhausted her strength to such a degree with expectation & gladness added to labour in our removal that I fear it will be Thursday before we can get away from this—City.' They would take the Petworth road and come through Eartham, which, Blake wrote: 'will be my first temple & altar. My wife is like a flame of many colours of precious jewels whenever she hears it named', for in her responsiveness she resembled Blake. He sends his 'Love & Respect', and adds to his letter: 'My fingers Emit sparks of fire with Expectation of my future labours.'

Blake's sister Catherine, unmarried and the youngest member of the family, went with them to live at Felpham. They 'set out between Six & Seven in the Morning of Thursday, with Sixteen heavy boxes & portfolios full of prints'—their luggage included a printing press, plates of the illuminated books and much paper—and 'travel'd thro' a most beautiful country on a most glorious day.' 'Our Journey,' Blake wrote to Flaxman, whom he called 'Dear Sculptor of Eternity', 'was very pleasant; & tho we had a great deal of Luggage, No Grumbling, All was Chearfulness & Good Humour on the Road, & yet we could not arrive at our Cottage before half past Eleven at night, owing to the necessary shifting of our Luggage from one Chaise to another; for we had Seven Different Chaises, & as many different drivers.' 'Our Cottage,' Blake wrote to Butts, 'is more beautiful than I thought it, & also more convenient, for tho' small it is well proportion'd. . . . Please to tell Mrs Butts that we have dedicated a Chamber for her service. . . .' Mrs Flaxman, too, the Blakes 'ardently desire to Entertain beneath our thatched roof of rusted gold' in the six-room cottage of two storeys, with its front door facing across the small garden towards cornfields, meadows and the sea-side.

Hayley received the Blakes 'with his usual brotherly affection'; Blake started work the day after they arrived, 'And Now Begins a New Life, because another covering of Earth is shaken off. . . . In my Brain are studies & Chambers fill'd with books & pictures of old, which I wrote & painted in ages of Eternity before my mortal life.' He wrote to Butts, 'Dear Friend of My Angels', three days after arriving:

My Wife & Sister are both very well, & courting Neptune for an Embrace, whose terrors this morning made them afraid, but whose mildness is often Equal to his terrors. The Villagers of Felpham are not meer Rustics; they are polite & modest. Meat is cheaper than in London, but the sweet air & the voices of winds, trees & birds, & the odours of the happy ground, makes it a dwelling for immortals. Work will go on here with God speed.

Blake, who perceived farm implements and a ploughboy's words to be symbols of artistic creation, continued: 'A roller & two harrows lie before my window. I met a plow on my first going out at my gate the first morning after my arrival, & the Plowboy said to the Plowman, "Father, The Gate is Open." ' Blake finds that he 'can work with greater pleasure than ever. . . . I shall wish for you,' he tells Butts, 'on Tuesday Evening as usual. . . . My Sister will be in town in a week, & bring with her your account & whatever else I can finish.'

Butts replied gratefully. He banteringly acknowledged that Blake's reference to angels had as usual perplexed him. Then, in earnest tones, he declared:

Whether you will be a better painter or a better poet from your change of ways and means I know not; but this I predict, that you will be a better man—excuse me, as you have been accustomed from friendship to do, but certain opinions imbibed from reading, nourished by indulgence, and riveted by a confined conversation, and which have been equally prejudicial to your interest and happiness, will now, I trust, disperse as a day-break vapour.

To the Archbishop of Canterbury himself—according to Butts—Blake signified 'dim incredulity, haggard suspicion, and bloated philosophy'.

Blake humbly accepted the criticism from his 'Friend of Religion & Order' (as he now called the patient, orthodox Butts) and wrote on 2 October to thank him for his 'reprehension of follies by me foster'd. Your prediction will, I hope, be fulfilled in me, & in future I am the determined advocate of Religion & Humility, the two bands of Society. Having been so full of the Business of Settling the sticks & feathers of my nest, I have not got any forwarder with "the three Marys" or with any other of your commissions': but Blake hoped, in his new life, to produce 'Improved Works'. He then described, in shimmering verse, his 'first Vision of Light' when he sat on the yellow sands at Felpham. His eyes expanded into regions of air and fire, until 'The jewels of Light' shone distinct and clear. Amazed, he saw each shining form as a man beckoning and saying that each grain of sand, herb and tree was a man, and all larger created things—mountain, sea and cloud—'Men Seen Afar'. To Blake's expanding vision 'the Jewels of Light' in the heavens then 'Appear'd as One Man' (Los, the Spirit of Prophecy) who enfolded Blake's limbs in beams of bright gold, purging away all the mire and clay of his body and in a mild voice saying to him: 'This is My Fold, O thou Ram horn'd with gold.'

Blake resumed his letter in prose, apologized for not having finished a miniature of Butts, and continued: 'Chichester is a very handsom City, Seven miles from us; we can get most Conveniences there. The Country is not so destitute of accomodations to our wants as I expected it would be . . . what we have seen is Most Beautiful, & the People are Genuine Saxons, handsomer than the people about London.'

Hayley's religious beliefs were suspect. His reputed unorthodoxy, not helped by his friendship with the infidel historian Edward Gibbon, cannot have encouraged Butts (or the Archbishop) to hope that Blake would find in the Turret a guiding light to the established Church. But Hayley's good deeds shone out. Though busily writing about Tom and faced with much work on Cowper, on 22 September he wrote a ballad about another victim of misfortune, 'Little Tom the Sailor', and set Blake to work to print and illustrate it with two designs. The ballad was to be sold as a broadsheet to relieve 'the Widow Spicer', mother of little Tom. Blake soon finished his relief etching of the text on copper, his woodcuts of the headpiece and tailpiece on pewter, and dated the work 5 October. Mrs Blake printed the broadsheet on the hand-press and some watercolour washes were then added.

An absorbing commission from Hayley was the painting in light tempera on canvas of a series of eighteen 'Heads of the Poets' to decorate the library at the Turret as a memorial to Tom. This room, although it occupied all the east side of the upper storey of the house, could not take all Hayley's remarkable collection of English and foreign books. In 1821, the year after he died, they were to be auctioned in 2,649 lots, the sale lasting thirteen days. Homer and Milton were the authors of whom he owned most editions.

His knowledge of Italian, Spanish and Portuguese literature was exceptional in the England of his day, and Dante had never been translated into English before Hayley translated the first three cantos of the *Inferno*. Blake's subjects reflected Hayley's wide tastes and included Homer, Cicero, Dante, Chaucer, Camõens, Ercilla, Spenser, Milton, Dryden, Otway, Pope and Cowper. Carefully drawn leaves, flowers and berries were subtly varied by Blake to suit the heads that they were to wreathe.

Tom was to be commemorated not only by the fireplace which he had himself designed and by Blake's portrait of him, but by some of the figures in the backgrounds of other canvases. Tom's pencil drawing of the death of Demosthenes—'conceived', Flaxman had said, 'with a truly Grecian greatness and simplicity'—was faithfully copied by Blake alongside the heavily wreathed head of Demosthenes. Tom's work may also be reflected in pictures accompanying Shakespeare, Tasso, Voltaire and Klopstock, who was known as 'the Milton of Germany'. Klopstock's complaints about the coarseness of English verse, which he traced to Swift, had been repaid by Blake in a ribald comic poem in his notebook. 'When Klopstock England defied', the traditional deity, 'old Nobodaddy aloft [roughly equivalent to Urizen, and probably named from 'Nobody's Daddy'] Farted & Belch'd & cough'd' and called to 'English Blake', who was sitting in the privy under the poplar trees at Lambeth, 'giving his body ease'. Blake 'turned himself round three times three' and used the astral medicine of Paracelsus to cast a spell on Klopstock's bowels, so that Klopstock's soul could not be unlocked from its body 'Till to the last trumpet it was farted.' Old Nobodaddy, who had never seen such a thing since creation, 'beg'd me to turn again And ease poor Klopstock's ninefold pain.' In pity, Blake unwound the spell.

Hayley's comprehensive library and print-collection supplied Blake with all the pictures he needed of the writers he was going to portray. By November 1800 he was busy on the series, which he presumably painted in his cottage, although its windows were small and the light cannot have been good. Dampness from a spring seeped up through the earth floor and the single layer of floor-boards, and Mrs Blake became ill. On 26 November, when Hayley was away, Blake wrote to him:

Absorbed by the poets Milton, Homer, Camoens, Ercilla, Ariosto, and Spenser, whose physiognomies have been my delightful study, *Little Tom* has been of late unattended to, and my wife's illness not being quite gone off, she has not printed any more since you went to London. . . . We mean to begin printing again tomorrow. Time flies very fast and very merrily. I sometimes try to be miserable that I may do more work, but find it is a foolish experiment. . . .

In February 1801, Hayley wrote to Romney that Blake was engraving Romney's portrait of Cowper, for Hayley's *Life*. Blake 'says I have taught him to paint in miniature and, in truth, he has improved his excellent versatile talents very much.' One of Blake's miniatures was of Cowper's lively young cousin, the Rev. John Johnson. 'Johnny of Norfolk', as he was called, visited Felpham and, when writing to Hayley on 17 March, added: 'Remember me most kindly to our dear friend Blake, and the duck to whom he is a drake!—Also to the incomparable inhabitant of the peerless villa of Lavant'—the delightful Miss Harriet Poole, Hayley's friend who lived some three miles north of Chichester. Hayley had already introduced Blake to her and to other notable people in the neighbourhood, potential patrons of a miniaturist.

When Lady Hesketh received, from Hayley, Blake's miniature of Cowper painted from Romney's portrait, she was horrified. 'This fatal resemblance' was, she wrote, *'dreadful! shocking!'* because—although she did not say so—Blake had caught Romney's hint of her cousin's madness. Hayley tried to soothe her, but he did not change his plan of publication.

On 10 May, Blake wrote to Butts: 'Mr Hayley acts like a Prince. I am at complete Ease, but I wish to do my duty, especially to you, who were the precursor of my present Fortune. I never will send you a picture unworthy of my present proficiency. I soon shall send you several; my present engagements are in Miniature Painting. Miniature is become a Goddess in my Eyes, & my Friends in Sussex say that I Excel in the pursuit. I have a great many orders, & they Multiply.' He pressed the Buttses to visit him.

Three days later, on 13 May, enclosing a miniature—long overdue and freshly painted—of his dead wife Eliza, Hayley complacently wrote to a friend: 'I have recently formed a new artist for this purpose by teaching a worthy creature (by profession an engraver) who lives in a little cottage very near me to paint in miniature.' The *Life of Cowper* and its engravings would, Hayley hoped, be ready for the printer by Christmas. In September, Blake was engraving a portrait of Cowper's mother. Hayley's friends quickly took a liking to Blake and, as Johnny Johnson had done, sent him greetings in letters to Hayley.

On 11 September, Blake sent Butts the miniature that had been unfinished eleven months before and wrote: 'I labour incessantly & accomplish not one half of what I intend, because my Abstract folly hurries me often away while I am at work, carrying me over Mountains & Valleys, which are not Real, in a Land of Abstraction where Spectres of the Dead wander.' (By these spectres, Blake seems to mean abstract ideas which only inspiration can bring to life.) This folly, Blake continued, 'I endeavour to prevent & with my whole might chain my feet to the world of Duty & Reality; but in vain! the faster I bind, the better is the Ballast, for I, so far from being bound down, take the world with me in my flights, & often it seems lighter than a ball of wool rolled by the wind.' Though Blake must seem to have neglected Butts's most pleasant orders for pictures from the Bible, 'I have not neglected them, & yet a Year is rolled over.' Soon Blake will send, on the coach which goes three times a week to London, several pictures together, some of which are not yet completed. He adds, after his signature: 'Next time I have the happiness to see you, I am determined to paint another Portrait of you from Life . . . for I have now discover'd that without Nature before the painter's Eye, he can never produce any thing in the walks of Natural Painting.'

Hayley pressed Johnny Johnson to visit the Turret in October, and wrote to him: 'the warmhearted, indefatigable Blake works daily by my side, on the intended decorations of our biography. Engraving, of all human works, appears to require the largest portion of patience, and he happily possesses more of that inestimable virtue than I ever saw united before to an imagination so lively and so prolific!'

To Flaxman, Blake wrote in October, rejoicing at the prospect of peace now that negotiations had opened with Napoleon (they were to be concluded in March 1802): 'The Kingdoms of this World are now become the Kingdoms of God & his Christ, & we shall reign with him for ever & ever. The Reign of Literature & the Arts Commences. Blessed are those who are found studious of Literature & Humane & polite accomplishments. Such have their lamps burning & such shall shine as the stars.' Blake goes on to write that the Rev. Joseph Thomas of Epsom, a new patron whom he owed to Flaxman's unfailing care and who was to prove very generous,

has been at Felpham & did me the favor to call on me. I have promis'd him to send my designs for Comus when I have done them, directed to you.

Now I hope to see the Great Works of Art, as they are so near to Felpham, Paris being scarce further off than London.

Blake's hope of going abroad was never to be fulfilled. For his knowledge of works of art outside a limited area round Felpham and London, where he probably saw many privately owned pictures exhibited from time to time, he had to depend, all his life, on engravings, copies, written descriptions and travellers' tales.

His only book-engraving in 1801 was a portrait of Michelangelo, for the Royal Academy *Lectures on Painting* by Fuseli, whose old friend of student days, Lavater, had died in January. In contrast to Blake's faith in spirits was the disbelief of Fuseli, who said: 'I hate superstition. When I was in Switzerland [1778–9], talking with Lavater upon the appearance of the spirit after death, it was agreed between us, that if it were allowed by the Deity to visit earth, the first who died should appear to the other; my friend was the most scrupulous man in existence with regard to his word; he is dead, and I have not seen him.'

While Blake was at Felpham, his life-long intimacy with Milton developed in intensity. The fine library of Milton's works at the Turret helped to stimulate this, and so did Hayley's plan for Blake to illustrate Milton's Latin poems in Cowper's translation. Subjects from Milton were popular with artists in Blake's time. Barry, Flaxman, Mortimer, Romney, Smirke, Stothard and Wright of Derby all, in varying degrees, illustrated

Milton, though Fuseli's passionate dedication was approached by none of them. Blake is exceptional in his broad but detailed understanding of Milton, his fidelity to Milton's poetry and the copious originality of his illustrations. He began with the masque *Comus* (a work far less often illustrated than *Paradise Lost*), and painted two sets of eight watercolour illustrations: one set was for Thomas, the other was bought later by Butts. In designs that are enigmatic, chaste but erotic, statuesque but mobile, Blake reinterprets the poetic sophistication and dramatic naïvety of *Comus* (35).

Towards the end of 1801, Hayley, despite all his biographical work (his *Life of Cowper* was not ready for the printer until the following March) wrote some children's ballads about animals, for Blake to illustrate. Like the *Life*, they would be printed by Seagrave, a Chichester printer and friend of Hayley, and the ballads would be sold as broadsheets entirely for Blake's benefit. Every evening that winter, in the Turret library, Hayley played the schoolmaster—a role which he had always enjoyed—and taught Blake Greek. The forty-four-year-old student, who as a boy had escaped ordinary schooling, possessed a natural flair for languages. Together, teacher and pupil collated Homer's *Odyssey* with the first edition of Cowper's translation and the new edition, which Johnny Johnson was preparing, of Cowper's poems. Blake's heads of Homer, Cowper and Tom, and Romney's portraits of Cowper and 'Lady Hamilton as Sensibility', were notable among the many painted faces that gazed across the candlelit table where the two men worked.

Blake would often ride with Hayley to visit Miss Poole at Mid Lavant, a good ten miles away: Blake on the pony Bruno (probably Tom's, which had been looked after by Miss Poole since Tom's death and was now lent to Blake) and Hayley on Hidalgo, his favourite white charger. Hayley enjoyed riding high-spirited horses despite his faulty hip-joint, and he always added to the risk by carrying an umbrella, which he used in bright light as a parasol to protect his weak eyes. Not surprisingly he was often thrown, and he alarmed his friends by his persistence.

Hayley continued to write about Blake during that winter as 'an excellent creature with admirable talents', 'our worthy friend Blake', 'our good Blake'. At the cottage, however, the winter was not happy. On 10 January 1802 Blake wrote to thank Butts for a letter. After referring to his wife's constant 'Ague and Rheumatism' and his own illness at Felpham, he goes on:

When I came down here, I was more sanguine than I am at present; but it was because I was ignorant of many things which have since occurred, & chiefly the unhealthiness of the place. Yet I do not repent of coming on a thousand accounts; & Mr H., I doubt not, will do ultimately all that both he & I wish—that is, to lift me out of difficulty; but this is no easy matter to a man who, having Spiritual Enemies of such formidable magnitude, cannot expect to want natural hidden ones.

Thus wept the Angel voice & as he wept the terrible blasts
Of trumpets, blew a loud alarm across the Atlantic deep.
No trumpets answer; no reply of clarions or of fifes,
Silent the Colonies remain and refuse the loud alarm.

On these vast shady hills between America & Albions shore;
Now barr'd out by the Atlantic sea: call'd Atlantean hills;
Because from their bright summits you may pass to the Golden world
An ancient palace, archetype of mighty Emperies,
Rears its immortal pinnacles, built in the forest of God
By Ariston the king of beauty for his stolen bride.

Here on their magic seats the thirteen Angels sat perturb'd
For clouds from the Atlantic hover oer the solemn roof.

1 Plate from *America*, 1792–1820; relief-etching finished in pen and watercolour
heightened with gold paint. Orc, the springing, fiery adolescent, red-haired like
Blake, inflames the American colonies to rebel

Plates from *Songs of Innocence* (1789–94). Blake's processes of creating a plate—writing, relief-etching, printing and colouring—often spanned many years. Examples 2, 3, 4 and 5 are relief-etchings finished in pen and water-colour, here reduced slightly from actual size.

2 (*Right*) 'Infant Joy'; in most copies (compare that reproduced on the jacket of this book), the womb-like impregnated flower and flaccid bud are coloured scarlet or vermilion

3 (*Left*) 'Laughing Song'; at the open-air feast, the standing boy waves his hat, holds up his glass and sings

Plates from *Songs of Experience*, 1794

4 (*Left*) 'London'; a boy leads an old man with a crutch and, below, maintains the fire of life

5 (*Right*) 'The Tyger'; the poem is built of awe-inspired questions, unlikely to be prompted by the tiger shown below them

6   Plate from *The Book of Urizen*, 1794–1815; relief-etching finished in watercolour (actual size). In Air, one of the four elements illustrated full-page, Urizen tumbles on rocks or clouds

7   (*Opposite top*) Watercolour, 1796–7: title-page, 'Night the Eighth', *Night Thoughts* (Edward Young); the Whore of Babylon dominates worldly powers, a seven-headed monster

8   (*Opposite below*) Wool and silk embroidery, c. 1800, Mrs T. Butts: 'Two Hares in Long Grass'. Designer unknown: unconventional style and colour suggest Blake

THE
COMPLAINT.
OR,
Night-Thoughts
ON
LIFE, DEATH, and IMMORTALITY.

NIGHT the EIGHTH.
VIRTUE's APOLOGY:
OR,
The MAN of the WORLD Answer'd.

In which are Considered,
The LOVE of This LIFE;
The AMBITION and PLEASURE, with the WIT
and WISDOM of the WORLD.

LONDON:
Printed for G. HAWKINS, at Milton's Head, between the Two Temple-
Gates, Fleet-street, near Temple-Bar.
And Sold by M. COOPER, at the Globe, in Pater-noster Row.
MDCCXLV.

9   Watercolour, c. 1800–3: 'Jacob's Ladder', Genesis 28:12; angels descend to dreaming Jacob, bringing bread, wine, scroll of vision, book and scientific compasses

10   Plate from *Milton*, 1808–15; relief-etching finished in watercolour,
heightened in gold paint (actual size). His sandals bound on, Blake turns
to become 'One Man' with Los and 'walk forward thro' Eternity'

11 Frontispiece, *Europe*, 1794; relief-etching finished in watercolour, black ink
and gold paint in 1827, for Frederick Tatham; 'Urizen Creating the Universe'.
Urizen's compasses cannot bind the infinite: they impose rational order on a
material world

Your approbation of my pictures is a Multitude to Me. . . . Your kind offer of pecuniary assistance I can only thank you for at present, because I have enough to serve my present purpose here; our expenses are small, & our income, from our incessant labour, fully adequate to them at present. I am now engaged in Engraving 6 small plates for a New Edition of Mr Hayley's Triumphs of Temper, from drawings by Maria Flaxman, sister to my friend the Sculptor, and it seems that other things will follow in course, if I do but Copy these well. . . . One thing of real consequence I have accomplish'd by coming into the country, which is to me consolation enough: namely, I have recollected all my scatter'd thoughts on Art & resumed my primitive & original ways of Execution in both painting & engraving, which in the confusion of London I had very much lost & obliterated from my mind. . . .

But you have so generously & openly desired that I will divide my griefs with you, that I cannot hide what it is now become my duty to explain.—My unhappiness has arisen from a source which . . . might hurt my pecuniary circumstances, As my dependence is . . . particularly on the Engravings I have in hand for Mr H.: & I find on all hands great objections to my doing any thing but the meer drudgery of business, & intimations that if I do not confine myself to this, I shall not live; this has always pursu'd me. You will understand by this the source of all my uneasiness. This from Johnson & Fuseli brought me down here, & this from Mr H. will bring me back again; for that I cannot live without doing my duty to lay up treasures in heaven is Certain & Determined, & to this I have long made up my mind. . . . The Thing I have most at Heart—more than life, or all that seems to make life comfortable without—Is the Interest of True Religion & Science, [inspired art and spiritual knowledge, revelations of Christ] & whenever any thing appears to affect that Interest (Especially if I myself omit any duty to my Station as a Soldier of Christ), It gives me the greatest of torments. I am not ashamed, afraid, or averse to tell you what Ought to be Told: That I am under the direction of Messengers from Heaven, Daily & Nightly. . . . Temptations are on the right hand & left; behind, the sea of time & space roars & follows swiftly; he who keeps not right onward is lost, & if our footsteps slide in clay, how can we do otherwise than fear & tremble? but . . . if we fear to do the dictates of our Angels, & tremble at the Tasks set before us; if we refuse to do Spiritual Acts because of Natural Fears or Natural Desires! Who can describe the dismal torments of such a state!—I too well remember the Threats I heard!—If you, who are organised by Divine Providence for Spiritual communion, Refuse, & bury your Talent in the Earth, even tho' you should want Natural Bread, Sorrow & Desperation pursues you thro' life, & after death shame & confusion of face to eternity. Every one in Eternity will leave you, aghast at the Man who was crown'd with glory & honour by his brethren, & betray'd their cause to their enemies. You will be call'd the base Judas who betray'd his Friend! —Such words would make any stout man tremble, & how then could I be at ease? But I am now no longer in That State, & now go on again with my Task, Fearless, and tho' my path is difficult, I have no fear of stumbling while I keep it.

Blake expresses his own and his wife's frequent wish to be with Mr and Mrs Butts again, and he is 'determin'd not to remain another winter here, but to return to London'.

Blake's vital need to fulfil his prophetic mission was far beyond the comprehension of Hayley. That well-intentioned, unspiritual, possessive patron, from a mixture of kindly and selfish motives, hoped to bind Blake to him by pedestrian commissions for engravings and miniatures. Blake intensely resented this restriction. Perhaps he had already shown Hayley the developing manuscript of *Vala* or some pages of his new epic, *Milton*, begun at Felpham though not engraved until later; or he may have told Hayley his plans for a third epic, *Jerusalem*, which was conceived at Felpham though not written there. Hayley would obviously have regarded such astonishing works as a waste of time, and possibly he said so. His threats of unemployment profoundly disturbed and tormented Blake, who revealed his anguish only to his wife—and to Butts when that concerned and wonderfully sympathetic friend pressed him to do so. Blake successfully hid his real feelings and purposes from Hayley. 'The zealous, indefatigable Blake', 'our kind Blake', 'the good Blake' continued to work daily by Hayley's side. On 3 February 1802, 'Here', wrote Hayley, contributing to Johnny Johnson's edition of Cowper's *Odyssey*, 'is instantaneously a title page for thee, and a Greek motto, which I and Blake, who has just become a Grecian and literally learning the language, consider as a happy hit!'

On 16 May Hayley wrote to Johnny Johnson about Blake: 'he is at this moment by my side, representing on copper an Adam, of his own, surrounded by animals, as a frontispiece to the projected ballads.' These animal ballads, beginning with *The Elephant*, were planned, Hayley told Lady Hesketh, as a fifteen-part series, one ballad 'every month with three prints annexed to it, for the moderate price of half a crown', the sales to be boosted by Hayley's friends. Johnson and Lady Hesketh liked the elephant at first sight and were hopeful about sales, but the latter wrote that an eighty-two-year-old man of taste and a woman of quality were critical of the illustrations. To stimulate the artist's 'endeavours after perfection', Lady Hesketh—who had not met Blake—gave details. Perhaps Blake remembered this episode when he wrote some years later: 'The Enquiry in England is not whether a Man has Talents & Genius, But whether he is Passive & Polite & a Virtuous Ass & obedient to Noblemen's Opinions in Art & Science. If he is, he is a Good Man. If Not, he must be Starved.'

On 15 July Hayley wrote to Lady Hesketh, boldly comparing Blake with Cowper. Despite her horror of the subject of her cousin's madness, Hayley dared to refer to it:

my diligent and grateful artist [Blake] resembles our beloved bard [Cowper] in the tenderness of his heart, and in the perilous powers of an imagination utterly unfit to take due care of himself. With admirable faculties, his sensibility is so *dangerously acute*, that the common rough treatment which true genius often receives from *ordinary minds* in the commerce of the world, might not only wound him *more than it should do*, but really reduce him to the incapacity of an idiot without the consolatory support of a considerate friend.

There is, Hayley claims, true genius even in Blake's wildest works and he has the capacity to draw pictures 'almost as excellent and original' as Cowper's poetry. Of Cowper, Blake

often reminds me of little touches of *nervous infirmity*, when his mind is darkened with any unpleasant apprehension. He reminds me of him also by being a most fervent admirer of the Bible, and intimately acquainted with all its beauties. . . . Heaven has bestowed on this extraordinary mortal perhaps the only female on earth, who could have suited him *exactly*. They have been married more than seventeen years and are as fond of each other, as if their honey moon were still shining. . . . The good woman not only does all the work of the house, but she even makes the greatest part of her husband's dress, and assists him in *his art*— she draws, she engraves, and sings delightfully and is so truly the half of her good man, that they seem animated by one soul, and that a soul of indefatigable industry and benevolence: it sometimes hurries them both to labour *rather too much*, and I had some time ago the pain of seeing both confined to their bed.

Some seventeen years later, Blake noted in a book about madness, by Spurzheim, with reference to insanity caused by religion: 'Cowper came to me and said: "O that I were insane always. I will never rest. Can you not make me truly insane? I will never rest till I am so. O that in the bosom of God I was hid. You retain health and yet are as mad as any of us all—over us all—mad as a refuge from unbelief—from Bacon, Newton and Locke." '

As the summer of 1802 wore on, Blake recovered from another bout of illness. He began the first of two revealing letters to Butts on 22 November, by mentioning his elder brother, James, the hosier:

My Brother tells me that he fears you are offended with me. I fear so too, because there appears some reason why you might be so. But when you have heard me out, you will not be so.

I have now given two years to the intense study of those parts of the art which relate to light & shade & colour, & am Convinc'd that either my understanding is incapable of comprehending the beauties of Colouring, or the Pictures which I painted for you Are Equal in Every part of the Art, & superior in One, [simplicity of colour] to any thing that has been done since the age of Rafael. . . . I look upon you as the Chief of my Friends, whom I would endeavour to please, because you, among all men, have enabled me to produce these things. I would not send you a Drawing or a Picture till I had again reconsider'd my notions of Art, & had put myself back as if I was a learner. I have proved that I am Right, & shall now Go on with the Vigour I was in my Childhood famous for. . . .

But You will justly enquire why I have not written all this time to you? I answer I have been very Unhappy, & could not think of troubling you about it, or any of my real Friends. (I have written many letters to you which I burn'd & did not send). . . . Tho' I have been very unhappy, I am so no longer. I am again Emerged into the light of day; I still & shall to Eternity Embrace Christianity and Adore him who is the Express image of God; but I have travel'd thro' Perils & Darkness not unlike a Champion. I have Conquer'd, and shall still Go on Conquering. Nothing can withstand the fury of my Course among the

Stars of God & in the Abysses of the Accuser. My Enthusiasm is still what it was, only Enlarged and confirm'd.

I now Send Two Pictures. . . .

No sooner had Blake finished that letter than he began another to Butts: 'I found that I had not said half what I intended to say. . . .' One canvas is left: what subject does Butts choose to be painted on it? and 'the remaining Number of Drawings which you gave me orders for is Eighteen. I will finish these with all possible Expedition. . . .' Blake's illustrations to the Bible, which began as this series of fifty for Butts, eventually numbered nearly two hundred, hardly any of them larger than two feet square, some in tempera, some in colour-print, others in watercolour. The temperas are on canvas, wood or copper. In the best of his Bible paintings, Blake's flowing forms and clear colours impart a sense of living vision (37, 9). His letter goes on to recount a visionary experience described in 'some Verses which My Wife desires me to Copy out & send you with her kind love & Respect; they were Composed above a twelve-month ago, while walking from Felpham to Lavant to meet my Sister.' The vivid poem presents, in narrative, Blake's internal conflicts, external torments, defiance of worldly standards and faith in multiple vision. A world ecstatically alive with fairy elves, silver angels, golden demons 'And God himself in the passing hours' surrounds Blake. As he walks onward under 'a mild sun that mounts & sings', he remembers Tasso's lines on the creation of the world, which Hayley had translated and Blake transcribed: when Hayley read them aloud 'my heart knock'd against the root of my tongue.' Now there appear Blake's father hovering upon the wind, Blake's favourite brother Robert and their reckless brother 'John the evil one In a black cloud making his mone'. (John had been apprenticed to a gingerbread-maker, was reduced to begging at Blake's door, enlisted as a soldier and died in his thirties.) Though dead, they invade Blake's path, 'Notwithstanding my terrible wrath'. They beg him to stop, while angels try to drive them off. 'A frowning Thistle' in Blake's way implores him to persist. Blake always sees with double vision. The material thistle is, to his inward eye (his intellect), 'an old Man grey' who threatens that retreat would betray Blake 'to endless woe': Los, the spirit of prophecy, has sworn that:

> Poverty, Envy, old age & fear
> Shall bring thy Wife upon a bier;
> And Butts shall give what Fuseli gave,
> A dark black Rock & a gloomy Cave.

The agony of conflicting duties and loyalties forces Blake to ask: must Butts feel neglected because I give due respect to Hayley? must Flaxman think me wild? 'Must my Wife live in my Sister's bane [destruction] Or my Sister survive on my Love's pain?'—questions which imply prolonged discord between the two women. Blake kicked and broke the thistle. Then Los appeared, descending: to Blake's double sight ' 'Twas outward a Sun: inward Los in his might.' Blake defiantly declares that he and Mrs Blake labour day and night, eat little and drink less: 'This Earth breeds not our happiness.' Therefore he rejects the outward sun, source of earthly comfort and prosperity, and declares his faith in the spiritual sun, Los. Triumphant 'With the bows of my Mind & the Arrows of Thought', Blake marches on along his path where Los now flames and 'My brothers & father march before.' Blake has achieved not only the threefold vision, which is emotional, but the fourfold vision, which is spiritual.

Hayley's letters to his friends ceased to mention Blake, so that on 3 December 1802 Johnny Johnson wrote: 'By the bye is our dear Blake *dead*? You are as silent about him as the *grave*!' At last the first two volumes of the *Life of Cowper*, with Blake's five engravings—four of them portraits— were ready for publication. Lady Hesketh was full of admiration for Hayley's work, and she liked Blake's. Blake's sense of relief is evident from his letter of 30 January 1803 to his brother James, the hosier: 'to please Lady H. was a doubtful chance who almost ador'd her Cousin the poet & thought him all perfection, & she writes that she is quite satisfied with the portraits & charm'd by the great Head in particular, tho' she never could bear the original Picture.' Earlier in this long letter to James, Blake wrote:

You know that it is my way to make the best of every thing. I never make myself nor my friends uneasy if I can help it. My Wife has had Agues & Rheumatisms almost ever since she has been here, but our time is almost out that we took the Cottage for. . . .

The Blakes have determined

To leave This Place, because I am now certain of what I have long doubted, Viz that H. is jealous as Stothard was. . . . The truth is, As a Poet he is frighten'd at me & as a Painter his views & mine are opposite; he thinks to turn me into a Portrait Painter . . . but this he nor all the devils in hell will never do. I must own that seeing H. like S., Envious . . . made me very uneasy, but it is over & I now defy the worst & fear not while I am true to myself which I will be. This is the uneasiness I spoke of to Mr Butts, but I did not tell him so plain & wish you to keep it a secret & to burn this letter because it speaks so plain. . . . Be not . . . uneasy on any account & tell my Sister not to be uneasy, for I am fully Employ'd & Well Paid. . . . The Profits arising from Publications are immense. . . .

Blake believes that he has learnt, by knowing 'H. & his connexions & his method of managing', how to make his own fortune by publishing 'many very formidable works, which I have finish'd & ready'. Perhaps Blake thought that he could make as much money from publishing his own poems as Hayley had made from *Triumphs of Temper*, for the twelfth edition of which Blake was still engraving six little plates after Maria Flaxman for ten guineas each. 'But I again say as I said before, We are very Happy sitting at tea by a wood fire in our Cottage, the wind singing above our roof & the sea roaring at a distance, but if sickness comes all is unpleasant.' Blake had been 'really very ill' when he wrote to Butts the last time, but was not then persuaded—as he is now—that the Felpham 'air tho' warm is unhealthy.'

The ballads, Blake declares, 'are likely to be Profitable, for we have Sold all that we have had time to print. Evans the Bookseller in Pallmall says they go off very well. . . .' In fact, friends and booksellers had managed to sell very few copies of the four published broadsheets; and the generosity of Lady Hesketh, who deliberately overpaid, was exceptional. Hayley was worried. In April, he wrote anxiously about his 'worthy friend Blake' to the bookseller, Evans: 'I am very desirous of not leading him into *an unprofitable adventure*. He has paid a bill of £30 for paper and the copies he has disposed of in the country have not produced more than half that sum to reimburse him. What cash have you for him? He is an excellent creature, but not very fit to manage pecuniary concerns to his own advantage.' Hayley's fears were justified. The project failed and petered out. In the end, only about 115 broadsheets had been sold by his Sussex friends, and even fewer by booksellers. Blake was left with a clear loss and a stock of copies printed on expensive paper by Seagrave, to whom he was in debt.

Blake's letter to James of 30 January continued with defiant hope about 'various projected works' in engraving:

These are works to be boasted of, & therefore I cannot feel depress'd, tho' I know that as far as Designing & Poetry are concern'd I am Envied in many Quarters, but I will cram the dogs, for I know that the Public are my friends & love my works & will embrace them whenever they see them. My only Difficulty is to produce fast enough.

I go on Merrily with my Greek & Latin; am very sorry that I did not begin to learn languages early in life as I find it very Easy; am now learning my Hebrew. . . . I read Greek as fluently as an Oxford scholar & the Testament is my chief master. . . .

Hayley was still indefatigable in his efforts on behalf of Blake's material welfare. As Flaxman, who had heard of their impending move, wrote to Hayley on 28 May, 'you have always acted with the same bounty and kindness by them as you do by all.' Blake, disenchanted by Hayley's spiritual deadness and stifling in his possessive embrace, longed to be away: and he could go without an open quarrel! 'Congratulate me,' Blake wrote to Butts on 25 April, on the prospect of 'my return to London, with the full approbation of Mr Hayley'. There:

I may converse with my friends in Eternity, See Visions, Dream Dreams & prophecy & speak Parables unobserv'd & at liberty from the Doubts of other Mortals; perhaps Doubts proceeding from Kindness, but Doubts are always pernicious, Especially when we Doubt our Friends . . . & if a Man is the Enemy of my Spiritual Life while he pretends to be the Friend of my Corporeal, he is a Real Enemy—but the Man may be the friend of my Spiritual Life while he seems the Enemy of my Corporeal, but Not Vice Versa.

Further on in his letter, Blake alludes to his new long poem, *Milton*, when he asserts:

But none can know the Spiritual Acts of my three years' Slumber on the banks of the Ocean, unless he has seen them in the Spirit, or unless he should read My long Poem descriptive of those Acts; for I have in these three years composed an immense number of verses on One Grand Theme, Similar to Homer's Iliad or Milton's Paradise Lost. . . . I have written this Poem from immediate Dictation, twelve or sometimes twenty or thirty lines at a time, without Premeditation & even against my Will; the Time it has taken in writing was thus render'd Non Existent, & an immense Poem Exists which seems to be the Labour of a long Life, all produc'd without Labour or Study. I mention this to shew you what I think the Grand Reason of my being brought down here.

On 6 July Blake wrote more to Butts about his new epic,

a Sublime Allegory, which is now perfectly completed into a Grand Poem. I may praise it, since I dare not pretend to be any other than the Secretary; the Authors are in Eternity. I consider it as the Grandest Poem that this World Contains. Allegory address'd to the Intellectual powers, while it is altogether hidden from the Corporeal Understanding, is My Definition of the Most Sublime Poetry. . . . This Poem shall, by Divine Assistance, be progressively Printed & Ornamented with Prints & given to the Public. But of this work I take care to say little to Mr H., since he is as much averse to my poetry as he is to a Chapter in the Bible. . . . I have shewn it to him, & he has read Part by his own desire & has looked with sufficient contempt to inhance my opinion of it. But I do not wish to irritate by seeming too obstinate in Poetic pursuits. . . .

Mr H. approves of My Designs as little as he does of my Poems, and I have been forced to insist on his leaving me in both to my own Self Will; for I am determin'd to be no longer Pester'd with his Genteel Ignorance & Polite Disapprobation. I know myself both Poet & Painter . . . but his imbecile attempts to depress Me only deserve laughter.

This summer, Blake asserted himself and startled Hayley by demanding an increase in pay for two engravings of Romney, whose *Life* Hayley was going to write. Blake claimed further on in his letter: 'my antagonist is silenc'd completely, & I have compell'd what should have been of freedom —My Just Right as an Artist & as a Man.' Blake insists on being altogether left to his own judgment 'As you, My dear Friend, have always left me, for which I shall never cease to honour & respect you.' Flaxman responded to Hayley's news of the friction: 'I am heartily grieved for Blake's irritability, and your consequent trouble.'

Blake dated his 'Grand Poem', *Milton*, 1804 on his etched title page. He seems to have intended to present his great work as an epic in twelve books, but he later reduced that number to two. Like the author of *Paradise Lost*, Blake claims that he is writing 'to Justify the Ways of God to Men': but this implies a fundamental conflict, because Milton's god was Urizen and Blake's is 'the Poetic Genius Who is the eternal all-protecting Divine

Humanity'. Part of Blake's Preface is the superb lyric which begins 'And did those feet in ancient time', but in *Milton* itself some of the descriptive passages, written in unrhymed septenaries, are in their way no less evocative and thrilling than that lyric, now popularly called 'Jerusalem'.

Blake's epic tells of Milton's return to earth after he has been dead for a hundred years. Milton erred in his seventeenth-century life by placing reason above imagination and by denying to sex, after the Fall, the quality of divine inspiration. These errors led him to endorse religious war, to debase sex and to experience unhappiness in family life. In Blake's poem, Milton attempts and achieves redemption. To purge himself of self-righteousness and to redress his relationships with women, Milton's shadow (the residue of his suppressed desires) must re-enter earthly life and come to terms with his Emanation and his Spectre. Milton's Emanation is Ololon, 'a Virgin of twelve years' and therefore old enough for sexual experience. This one figure embodies the three wives and three daughters of Milton. His Spectre is Satan. The consummation of Milton's shadow, his Emanation and his Spectre is achieved in Blake's garden at Felpham. 'I beheld Milton with astonishment . . . descending down into my Cottage Garden, clothed in black, severe & silent he descended.' Blake's path becomes a solid fire '& Milton silent came down on my Path'. Ololon, too, descends into the garden. She 'Stood trembling in the Porch' on the seaward side of Blake's cottage. Beyond the shore, 'loud Satan thunder'd on the stormy Sea.' Milton declares his purpose to destroy his negation, his reasoning power, his Spectre: Satan.

> To bathe in the Waters of Life, to wash off the Not Human,
> I come in Self-annihilation & the grandeur of Inspiration,
> To cast off Rational Demonstration by Faith in the Saviour. . . .

Milton is moved to sacrifice himself for wholeness when he hears a bard in eternity sing the story of the conflict between Satan and Palamabron, visionary forms of Hayley (Milton's biographer) and Blake (poet and artist, creatively concerned with Milton). In the bard's song, Blake indignantly tells a tale of Hayley's interference with his creative work, and justifies the prayer: 'O God, protect me from my friends, that they have not power over me.' Satan lovingly cajoles Palamabron into letting him take over Palamabron's work and use the poet's harrow. Disaster follows: 'the horses of the Harrow Were madden'd with tormenting fury, & the servants of the Harrow, The Gnomes', spirits of the earth (whose name—'gnome'—also means a wise saying), accuse Satan with indignation, fury and fire. Palamabron appeals to Los, whose judgment is that Satan and Palamabron should not intrude on each other's work:

> let each his own station
> Keep: nor in pity false, nor in officious brotherhood, where
> None needs, be active.

Blake shows, in his subtle characterization of Hayley as Satan, how extremely difficult it must have been for Blake to oppose a patron as benevolent, sentimental and shallow as Hayley. In reversed writing, at the beginning of the second book, Blake printed: 'How wide the Gulf & Unpassable between Simplicity & Insipidity': such a gulf seemed to divide Blake from Hayley.

As a shooting star, Milton descends into Blake's left foot, inspires him, and corrects the errors which have disturbed the enlightened devotee of Milton. The errors are redeemed in the writing of this poem which is, on one level, about its own composition. When Milton has achieved wholeness, at the end of the poem, and 'Jesus wept & walked forth From Felpham's Vale clothed in Clouds of blood', the immortal sound of the four Zoas' apocalyptic trumpets strikes Blake with terror. 'My bones trembled, I fell outstretch'd upon the path A moment.' When he recovers from his faint, Mrs Blake—his 'sweet Shadow of Delight'—stands trembling by his side.

> Immediately the Lark mounted with a loud trill from Felpham's Vale,
> And the Wild Thyme from Wimbleton's green & impurpled Hills.

The lark's song and the thyme's scent have inspired Blake in his poem. They are Los's messengers: 'The Wild Thyme is Los's Messenger to Eden' and 'the Lark's Nest is at the Gate of Los.' In lines as ecstatic as any that Blake ever wrote, he describes the song of the lark who leads the choir of day, and the 'precious Odours' of the opening flowers: at their sweet fragrance, 'Men are sick with Love. . . .' From wild thyme, messenger of Time (as mortals name Los), comes a perfume symbolic of creative time, and punningly apt. 'Every Time less than a pulsation of the artery Is equal in its period & value to Six Thousand Years,'—that is, it equals all time— 'For in this Period the Poet's Work is Done'. In describing the creative moment, Blake probably drew on his wide knowledge of folklore, which enriched his poetry at many points. According to folklore, the boundary between day and night is a time of supernatural power. 'There is a Moment in each Day that Satan cannot find, Nor can his Watch Fiends find it . . . & when it once is found It renovates every Moment of the Day if rightly placed.' *Milton* vibrates with simultaneous actions. The intricate structure shows a world incandescent with creatures sensuously alive. It is thronged with figures in a kaleidoscopic motion, exposed to agony as to ecstasy. This is how the world must have looked to Blake. No wonder he resented Hayley's attempt to deflect him from such a re-creation of it!

When, after leaving Felpham, Blake illuminated this prophetic book, he made some full-page plates of great splendour and extreme interest, and some fascinating small pictures. A number of the plates of text have only tiny decorations. Much of the poetic imagery in *Milton* is, in itself, visually complete:

When Luvah's bulls each morning drag the sulphur Sun out of the Deep
Harness'd with starry harness, black & shining, kept by black slaves
That work all night at the starry harness, Strong and vigorous
They drag the unwilling Orb. . . .

On 10 May 1803, war with France had been renewed and with it the fear
of invasion. Against this nervous background, an incident in Blake's
garden on Friday 12 August assumed dramatic intensity. William, the
ostler from the Fox Inn, was doing some gardening for Blake. Without
Blake's knowledge, he invited a soldier, Private John Scofield, who was
quartered along the road at the Fox Inn, to help him. So far as Blake knew,
Scofield had no business to be in the cottage garden. On 16 August Blake
sent Butts seven drawings (which 'about balances our account') and a
description of what happened when Scofield apparently intruded:

I desired him, as politely as was possible, to go out of the Garden; he made me
an impertinent answer. I insisted on his leaving the Garden; he refused. I still
persisted in desiring his departure; he then threaten'd to knock out my Eyes,
with many abominable imprecations & with some contempt for my Person; it
affronted my foolish Pride. I therefore took him by the Elbows & pushed him
before me till I had got him out; there I intended to have left him, but he,
turning about, put himself into a Posture of Defiance, threatening & swearing at
me. I, perhaps foolishly & perhaps not, stepped out at the Gate, &, putting aside
his blows, took him again by the Elbows, &, keeping his back to me, pushed him
forwards down the road about fifty yards—he all the while endeavouring to turn
round & strike me, & raging & cursing, which drew out several neighbours; at
length, when I had got him to where he was Quarter'd, which was very quickly
done, we were met at the Gate by the Master of the house, The Fox Inn (who
is the proprietor of my Cottage), & his wife & Daughter & the Man's Comrade
& several other people. My Landlord compell'd the Soldiers to go in doors, after
many abusive threats against me & my wife from the two Soldiers; but not one
word of threat on account of Sedition was utter'd at that time.

Nevertheless, Scofield and his comrade, Private John Cock, had taken out
a warrant against Blake for an assault and seditious words. 'This method of
Revenge', Blake told Butts, 'was Plann'd between them after they had got
together into the Stable. This is the whole outline.'

Blake could not be convicted of sedition on Scofield's unsupported
testimony. No-one had overheard Blake utter sedition in the garden. None
of the witnesses who gathered at the door of the Fox heard Scofield accuse
Blake of sedition; and at the only time when Blake could have damned the
King in the presence of both Scofield and Cock, the witnesses were all
listening at the door of the Fox and they apparently vouched that Blake did
not utter sedition. While there is no doubt that Blake held seditious views,
there is no evidence that he expressed them on this occasion; and he certainly did not do so before two witnesses.

On Monday 15 August, Scofield swore his information and complaint before a Justice of the Peace in Chichester and Cock testified that he had heard Blake damn the King, at the door of the inn. Besides quoting sentiments which might plausibly be attributed to Blake, Scofield reinforced his accusation with obvious inventions. The next day, Tuesday, Blake duly appeared in response to the charges of assault and sedition. He brought William the ostler with him, to swear that Blake had uttered no seditious word. 'I have', Blake told Butts,

been before a Bench of Justices at Chichester this morning; but they, as the Lawyer who wrote down the Accusation told me in private, are compell'd by the Military to suffer a prosecution to be enter'd into: altho' they must know, & it is manifest, that the whole is a Fabricated Perjury. I have been forced to find Bail. Mr Hayley was kind enough to come forwards, & Mr Seagrave, Printer at Chichester; Mr H. in 100£, & Mr S. in 50£; & myself am bound in 100£ for my appearance at the Quarter Sessions, which is after Michaelmass. So I shall have the satisfaction to see my friends in Town before this Contemptible business comes on. I say Contemptible, for it must be manifest to every one that the whole accusation is a wilful Perjury.

Hayley wrote to Lady Hesketh that Blake was involved 'in as vexatious and unjust a persecution as an innocent, well-meaning creature could possibly fall into.' Blake continued to Butts:

Thus, you see, my dear Friend, that I cannot leave this place without some adventure; it has struck a consternation thro' all the Villages round. Every Man is now afraid of speaking to, or looking at, a Soldier; for the peaceable Villagers have always been forward in expressing their kindness for us, & they express their sorrow at our departure as soon as they hear of it. Every one here is my Evidence for Peace & Good Neighbourhood; & yet, such is the present state of things, this foolish accusation must be tried in Public. Well, I am content, I murmur not & doubt not that I shall recieve Justice, & am only sorry for the trouble & expense. I have heard that my Accuser is a disgraced Sergeant; his name is John Scholfield; perhaps it will be in your power to learn somewhat about the Man. . . .

Blake suspected that Scofield might be a government informer sent to entrap him for being a radical. However, although Butts was concerned professionally with the registration of troops, he does not seem to have found out anything about Scofield.

Blake, anxious and 'in a Bustle to defend' himself, was moved to gratitude and remorse by Hayley's loyal, practical concern for him. The friction between them, Blake now suspected, must have been caused by his own simple personality. He ended his letter to Butts:

Dear Sir, This perhaps was suffer'd to Clear up some doubts, & to give opportunity to those whom I doubted to clear themselves of all imputation. If a Man offends me ignorantly & not designedly, surely I ought to consider him with favour & affection. Perhaps the simplicity of myself is the origin of all offences committed against me. If I have found this, I shall have learned a most valuable thing, well worth three years' perseverance. I have found it. It is certain that a too passive manner, inconsistent with my active physiognomy, had done me much mischief. I must now express to you my conviction that all is come from the spiritual World for Good, & not for Evil.

Give me your advice in my perilous adventure; burn what I have peevishly written about any friend. I have been very much degraded & injuriously treated; but if it all arise from my own fault, I ought to blame myself.

O why was I born with a different face?
Why was I not born like the rest of my race?
When I look, each one starts! when I speak, I offend;
Then I'm silent & passive & lose every Friend. . . .

. . . My much terrified Wife joins me in love to you & Mrs Butts & all your family. I again take the liberty to beg of you to cause the Enclos'd Letter to be deliver'd to my Brother, & remain Sincerely & Affectionately Yours. . . .

There was some cause for terror. Although a jury would very probably acquit Blake of assault, the charge of sedition was more serious, especially at this time of national emergency. If he was found guilty, Blake could be sentenced to some months in prison. Hayley generously arranged for a lawyer friend of his, Samuel Rose, to represent Blake at the trial. This would not occur until January 1804, because it was customary to prefer an indictment at one quarter sessions but not to try the case until the next. To help in his defence when the time came, without delay Blake wrote an efficient memorandum refuting Scofield's accusations.

With this trouble hanging over them, exactly three years after their joyous arrival at Felpham, the Blakes returned, in September 1803— worried, upset, but in some ways relieved—to London, from the coast on to which Napoleon's thousands of soldiers, horses and cannons were expected to pour out of flat-bottomed landing-craft. In London, handbills called on Britons to seize the musket and slay the French, and sweet shops sold 'Boney's Ribs' for children to chew. For three weeks, the Blakes probably stayed in the family home, 28 Broad Street, with James who—as Cumberland noted—still kept 'a stocking shop' there. Blake called on Flaxman as soon as possible, and was full of admiration for his genius and industry. On 7 October Blake wrote to Hayley:

I fear that you have & must suffer more on my account than I shall ever be worth—Arrived safe in London, my wife in very poor health, still I resolve not to lose hope of seeing better days.

Art in London flourishes. Engravers in particular are wanted. . . . Yet no one brings works to me. I am content that it shall be so as long as God pleases. I know that many works of a lucrative nature are in want of hands; other Engravers are courted. I suppose that I must go a Courting, which I shall do awkwardly. . . .

Blake, 'a Man almost 50 Years of Age, who has not lost any of his life since he was five years old without incessant labour & study', finds that he is considered:

inferior to a boy of twenty, who scarcely has taken or deigns to take a pencil in hand, but who rides about the Parks or Saunters about the Playhouses, who Eats & drinks for business not for need. . . . Yet I laugh & sing, for if on Earth neglected I am in heaven a Prince among Princes, & even on Earth beloved by the Good as a Good Man; this I should be perfectly contented with, but at certain periods a blaze of reputation arises round me in which I am consider'd as one distinguish'd by some mental perfection, but the flame soon dies again & I am left stupified and astonish'd.

On 4 October Blake duly appeared at the Michaelmas Quarter Sessions in Petworth. The bills of indictment against him for using seditious words and for assault were presented. The jury returned a true bill, Blake pleaded not guilty and entered into recognizances for his appearance at the next Quarter Sessions. The mood of the times is shown in the *Sussex Weekly Advertiser*'s report, immediately under its account of Blake's case: 'A bill of indictment was also found against ten men at Littlehampton, for creating a riot and rescuing a man from the custody of a pressgang.'

In London, Blake tracked down some of Romney's paintings on Hayley's behalf and in a letter about them, on 26 October, he mentioned a commission from Fuseli for two plates (for Chalmers's illustrated edition of Shakespeare) besides the head of Romney that he was engraving for Hayley's *Life*:

I have got to work after Fuseli for a little Shakespeare. Mr Johnson, the bookseller, tells me that there is no want of work. So far you will be rejoiced with me, and your words, '*Do not fear you can want employment!*' were verified the morning after I received your kind letter. . . .

The Blakes were now in their new home, 17 South Molton Street, a turning off the south side of Oxford Street. It is about a mile north-west of Golden Square and a few minutes' walk from the old Tyburn gallows, now Marble Arch, and from 'Hyde Park on Tyburn's awful Brook'. They rented rooms on the first floor of this four-storey terrace-house that also accommodated other lodgers, among them the young, friendly Mrs Enoch. There was no garden and no tree, but open meadows were still only a short walk away north of Oxford Street, formerly Tyburn Road. The Blakes stayed in this house for nearly seventeen years, until 1821.

Thanks to Flaxman, who continued to recommend Blake as an engraver, a commission for two plates came from the secretary for foreign correspondence of the Royal Academy, Prince Hoare, painter of portraits and historical pictures. Blake continued to act as Hayley's agent in London, and engraved two plates for volume three of his *Life of Cowper*.

On 1 January 1804, Hayley wrote to Johnny Johnson: 'When will you reach the Turret? in time I hope to hear our beloved Rose eloquently and successfully defend our interesting artist, whose trial is to take place on Tuesday the 10th of this month.' On 2 January Hayley added a postscript to tell the news of his latest toss from the saddle: 'a new, stout and tall horse fell suddenly in his canter and had I not luckily had on a new strong hat, my skull would have been smashed by a flint—as it is I have a little cut on the forehead.' Dr Guy was called and Hayley told him: 'you must patch me up very speedily; for, living or dying, I must make a public appearance within a few days at the trial of our friend Blake.' Johnson sent Hayley greetings for Blake's thirty-seven-year-old advocate (who had been a friend of Cowper), Samuel Rose, a barrister of some achievement and brilliant promise but wavering health: 'Success to the Rose! Amen.' A few days before the trial, while Mrs Blake stopped at South Molton Street with the kind Mrs Enoch to befriend her, Blake probably went to stay with Hayley, who had been adequately patched up by Dr Guy, at Felpham.

The trial of Rex *v* Blake took place, after a day's postponement, on Wednesday 11 January 1804 at Chichester Guildhall. This gaunt, grey medieval building, formerly the chancel of a church of the Grey Friars' convent, set among lawns just inside the old city walls, had been equipped for use as a courtroom but was probably very cold in January. Charles Lennox, third Duke of Richmond, aged sixty-nine, presided at the Quarter Sessions. A staunch Tory, he was naturally opposed to Hayley, a Whig and an admirer of Voltaire and Rousseau.

One of the anonymous spectators, who came to the Guildhall chiefly to see Hayley, 'the great man' of the neighbourhood, was a lad who—according to Gilchrist—remembered to the end of his long life only one thing from the trial: Blake's flashing eye. The active physiognomy of the accused, his 'different' face and republican forehead were tell-tale signs of radicalism more obvious to Blake than to the court. He was accused of having said: 'Damn the King and his country; his subjects and all you soldiers are sold for slaves. . . .' Such sentiments about the King and his soldiers do sound authentic. Under the rules of evidence in 1804, neither Blake nor his wife could be called to testify: but in the middle of the trial, when Scofield invented something to support his case, Blake—in a tone which electrified the whole court and carried conviction—called out with his usual vehemence: 'False!'

As described to the gentlemen of the jury by Rose, however, Blake was not only a monarchist but mildness personified. Rose's Blake 'felt as much indignation at the idea of exposing to contempt or injury the sacred person of the sovereign as any man'! And Rose's Hayley, 'whose patriotism and loyalty have never been impeached', would certainly not have encouraged a 'seditious character' or brought one to Sussex. Hayley testified to Blake's placid disposition and so did village witnesses. Like other artists, Rose eloquently claimed, Blake was, by the nature of art, softened and smoothed in character and likely to be exempted from angry passions, factions and disputes. Fortunately for Blake, neither the political content of his writings nor his connection with the Paine set was known to the court, nor did any political basis for his quarrel with Scofield emerge. In the garden, Blake's fury may have been caused by a suspicion that Hayley, or an army captain, had sent Scofield to ensnare him. At once, however, Hayley had proved his sterling loyalty to Blake.

Rose, who set out to prove that Scofield had fabricated the charge in revenge for being ejected from the garden, stressed the unreliability of a sergeant degraded to the ranks—as Scofield had been—for drunkenness. Neither Scofield nor Cock stood up well to cross-examination. Blake was supported by people whom Hayley called 'a little host of honest and friendly rustic witnesses', the most effective being Mrs Haynes, wife of a miller's servant. Her garden adjoined the Blakes' and she 'by her shrewd remarks clearly proved *several impossibilities* in the *false accusation.*' During the trial, the old Duke, who seemed to Hayley to be bitterly prejudiced against Blake, made some 'unwarrantable observations' which might have biassed the jury. Rose was attacked by a most severe cold on that very day. He valiantly struggled to keep going, but illness compelled him to abandon his speech unfinished. He had been an eloquent advocate. Later, the Duke, complimented him highly on his defence of Blake.

Night fell before the trial ended. The *Sussex Weekly Advertiser* described the outcome for Blake: 'After a very long and patient hearing he was by the jury acquitted, which so gratified the auditory, that the court was, in defiance of all decency, thrown into an uproar by their noisy exultations.' Blake was, for once in his life, a popular hero. In the tumult, Hayley went up to the Duke and said: 'I congratulate your Grace, that . . . you have at last had the gratification of seeing an honest man honourably delivered from an infamous persecution. Mr Blake is a pacific, industrious and deserving artist.' The Duke replied rather impolitely: 'I know nothing of him.' 'True, my Lord,' rejoined Hayley, 'your Grace knows nothing of him; and I have therefore given you this information: I wish your Grace a good night.' Hayley and Blake at once left Chichester for Mid Lavant, to rejoice and sup with Miss Poole, who had been too ill to attend the trial and was anxiously awaiting news. As for Rose—friendly, amiable and delicate—his cold rapidly turned to consumption.

6

Exhibition and Scorn
1804–09

'my restoration to the light of Art'

From London, Blake wrote to Hayley on 14 January 1804, in anxiety and
with humane concern:

I write immediately on my arrival. Not merely to inform you that I am safe
arriv'd, but also to inform you that in a conversation with an old Soldier who
came in the Coach with me I learned: that no one: not even the most expert
horseman: ought ever to mount a Trooper's Horse; they are taught so many
tricks . . . that it is a miracle if a stranger escapes with Life,—All this I learn'd
with some alarm . . . & entreat you never to mount that wicked horse again, nor
again trust to one who has been so Educated. God our Saviour watch over you
& preserve you.

The Flaxmans have already:

welcom'd Me with kind affection & generous exultation in my escape from the
arrows of darkness. . . . My poor wife has been near the Gate of Death as was
supposed by our kind & attentive fellow inhabitant, the young & very amiable
Mrs Enoch, who gave my wife all the attention that a daughter could pay to a
mother, but my arrival has dispell'd the formidable malady & my dear & good
woman again begins to resume her health & strength. . . . Gratitude is Heaven
itself; there could be no heaven without Gratitude. I feel it & I know it.

A violent cold kept Blake in his room for a week. Then he went about on
Hayley's behalf in busy pursuit of Romney's works. Hayley generously
sent an ample cheque to Rose for his legal work, with a complimentary
sonnet written out by Blake in his best copperplate hand. Rose was out
when Blake delivered the packet to his London address. All was 'in a good
train', Blake assured Hayley on 27 January:

Work in Abundance; & if God blesses me with health doubt not yet to make a
Figure in the Great dance of Life that shall amuse the Spectators in the Sky. . . .
My Wife gets better every Day: hope earnestly that you have entirely escaped

the brush of my Evil Star, which I believe is now for ever fallen into the Abyss—
God bless & preserve You . . . & with you my much admired & respected
Edward the Bard of Oxford [Edward Garrard Marsh, who was about to become a
Fellow of Oriel College: his poems are now forgotten, but he spoke poetry so
beautifully that Blake rejoiced to remember hearing him] whose verses still
sound upon my Ear like the distant approach of things mighty & magnificent;
like the sound of harps which I hear before the Sun's rising, like the remembrance of Felpham's waves & of the Glorious & far beaming Turret, like the
Villa of Lavant, blessed & blessing. Amen.

On 22 February Blake called on Rose who 'Alas! was ill in bed . . . & the
servant said that he remains very ill indeed.' Flaxman was, Blake told
Hayley, 'so busy that I believe I shall never see him again but when I call
on him, for he has never yet, since my return to London, had the time or
grace to call on me.' Prince Hoare proved to be a responsive, friendly artist
to engrave for: a 'good & excellent Man'. The plates of Cowper's monument
seemed never to get finished, for Blake dawdled. 'Engraving is Eternal
work. . . . I curse & bless Engraving alternately, because it takes so much
time & is so untractable, tho' capable of such beauty & perfection.' Hayley
chivvied him into sending the prints on 2 April: Hayley thought them well
executed.

To the detriment of Blake's own work, he devoted much time and
trouble in 1804 to research for Hayley into Romney's art. Blake expected
that Hayley would commission him to engrave several plates for the *Life*
from Romney's pictures, which, Blake thought, 'deserve to be Engraved by
the hands of Angels.'

Advising Hayley to employ Seagrave rather than Johnson to print the
Life, Blake wrote on 28 May:

in London you will be cheated every way . . . every calumny and falsehood
utter'd against another of the same trade is thought fair play. Engravers, Painters,
Statuaries, Printers, Poets, we are not in a field of battle, but in a City of Assas-
sinations. This makes your lot truly enviable, and the country is not only more
beautiful on account of its expanded meadows, but also on account of its benevolent minds.

Hayley thought Blake was asking too much for engravings but James
Parker, Blake's old friend and former partner, 'whose Eminence as an
Engraver makes his opinion deserve notice' Blake claimed in June, supported Blake's prices. These were from thirty guineas, whereas Caroline
Watson was asking twenty-five guineas for a finished plate and half as much
for an engraved sketch. Hayley eventually commissioned twelve plates for
the *Life*: seven are by Caroline Watson and only one, 'The Shipwreck', is
by Blake. Even for this one, Hayley confided to Flaxman that he wanted to
employ Robert Hartley Cromek, Flaxman's favourite engraver, but would
be sorry to risk wounding the feelings of 'our quick-spirited friend'.

By August, Blake needed cash: 'Money flies from me,' he wrote to Hayley. 'Profit never ventures upon my Threshold, tho' every other man's doorstone is worn down into the very Earth by the footsteps of the fiends of commerce.' Three months later he wrote again to Hayley: 'I must now tell my wants, & beg the favour of some more of the needful: the favor of ten Pounds more will carry me thro' this Plate & the Head of Romney, for which I am already paid'—but which Hayley never used.

John Birch, a surgeon friend of the Blakes and the Buttses, had been giving Mrs Blake electrical treatment and on 23 October Blake was able to tell Hayley that she 'is surprisingly recovered. Electricity is the wonderful cause; the swelling of her legs and knees is entirely reduced. She is very near as free from rheumatism as she was five years ago, and we have the greatest confidence in her perfect recovery.' Moreover, Blake had himself experienced a spiritual regeneration. After three years at Felpham, hungry for pictures, he had feasted the eyes of his spirit at an exhibition in Marylebone of paintings belonging to Joseph, Count Truchsess. The thousand pictures, by old masters such as Dürer, Michelangelo and Leonardo, were valued by the German Count at £60,000 though Sir Thomas Lawrence, who claimed he could find scarcely an original work by a great master among them, priced the collection at less than £2,000. But their spiritual worth to Blake was incalculable. They shed upon him the true light of art: and twenty years of torment by the rationalizing Spectre—those twenty years since Blake first set up shop—ended in the fresh light of Innocence.

For now! O Glory! and O Delight! I have entirely reduced that spectrous Fiend to his station, whose annoyance has been the ruin of my labours for the last passed twenty years of my life. He is the enemy of conjugal love and is the Jupiter of the Greeks, an iron-hearted tyrant, the ruiner of ancient Greece. . . . Suddenly, on the day after visiting the Truchsessian Gallery of Pictures, I was again enlightened with the light I enjoyed in my youth, and which has for exactly twenty years been closed from me as by a door and by window-shutters. . . . O the distress I have undergone, and my poor wife with me: incessantly labouring and incessantly spoiling what I had done well. Every one of my friends was astonished at my faults, and could not assign a reason; they knew my industry and abstinence from every pleasure for the sake of study, and yet—and yet—and yet there wanted the proofs of industry in my works. I thank God with entire confidence that it shall be so no longer—he is become my servant who domineered over me, he is even as a brother who was my enemy. Dear Sir, excuse my enthusiasm or rather madness, for I am really drunk with intellectual vision whenever I take a pencil or graver into my hand, even as I used to be in my youth, and as I have not been for twenty dark, but very profitable years. I thank God that I courageously pursued my course through darkness.

The tormenting power of Greek thought has finally dissolved in that profounder wisdom, Biblical wisdom, oriental in origin, into which elements of classical wisdom were long ago absorbed.

This ecstatic mood shines out again in Blake's letter of 4 December: 'For O happiness never enough to be grateful for! I have lost my Confusion of Thought while at work & . . . now no longer Divided nor at war with myself I shall travel on in the strength of the Lord God as Poor Pilgrim says.' More soberly, Blake tells Hayley a fortnight later, 'I must solicit for a supply of money, and hope you will be convinced that the labour I have used on the two plates has left me without any resource but that of applying to you. I am again in want of ten pounds. . . .' The Blakes remember their 'happy Christmas at lovely Felpham. . . . We are often sitting by our cottage fire, and often we think we hear your voice calling at the gate. Surely these things are real and eternal in our eternal mind and can never pass away. My wife continues well, thanks to Mr Birch's Electrical Magic, which she has discontinued these three months.'

'The Death of so Excellent a Man as my Generous Advocate', Rose, from consumption at the age of thirty-seven, marked the year's end. On 28 December, in his letter to thank Hayley 'for the transmission of ten Pounds to the Dreamer over his own Fortunes: for I certainly am that Dreamer', Blake wrote: 'Farewell, Sweet Rose! thou hast got before me into the Celestial City. I also have but a few more Mountains to pass; for I hear the bells ring & the trumpets sound to welcome thy arrival among . . . Spirits of Just Men made Perfect.'

In January 1805, Blake was deep in negotiations with a London publisher, Richard Phillips, on Hayley's behalf. As a go-between, Blake showed patience and some diplomacy. Phillips seemed keen to publish Hayley's works and advised that the broadsheet animal *Ballads* 'should be published *all together* in a volume the size of the small edition of the *Triumphs of Temper*, with six or seven plates. . . . And', Blake told Hayley, 'he will go equal shares with me in the expense and the profits, and that Seagrave is to be the printer. . . . I consider myself as only put in trust with this work, and that the copyright is for ever yours. . . . Truly proud I am to be in possession of this beautiful little estate; for that it will be highly productive I have no doubt, in the way now proposed. . . .' Seagrave proved to be a fortunate choice of printer, because by 25 April 'The Journeyman Printers throughout London are at War with their Masters & are likely to get the better. Each Party meet to consult against the other; nothing can be greater than the Violence on both sides. Printing is suspended in London Except at private Presses. I hope this will become a source of Advantage to our Friend Seagrave. . . .'

Since returning to London, Blake had engraved from Fuseli's designs only the two small plates for Chalmers's Shakespeare. Fuseli, who knew precisely what he wanted from an engraver, had formerly relied on his intimate friend Blake to share his vision and interpret it on the engraver's plate. Now, although the old friends did not quarrel, they were less close than they had been before 1799, and Fuseli gave Blake only enough commissions to maintain their friendship. The reputation of Fuseli, now in his mid-sixties, was terrifying: but an apprehensive young visitor, Haydon, calling on the supposedly diabolical Fuseli for the first time, found him to be only 'a little white-headed, lion-faced man in an old flannel dressing-gown, tied round his waist with a piece of rope, and upon his head the bottom of Mrs Fuseli's work-basket'. In 1804 he was elected Keeper of the Royal Academy Schools, as Blake goes on to mention without any professional jealousy in his letter to Hayley of 25 April 1805: 'Fuseli is made Master of the Royal Academy. Banks the Sculptor is Gone to his Eternal Home. I have heard that Flaxman means to give a Lecture on Sculpture at the Royal Academy on the Occasion of Banks' Death. . . . Now I concieve Flaxman stands without a competitor in Sculpture.'

In late September, Blake was visited by Cromek (40), one of Bartolozzi's ex-pupils. Cromek had engraved many of Stothard's book-plates, lived near him in Newman Street, and was now a special friend of the Flaxmans. 'A man of independent spirit', Flaxman called him, 'very handsomely employed, as he well deserves.' Cromek was beginning to promote other men's work. He looked at some of Blake's designs and commissioned him—as Flaxman told Hayley on 18 October—'to make a set of forty drawings from Blair's poem of *The Grave*, twenty of which he proposes to have engraved by the designer and to publish them with the hope of rendering service to the artist.'

The Grave is a blank-verse poem somewhat longer than the second book of Blake's *Milton*, by Robert Blair, an eighteenth-century Scottish parish priest. Written before Young's *Night Thoughts*, it was published in 1743. Copies of it soon lay with *The Pilgrim's Progress* and *Robinson Crusoe* on the window-sills of cottages and the tables of wayside inns. This surprisingly energetic poem—strong in its images, its sense of drama and conviction of resurrection—had qualities to attract Blake. By 18 October, Flaxman and several other Royal Academicians had already seen some of his designs, found them striking, and meant to give encouragement. Flaxman told Hayley on 14 November: 'Blake has his hands full of work for a considerable time to come, and if he will only condescend to give that attention to his worldly concerns which everyone does that prefers living to starving, he is now in a way to do well.' On 27 November Blake wrote to Hayley about Cromek: 'I produced about twenty Designs which pleas'd so well that he . . . has now set me to Engrave them. He means to Publish them by Subscription with the Poem as you will see in the Prospectus which he sends you in the same Pacquet with the Letter.' Moreover, the book of animal *Ballads*, now duly published for Blake's benefit by Phillips, was said to be 'approved by the best, that is, the most serious people'. Blake gave this letter to Cromek himself to enclose with the prospectus and to post.

Blake had not seen Cromek's prospectus. In it, where he expected his *own* engravings to be announced, it advertised 'Twelve Very Spirited Engravings by Louis Schiavonetti, from Designs Invented by William Blake'. Subscribing patrons to the edition included Cosway, Flaxman, Lawrence, Stothard and Fuseli, who recommended it in five eloquent, sombre paragraphs. Fuseli wrote that the illustrations 'claim approbation, sometimes excite our wonder, and not seldom our fears', when we see the artist 'play on the very verge of legitimate invention': artists of every sort, 'from the student to the finished master . . . will find here materials of art and hints of improvement!' Only for his friend Blake would Fuseli have appealed to the public in his own name: but Fuseli's generosity could not heal the stab-wound inflicted by Cromek. It is likely that Blake had already begun to engrave 'Death's Door' for *The Grave*, in an uncompromisingly rough style, when Cromek unscrupulously switched the job to Schiavonetti, a successful imitator and outstripper of Bartolozzi. Blake was mortified by Cromek's callous deceit. The wound was still festering two or more years later:

> Cr— loves artists, as he loves his Meat
> He loves the Art, but 'tis the Art to Cheat.

he wrote in his notebook.

On 1 December 1805, Flaxman wrote to Hayley: 'Blake is going on gallantly with his drawings from *The Grave* . . . he has good employment besides, but still I very much fear his abstracted habits are so much at variance with the usual modes of human life, that he will not derive all the advantage to be wished from the present favourable appearances.' On the same day, an anonymous reviewer of the *Ballads* in *The Eclectic Review* noted that the plates 'mark the genius, if not the taste, of an artist. . . .' Blake's dynamic style of engraving seemed coarse in 1805.

Hayley encouraged Blake's projected work on *The Grave*, for which Blake thanked him on 11 December and remarked 'It bids fair to set me above the difficulties I have hitherto encounter'd. But my Fate has been so uncommon that I expect Nothing.' Referring to powerful publishers who disdained his burin, he tells Hayley:

I was alive & in health & with the same Talents I now have all the time of Boydell's, Macklin's, Bowyer's, & other Great Works. I was known by them & was look'd upon by them as Incapable of Employment in those Works; it may turn out so again, notwithstanding appearances. . . . You, Dear Sir, are one who has my Particular Gratitude, having conducted me thro' Three that would have been the Darkest Years that ever Mortal Suffer'd, which were render'd thro' your means a Mild & Pleasant Slumber. I speak of Spiritual Things, Not of Natural. . . . It will not be long before I shall be able to present the full history of my Spiritual Sufferings to the Dwellers upon Earth & of the Spiritual Victories obtain'd for me by my Friends.

Blake was creating this history not only in *Milton* and his third epic, *Jerusalem*, but also in radically re-writing vital parts of *Vala*, notably its beginning and end. Enlightened by his Truchsessian experience, he introduced Christ the redeemer in the place of Luvah:

> For when Luvah sunk down, himself put on the robes of blood
> Lest the state call'd Luvah should cease; & the Divine Vision
> Walked in robes of blood till he who slept should awake.

When Blake incorporated this Christian scheme into his poem, it was often at the cost of rhythm and line-length. Spiritual truth mattered more to him than the throb of poetry which, with care, he could have set pulsing.

'I am kept Happy,' Blake goes on to assure Hayley,

> as I used to be, because I throw Myself & all that I have on our Saviour's Divine Providence. O What Wonders are the Children of Men! Would to God that they would . . . know that Recieving a Prophet As a Prophet is a Duty which If omitted is more Severely Avenged than Every Sin & Wickedness beside. . . . I know that those . . . who mock'd & Despised the Meekness of True Art (and such, I find, have been the situations of our Beautiful, Affectionate Ballads) [which were being judged as if written for adults and ridiculed by some reviewers] I know that such Mockers are Most Severely Punish'd in Eternity. . . . The Mocker of Art is the Mocker of Jesus.

With the ardour of youth which never left Blake, he then exhorts Hayley to persist in spiritual labours. Often in their correspondence—of which this is apparently the last extant letter—Blake seems to be writing to record his own experiences and hopes, rather than to light a reflection in the tarnished, worldly understanding of Hayley, whose spiritual dimness Blake well knew.

Blake's sense of betrayal increased. By December 1805 he began to perceive that Hayley was transferring to other engravers further work which Blake had expected, including commissions for Cowper, Milton and Romney. Flaxman's close friend Cromek was not only reducing the number of designs for *The Grave* but also accepting a commission to engrave the frontispiece to Dr B. H. Malkin's *Memoirs of his Child*. Blake had designed this frontispiece and expected to engrave it. Probably through Cromek, Blake had met Malkin (headmaster of Bury Grammar School) whose son Thomas, an infant prodigy, had died at the age of six. Malkin, an art-lover and a radical in politics, quotes Blake's testimony that young Thomas's drawings show 'firm, determinate outline. . . . All his efforts prove this little boy to have had that greatest of all blessings, a strong imagination, a clear idea, and a determinate vision of things in his own mind.' Malkin's introductory letter of 4 January 1806 to the *Memoirs* is addressed to Thomas Johnes of Hafod and contains the earliest biographical and critical essay on Blake. It must have been based on information from Blake himself. According to Malkin, Blake the visionary artist has been thwarted by sceptics and rationalists who 'pursue and scare a warm and brilliant imagination, with the hue and cry of madness. . . . By them have the higher powers of this artist been kept from public notice, and . . . has he been stigmatised as an engraver, who might do tolerably well, if he was not mad.' As 1806 began, however, Blake was agonizingly aware that even his work as a commercial engraver was being eroded by Hayley, Cromek and—indirectly—Flaxman. Bitterly hurt by their rejection of him not only as a craftsman but also, Blake felt, as a friend, he broke away from them all and for nearly ten years he made no commercial engravings.

At this time of wretched isolation, he leaned yet more heavily on his sympathetic, generous patron, Butts. For him, in 1805, Blake had painted at least twelve watercolours (including 'Ezekiel's Vision of the Whirlwind' —41), many of them magnificent, and had sold him at least eight prints. In that year, Blake probably painted the apocalyptic temperas 'The Spiritual Form of Nelson Guiding Leviathan'—which Butts later owned—and 'The Spiritual Form of Pitt Guiding Behemoth'. During the next five years, Butts continued to enrich his house with Blake's pictures and books, paying more than £400 for them, while Blake did hardly any work for anybody else. On Christmas Day 1805, Blake also undertook, for twenty-five guineas a year, to teach engraving to Butts's son Tommy, aged seventeen, so that the boy could if necessary earn a living as a craftsman. The lessons probably lasted only a year, because at Christmas 1806 Tommy followed his elder brother, Joseph, into the office of the Commissary General of Musters, where their father was chief clerk. According to a family tradition, Butts benefited more than Tommy from the lessons.

Of Butts's work as chief clerk, his superior wrote: 'The employment is irksome, admits of little variety, and affords no mental improvement; exacting patience, unwearied application, and undivided attention.' Still, Butts found jobs in his office for his family and friends. There—apparently without scruple—he and his sons drew far more overtime pay than they are likely to have earned. Butts had an ample income. In the year ending 3 March 1806, he could afford to pay Blake a sixth of it: this amounted to £66, which was probably almost enough for the Blakes to live on.

Blake did not sever himself completely from the publication of *The Grave*. He asked his loyal friend Ozias Humphry (whose failing sight had forced him to give up miniature painting and who was now Painter in Crayons to His Majesty) to help him get—though he cannot have wholeheartedly wished for this—permission from old Queen Charlotte to dedicate to her his designs for *The Grave*. She duly accepted Blake's dedication and his verses, in which he described himself 'Bowing before my Sov'reign's Feet': a position hateful to a republican, but perhaps in a way soothing to Blake if anxieties about his Chichester trial still beset him.

That experience had left sores in his mind. They persisted, festering and spreading their poison. In *Jerusalem*, a great work of fifteen years or more, begun in 1804, two of the villains, sons of the giant Albion, are Scofield and

119

Cock, who 'accumulate A World in which Man is by his Nature the Enemy of Man.' They 'devour the Sleeping Humanity of Albion in rage & hunger' and they 'separate a Law of Sin' to punish Blake in his members. Blake's memory of Hayley suppurated too, while the years passed. Hyle—as Cockneys pronounce 'Hayley'—is another of the villainous sons of Albion in *Jerusalem*. A bad artist who uses 'Affections rent Asunder & opposed to Thought', Hyle is the agent of 'Rational Morality, deluding to death the little ones In strong temptations of stolen beauty.' So Blake brooded on wickedness and exposed, in a book which nobody read, the terrible significance of his enemies.

On 1 July 1806, a rousing letter from Blake was printed in *The Monthly Magazine* whose proprietor, Richard Phillips, was the publisher of Hayley's *Ballads*. 'My indignation,' Blake said in this letter, 'was exceedingly moved at reading a criticism . . . on the picture of Count Ugolino, by Mr Fuseli, in the Royal Academy Exhibition. . . .' Fuseli's treatment of his subject and his use of colour had been criticized. Blake praises, in detail, both aspects of Fuseli's picture. Then he appeals to the nation: 'our countrymen are easily brow-beat on the subject of painting; and hence it is so common to hear a man say: "I am no judge of pictures." But O Englishmen! know that every man ought to be a judge of pictures, and every man is so who has not been connoisseured out of his senses.' (In his notebook, Blake puns on 'The Cunning-sures & the aim-at-yours'.) A visitor has told Blake that Fuseli is a hundred years beyond the present generation. 'Though I am startled,' Blake acknowledges, 'at such an assertion, I hope the contemporary taste will shorten the hundred years into as many hours. . . .' This loyal, fervent letter is the counterpart of Fuseli's tribute to Blake's designs for *The Grave*.

Cut off from engraving those designs himself, Blake planned to make an engraving from Chaucer, an author then little read. At South Molton Street, Cromek saw Blake's pencil sketch for 'The Procession of Chaucer's Canterbury Pilgrims'. He appeared highly delighted with it and, so the unworldly Blake understood, commissioned him to engrave it. Cromek then went to Blake's old friend Stothard and, without mentioning Blake, suggested the subject as one which Cromek had always wanted to see depicted. For £60, Cromek commissioned Stothard to paint it in oils so that it could then be engraved—but not by Blake, who was told nothing of this. Stothard was a retiring, very hard-working, popular artist and a mild man. He accepted Cromek's commission in good faith: for Stothard wittingly to have wronged an old friend by stealing an idea from him would have been out of character. Blake called on Stothard at Newman Street one day, found him painting the picture, and—unaware that Cromek had anything to do with the coincidental choice of subject—politely praised Stothard's painting. When Blake discovered Cromek's involvement he was furious. For deliberately trying to thwart Blake's own project by a rival one, he blamed both

Cromek and Stothard. He spurned Stothard's friendship, abused him to strangers and fostered 'a poison tree' of hate. From Flaxman too, who believed in Stothard's innocence, Blake also withdrew yet further. He recorded in eight words in his notebook some terrible hours of Tuesday 20 January 1807: 'between Two & Seven in the Evening—Despair.'

Early in the year, he sat for his portrait to Thomas Phillips, an Associate of the Royal Academy, whose literary sitters eventually included Byron, Crabbe, Southey and Coleridge. Phillips, a fine painter, adept at conveying vigour of mind, was steadily gaining in reputation. At his studio in George Street he discussed with Blake, during a sitting, the sublime in art. Allan Cunningham writes that Blake told Phillips:

'I was one day reading Young's *Night Thoughts*, and when I came to that passage which asks "who can paint an angel?" I closed the book and cried, "Aye! who can paint an angel?" A voice in the room answered, "Michelangelo could." "And how do *you* know?" I said, looking round me; but I saw nothing save a greater light than usual. "I *know*," said the voice, "for I sat to him: I am the archangel Gabriel." "Oho!" I answered, "you are, are you . . . you may be an evil spirit." "Can an evil spirit do this?" asked the voice and I was aware of a shining shape, with bright wings, who diffused such light. As I looked, the shape dilated more and more: he waved his hands; the roof of my study opened; he ascended into heaven; he stood in the sun, and beckoning to me, moved the universe. An angel of evil could not have done that—it was the archangel Gabriel.'

Allan Cunningham adds that Phillips, as Blake spoke, caught his rapt expression. The portrait, which Mrs Blake never liked, is almost two-thirds life-size: it was shown at the Royal Academy in May 1807. Thomas Phillips then gave it to Cromek, who had it engraved by Schiavonetti.

Cromek made a lot of money by showing Stothard's painting of the *Canterbury Pilgrims*, from 1807, in all the large towns of England—admission one shilling—and by selling the original for £500. He raised Stothard's fee by £40, but never paid this addition to the original £60: so Blake was not the only artist who suffered from Cromek's meanness. In May 1807 Cromek refused Blake four guineas for a charming sketched vignette to accompany the dedication of *The Grave*. 'The Queen,' wrote Cromek scornfully to Blake, 'allowed *you*, not *me*, to dedicate the work to *her*!' Although the great increase in profits which her name could be expected to attract would all go to Cromek, he went on insultingly:

What public reputation you have, the reputation of eccentricity excepted, I have acquired for you. . . . *I also imposed on myself* when I believed what you so often have told me, that your works were equal, nay superior, to a Raphael or to a Michelangelo! Unfortunately for me as a publisher the public awoke me from this state of stupor, this mental delusion. That public is willing to give you credit for what real talent is to be found in your productions, *and for no more.* . . . Your drawings have had the *good fortune* to be engraved by one of the first artists in

Europe, and . . . your best work, the illustrations of *The Grave*, was produced when you and Mrs Blake were reduced so low as to be obliged to live on half-a-guinea a week!

From January to October 1805, Blake received at least four times as much as that: £2. 3s a week, a low but tolerable wage for a journeyman engraver. 'Why should you,' Cromek asks, 'so *furiously rage* at the success of the little picture of "The Pilgrimage"? 3,000 people have now *seen it and have approved of it.*'

Against the date 'Sunday August 1807', under 'South Molton Street', Blake wrote in his notebook: 'My Wife was told by a Spirit to look for her fortune by opening by chance a book which she had in her hand; it was Bysshe's Art of Poetry. She open'd the following . . .' and Blake quotes twenty-four lines by Mrs Aphra Behn describing the ecstasy of lovers. He continues about Mrs Blake's discovery: 'I was so well pleased with her Luck that I thought I would try my Own & open'd the following . . .': and he quotes from Dryden's *Virgil* ten lines describing the firmness of a storm-tossed mountain oak. Blake does not comment on this revelation.

For *Paradise Lost*, which Blake was ideally equipped to illustrate, he made two wonderful sets of watercolours, a dozen pictures in each: the first, for the Rev. Joseph Thomas in 1807; and the second, bought by Butts, in 1808. Twenty illustrated editions of *Paradise Lost* were published between 1740 and 1820, and besides Fuseli, such artists as Barry, Romney and a host of lesser painters based their pictures on it. Unlike those men, Blake had the intellectual and artistic genius to soar beyond the narrative poetry into the vital realm of Milton's ideas, to move at ease there, to express in symbolic form the essence of the poem and to enrich it with his own ideas, comparable in stature to Milton's. Blake worked with exceptional care on the design and detail of these illustrations. His emphasis is on Adam, Eve and hope for mankind. While Eve lies in bliss with Adam, Blake's sensuous Eden is lustrous, with the colour and firmness of jewels. In the picture of Adam and Eve being spied upon by Satan, the jealous intruder hovers in the air above and fondles his serpentine self with a gesture that echoes the lovers' embrace below him. In Milton's poem, however, Satan crouches in the form of a tiger to watch their innocent joy. Blake charmingly shows the natural beauty of Eden, lavish but innocent, in his painting of the sociable Archangel, Raphael, talking to Adam, while Eve serves food and drink (42). In 'Michael Foretells the Crucifixion', Blake painted a subject not previously illustrated on its own. It offers man hope of redemption.

On 18 January 1808, Blake wrote to his friend Ozias Humphry: 'The Design of The Last Judgment, which I have completed by your recommendation for The Countess of Egremont, it is necessary to give some account of. . . .' Blake then describes his magnificent, minutely detailed apocalyptic scene with its hundreds of figures (43). He finally tells Humphry: 'Such is the Design which you, my Dear Sir, have been the cause of my producing & which: but for you might have slept till the Last Judgment.' Humphry wrote about this picture:

The size of this drawing is but small—not exceeding twenty inches by fifteen or sixteen (*I guess*)—but then the grandeur of its conception, the importance of its subject, and the sublimely multitudinous masses, and groups, which it exhibits. . . . In brief, it is one of the most interesting performances I ever saw; and is, in many respects, superior to 'The Last Judgment' of Michelangelo and, to give due credit and effect to it, would require a tablet not less than the floor of Westminster Hall.

For the first time in eight years, Blake exhibited at the Royal Academy in 1808. He showed two watercolours, 'Jacob's Ladder' (9) and 'Angels Hovering Over Jesus's Body in the Sepulchre' (37), both of which belonged to Butts. Cromek advertised *The Grave* extensively, and used, as a puff, Fuseli's praise of Blake's designs. Most of the copies, about six hundred, had been sold to subscribers before publication. The lavish, well-printed book included descriptions of the plates, probably written by Malkin.

Fuseli had emphasized the moral worth of *The Grave*, a poem which impresses man with his destiny and contrasts the deaths of good and evil men. To Robert Hunt, the first reviewer of Cromek's edition—writing in *The Examiner*, a new journal produced by him and his brothers Leigh and John—Blair's poem showed 'original and vigorous thoughts' and Schiavonetti's engravings had 'done more than justice' to the designs: Blake's pictures of natural subjects, such as men dying, were powerful; but those of spirits were failures, absurd and indecent in their carnality. Three weeks later, in *The Examiner* of 28 August, Leigh Hunt included Blake (with Wordsworth) in a list of quacks and signed it with his editorial symbol, a pointing hand. To the three Hunt brothers, the Cerberus of the press who barked at 'Naked Beauty display'd', Blake therefore gave the composite name 'Hand' in *Milton* and *Jerusalem*. The eldest of Albion's twelve sons, Hand sits on Albion's cliffs, 'a mighty threat'ning Form . . . Plotting to devour Albion's Body of Humanity & Love'.

> His bosom wide & shoulders huge, overspreading wondrous,
> Bear Three strong sinewy Necks & Three awful & terrible Heads,
> Three Brains, in contradictory council brooding incessantly. . . .

In November, the anonymous critic of *The Antijacobin Review* wrote of Blake's designs for *The Grave* that in 'Death's Door', 'the feebleness of age is well depicted', whereas the old man's soul, 'renovated' above, is more like a naked madman than 'an inhabitant of the realms of bliss'. Blake's souls show 'all the fulness and rotundity of mortal flesh'. The ungraceful angel on the title-page 'might have been furnished with wings to infold his nakedness', because complete 'nudity, even in moral works, is not wholly desirable.' In general, the designs are 'the offspring of a morbid fancy', and what Fuseli praised as an attempt ' "to connect the visible with the invisible world, by a familiar and domestic atmosphere," has totally failed.' And Blake's verse dedication 'is one of the most abortive attempts to form a wreath of poetical flowers that we have ever seen'. Rather than let him try to write poetry again, his friends should restrain him in a 'strait waistcoat'. *The Monthly Magazine* of 1 December spoke more briefly and sympathetically of 'an air of ancient art' and 'a wildness of fancy and eccentricity' in Blake's designs, though his subjects 'admit of no just graphic representations.' Nevertheless, these designs for *The Grave* became better known to Blake's contemporaries than any of his other works.

About this time, Blake painted two sets of six watercolour illustrations for Milton's ode 'On the Morning of Christ's Nativity'. The peaceful joy of the Holy Family is beautifully conveyed in pictures which contrast it with the turmoil of pagan cults: Milton's poetic effect is made visible.

Blake pithily expressed some of his own views on art in his notes, probably begun about 1808, on the *Discourses* that Reynolds had delivered to Royal Academy students, 1769–90. 'This Man was Hired to Depress Art,' Blake begins. He goes on:

Having spent the Vigour of my Youth & Genius under the Opression of Sr Joshua & his Gang of Cunning Hired Knaves Without Employment & as much as could possibly be Without Bread, The Reader must Expect to Read in all my Remarks on these Books Nothing but Indignation & Resentment. . . . Reynolds & Gainsborough Blotted & Blurred one against the other & Divided all the English World between them. Fuseli, Indignant, almost hid himself. I am hid.

When Reynolds mentions artists contending for royal liberality, Blake cries: 'Liberality! we want not Liberality. We want a Fair Price & Proportionate Value & a General Demand for Art.' As for the tendency to generalize, which Reynolds calls 'the great glory of the human mind', Blake asserts: 'To Generalize is to be an Idiot. To Particularize is the Alone Distinction of Merit. General Knowledges are those Knowledges that Idiots possess.' Blake defines his fundamental quarrel with Reynolds: 'Reynolds's Opinion was that Genius May be Taught & that all Pretence to Inspiration is a Lie & a Deceit, to say the least of it. For if it is a Deceit, the whole Bible is Madness. This Opinion originates in the Greeks' Calling the Muses Daughters of Memory.' Blake amplifies this further on and quotes Milton: 'A work of Genius is a Work "Not to be obtain'd by the Invocation of Memory & her Syren Daughters, but by Devout prayer to that Eternal Spirit, who . . . sends out his Seraphim with the hallowed fire of his Altar to touch & purify the lips of whom he pleases." '

Some of Blake's notes are epigrams:

The difference between a bad Artist & a Good One Is: the Bad Artist Seems to Copy a Great deal. The Good one Really Does Copy a Great deal.

Drapery is formed alone by the Shape of the Naked.

Fresco Painting is Like Miniature Painting; a Wall is a Large Ivory.

As for Reynolds himself, 'he thinks he has proved that Genius & Inspiration are All a Hum.' Blake exults: 'I certainly do Thank God that I am not like Reynolds!'

On 1 December 1808, Cumberland sent with his daughter, Georgiana, who was coming to London, 'a few old tracings from Raphael's pictures in fresco' for Blake; her brothers, young George and Sydney, were living with the Cromeks. 'It is very unpleasant at Mrs Cromek's,' young George wrote to his father, 'they take great liberties with me, my home and abroad amusements and studies are frustrated by their selfish dispositions, *true Yorkshire.*' On 4 December George reported: 'Mr Blake was very much pleased with the tracings. I thought it a good opportunity to ask him for "The Holy Family", which he gave very readily.' Cumberland anxiously replied 'I hope you did not ask Blake for the picture very *importunately. . . .*' (It has since been lost.) On 18 December Cumberland wrote to Blake that an acquaintance wanted to buy a complete set of Blake's books 'coloured as mine are'. Blake replied gratefully, but explained that he could not return to his 'former pursuits of printing. . . . I have already involved my-self in engagements that preclude all possibility of promising any thing. I have, however . . . begun to print an account of my various Inventions in Art, for which I have procured a Publisher . . . I will send it you first of any body. . . .'

Blake's 'engagements' were probably his preparations to show his works at his brother James's house, 28 Broad Street, and his projected publication may have been *A Descriptive Catalogue* of them. In his printed advertise-ment of 15 May 1809 (an eccentric, amateurish announcement compared with the slick puffs of Cromek's professional advertising campaigns) Blake gave the reasons for his novel form of exhibition, a one-man show. 'The execution of my Designs, being all in Water-colours, (that is in Fresco) are regularly refused to be exhibited by the *Royal Academy*, and the *British Institution* has, this year, followed its example, and has effectually excluded me by this Resolution. . . .' He invited patrons of the British Institution 'to inspect what they have excluded: and those who have been told that my Works are but an unscientific and irregular Eccentricity, a Madman's Scrawls, I demand of them to do me the justice to examine before they decide.'

The first work he advertised was 'The Ancient Britons', a life-size picture of three men, the most beautiful, most strong and most ugly, 'overthrowing the Army of armed Romans', an episode adapted from a Welsh poem. This picture seems not to have survived. The second work advertised was 'The Canterbury Pilgrims', a fresco of 'Thirty Figures on

Horse-back, in a brilliant Morning Scene', with which Blake hoped to eclipse Stothard's famous and lucrative painting. Thirdly, Blake advertises his 'grand Apotheoses' of Nelson and Pitt, 'with variety' of frescoes and drawings. Blake sent one of these single-sheet advertisements to Ozias Humphry, who had spent some years in India and would appreciate the oriental aspects of Blake's work, with 'a ticket of admission if you should honour my Exhibition with a Visit.'

This exhibition of sixteen 'Poetical and Historical Inventions' (nine in tempera, seven in watercolour) opened in May 1809 on the first floor of the hosier's house, 'Admittance 2s.6d. each Person, a descriptive Catalogue included' or one shilling with only a list of exhibits included. In the catalogue, a pamphlet carelessly reproduced by a printer in Berwick Street, Blake declared his artistic creed, commented on his exhibits and criticized Stothard's painting from Chaucer. In his preface Blake attacked Titian and Correggio, Rubens and Rembrandt, and praised Raphael and Dürer, Michelangelo and Giulio Romano. Their works were still known to him chiefly through poor copies and prints, so that he confirmed his prejudices with limited knowledge. Few original works by old masters were available to him, although he would have seen some in the Earl of Egremont's collection at Petworth—accessible from Felpham—and in Cumberland's collection too. Blake reveals, in his comments on works exhibited, many of his fascinating beliefs about life and art. Here he declares his faith in the orient as the source of spiritual art, insists that the Greeks copied oriental works, 'terrific and grand in the highest degree', and himself longs to create comparable pictures in England:

The two pictures of Nelson and Pitt are compositions of a mythological cast, similar to those Apotheoses of Persian, Hindoo, and Egyptian Antiquity, which are still preserved on rude monuments, being copies from some stupendous originals now lost or perhaps buried till some happier age. The Artist having been taken in vision into the ancient republics, monarchies, and patriarchates of Asia, has seen those wonderful originals called in the Sacred Scriptures the Cherubim, which were sculptured and painted on walls of Temples, Towers, Cities, Palaces, and erected in the highly cultivated states of Egypt, Moab, Edom, Aram, among the Rivers of Paradise, being originals from which the Greeks and Hetrurians copied Hercules Farnese, Venus of Medicis, Apollo Belvidere, and all the grand works of ancient art. . . . The Artist has endeavoured to emulate the grandeur of those seen in his vision, and to apply it to modern Heroes, on a smaller scale.

The characters of Chaucer's pilgrims, Blake says,

compose all ages and nations: as one age falls, another rises, different to mortal sight, but to immortals only the same. . . . Names alter, things never alter. I have known multitudes of those who would have been monks in the age of monkery, who in this deistical age are deists. As Newton numbered the stars, and as Linneus numbered the plants, so Chaucer numbered the classes of men.

Blake then considers the individual pilgrims, their eternal significance (for 'Every age is a Canterbury Pilgrimage') and explains his grouping. His comments are sharp and stimulating. The Miller, for example, is 'a terrible fellow, such as exists in all times and places for the trial of men, to astonish every neighbourhood with brutal strength and courage, to get rich and powerful to curb the pride of Man. . . .'

The characters of Women Chaucer has divided into two classes, the Lady Prioress and the Wife of Bath. Are not these leaders of the ages of men? The lady prioress, in some ages, predominates; and in some the wife of Bath . . . she is also a scourge and a blight. I shall say no more of her, nor expose what Chaucer has left hidden; let the young reader study what he has said of her: it is useful as a scarecrow. There are of such characters born too many for the peace of the world.

Hitting out at Cromek and Stothard, Blake then 'courts comparison with his competitors, who, having received fourteen hundred guineas and more, from the profits of his designs in that well-known work, Designs for Blair's Grave, have left him to shift for himself.' Blake derides Stothard for placing Chaucer's Reeve—a carpenter—'a vulgar fellow', between his aristocratic Knight and Squire, 'as if he was resolved to go contrary in everything to Chaucer.' Stothard 'has jumbled his dumb dollies together' and depicted the Wife of Bath as 'a young, beautiful, blooming damsel' whereas (as Blake proves by quoting Chaucer) age has bereft her of beauty and she has already had four husbands. Stothard's scene is 'by Dulwich Hills, which was not the way to Canterbury. . . . All is misconceived, and its mis-execution is equal to its misconception. . . . I have been scorned long enough by these fellows, who owe to me all that they have; it shall be so no longer. . . .'

Blake turns to defend himself against critics of his 'spirits with real bodies' in *The Grave*. Greek statues of Gods immortal, 'embodied and organized in solid marble', represent spiritual existences 'to the mortal perishing organ of sight. . . . Mr B. requires the same latitude, and all is well. The Prophets describe what they saw in Vision as real and existing men, whom they saw with their imaginative and immortal organs; the Apostles the same; the clearer the organ the more distinct the object.'

Blake's life-sized tempera on canvas of 'The Ancient Britons' showed the victorious remnant of 'civilized men, learned, studious, abstruse in thought and contemplation: naked, simple, plain in their acts and manners; wiser than after-ages.' A young Royal Academy student, Seymour Kirkup, saw this sunset battle-piece, with Druid temples distant among the mountains. Many years later he remembered it as a masterpiece

which made such an impression on my mind that I could draw it now, after a lapse of fifty-five years or more. [The picture] must have been about fourteen feet by ten. In texture it was rather mealy, as we call it, and was too red; the sun seemed setting in blood. It was not Greek in character. Though the figures reminded one of Hercules, Apollo, and Pan, they were naked Britons. If you should ever hear of it, it is worth seeking. There is more power and drawing in it than in any of his works that I have known, even in Blair's *Grave*. . . .

Blake wrote of his country's ancient glory and of the legendary sources that formed his picture of 'The Ancient Britons': but its significance is in the fourfold nature of man. The Strong, Beautiful and Ugly victors 'were originally one man, who was fourfold; he was self-divided, and his real humanity slain on the stems of generation, and the form of the fourth was like the Son of God.' As for the last

of those naked Heroes in the Welch Mountains; they are there now, Gray saw them in the person of his bard on Snowdon; there they dwell in naked simplicity; happy is he who can see and converse with them above the shadows of generation and death. The giant Albion, was Patriarch of the Atlantic; he is the Atlas of the Greeks, one of those the Greeks called Titans. . . .

The antiquities of every Nation under Heaven, is no less sacred than that of the Jews. . . . All had originally one language, and one religion: this was the religion of Jesus, the everlasting Gospel. Antiquity preaches the Gospel of Jesus.

The highest poetry, music and visual art

is Inspiration, and cannot be surpassed; it is perfect and eternal. Milton, Shakspeare, Michael Angelo, Rafael, the finest specimens of Ancient Sculpture and Painting and Architecture, Gothic, Grecian, Hindoo and Egyptian, are the extent of the human mind. The human mind cannot go beyond the gift of God, the Holy Ghost.

Blake 'has considered his strong Man as a receptacle of Wisdom, a sublime energizer' who 'marches on in fearless dependance on the divine decrees, raging with the inspirations of a prophetic mind. The Beautiful Man acts from duty and anxious solicitude for the fates of those for whom he combats. The Ugly Man acts from love of carnage, and delight in the savage barbarities of war, rushing with sportive precipitation into the very teeth of the affrighted enemy.' The last bard 'capable of attending warlike deeds, is seen falling, outstretched among the dead and the dying, singing to his harp in the pains of death. . . . The Sun sets behind the mountains, bloody with the day of battle.' Blake's naked warriors show the 'flush of health in flesh exposed to the open air, nourished by the spirits of forests and floods in that ancient happy period.' No living model can help. Only imagination can show the artist the colours of this flesh. 'As to a modern Man, stripped from his load of cloathing, he is like a dead corpse.'

Some of the pictures shown had been 'painted at intervals, for experiment on colours without any oily vehicle'. Another, 'The Bramins', was 'an ideal design' of 'Mr Wilkin translating the Geeta' from the 'Hindoo Scriptures'. Four Bible pictures 'the Artist wishes were in Fresco on an enlarged scale to ornament the altars of churches, and to make England,

33 (*Above*) Catherine Blake, tempera: 'Agnes, from the Novel of the Monk'; given to Mrs Butts, c. September 1800

34 (*Right*) Sepia watercolour by Blake: 'The Waters Prevailed upon the Earth'; Genesis 7:24. Noah's Flood resulted in the Sea of Time and Space

35 (*Left*) Watercolour, 1805–10: 'The Magic Banquet', *Comus*. Lady seated, with transformed humans; a snake—Blake's addition to Milton—hisses at Comus's wand

36 (*Below*) Pencil and grey wash: 'A Vision'; the poet, in the innermost shrine of his imagination, writes from an angel's dictation

William Blake
I suppose it to be a Vision
Indeed I remember a
conversation with Mr Blake Frederick Tatham
about it

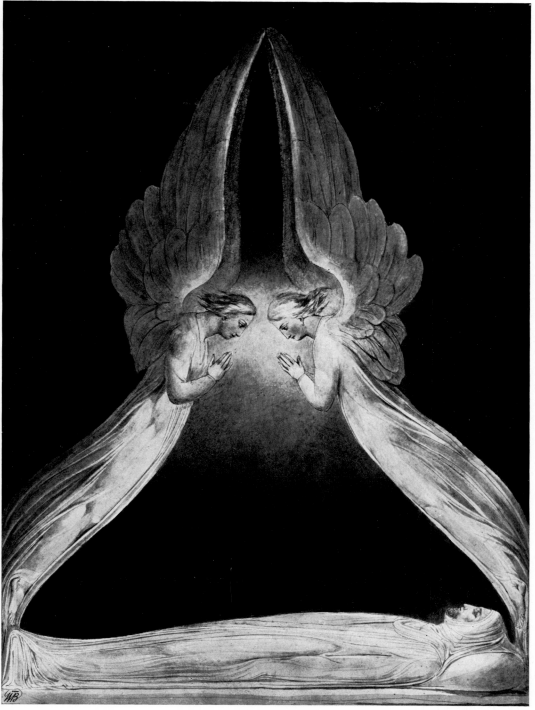

37 Watercolour, c. 1800: 'Angels Hovering over Jesus's Body in the Sepulchre'

38 Anon.: 'Tottenham Court Road Turnpike and St James's Chapel', after 1803 when Blake found London increasingly elegant, clean and neat, with widened streets

39 'Catherine Blake', about 1802, probably sewing or knitting. Blake drew on the back of a sheet of Hayley's 'Elephant' ballad

40 John Flaxman: 'Cromek', publisher of Robert Blair's *The Grave*

41   Watercolour, c. 1805: 'Ezekiel's Vision of the Whirlwind', Ezekiel I; a vast, fourfold revelation of eternity sweeps over the tiny prophet

42 Watercolour, 1808: 'Archangel Raphael with Adam and Eve', at mid-day
dinner of fruit and 'pleasant liquors', *Paradise Lost* 4: 492–511

43 Watercolour, 1808: 'The Last Judgment'. In the cloud rolling away from
Christ's throne are the 'Four Living Creatures filled with Eyes'

44 Blake, 1810: 'The Canterbury Pilgrims'. 'I defy any Man to Cut Cleaner Strokes than I do, or rougher where I please', Blake wrote of his engraving

45 Stothard, engraved Schiavonetti and Heath: 'Chaucer's Procession to Canterbury'; Stubbs praised the life and variety of Stothard's horses

Leaning against the pillars, & his disease rose from his skirts
Upon the Precipice he stood: ready to fall into Non-Entity.

Los was all astonishment & terror: he trembled sitting on the Stone
Of London: but the interiors of Albions fibres & nerves were hidden
From Los; astonishd he beheld only the petrified surfaces:
And saw his Furnaces in ruins, for Los is the Demon of the Furnaces;
He saw also the Four Points of Albion reversd inwards
He seizd his Hammer & Tongs, his iron Poker & his Bellows,
Upon the valleys of Middlesex, Shouting loud for aid Divine.

In stern defiance came from Albions bosom Hand, Hyle, Koban,
Gwantok, Peachy, Brereton, Slaid, Hutton, Skofeld, Kock, Kotope
Bowen: Albions Sons: they bore him a golden couch into the porch
And on the Couch reposd his limbs, trembling from the bloody field.
Rearing their Druid Patriarchal rocky Temples around his limbs.
All things begin & end, in Albions Ancient Druid Rocky Shore.)

46   Page from *Jerusalem*; relief-etching, 1804–20; Vala enticing Jerusalem and her daughters under the veil towards Babylonian St Paul's, away from Gothic West-minster Abbey

47 (*Right*) Visionary head, 1819, pencil: 'Caractacus'

48 (*Below left*) Engraving, c. 1818 (actual size): frontispiece, *For the Sexes: The Gates of Paradise*. Caterpillar and human chrysalis will evolve into butterflies—winged, eternal souls

49 (*Below right*) 'Head of the Ghost of a Flea', c. 1819, pencil; detail: mouth open

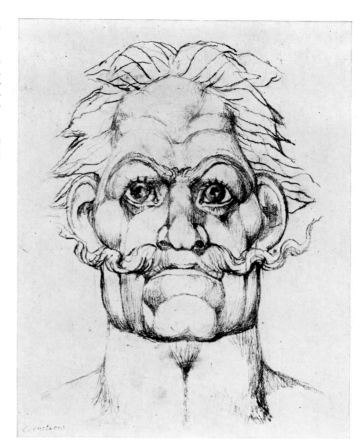

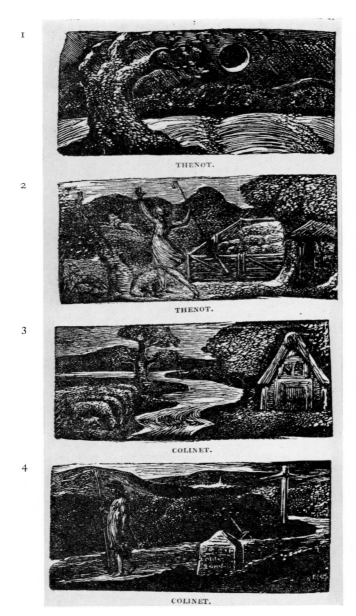

1

THENOT.

2

THENOT.

3

COLINET.

4

COLINET.

50   Wood engravings: a page from Thornton's *Virgil*, 1821 (actual size). Thenot, happy shepherd, commiserates with woeful Colinet, a shepherd born 'in hapless hour'. (1) mildewed corn, blasting winds, eclipsed moon; (2) defending the flock from fox, wolf and rot; (3) the river that Colinet regrets having left; (4) the shepherd restlessly wandering

51 John Linnell, pencil, 1821: 'Blake and Varley'

52 Life mask of Blake aged 66; heavy plaster probably dragged his mouth down, changing sensibility and sweetness of expression to severity

53 Samuel Palmer: self-portrait, c. 1826; black chalk heightened with white

54   Watercolour, c. 1826: 'Geryon Conveying Dante and Virgil Downwards',
Inferno 17

55   Unfinished engraving, 1827: 'The Whirlwind of Lovers', *Inferno* 5; Dante
fainting with compassion: Paolo and Francesca, slain lovers, arising in flame

Within the illustration:

Canst thou bind the sweet influences of Pleiades or loose the bands of Orion

14

Let there Be

Light

Let there be A

Firmament

Let the Waters be gathered together into one place

& let the Dry Land appear

And God made Two Great Lights

Sun

Moon

Let the Waters bring forth abundantly

Let the Earth bring forth

Cattle & Creeping thing & Beast

When the morning Stars sang together, & all the
Sons of God shouted for joy

WBlake   Inventut & Sc

56   Engraving, 1825: *Job*, plate 14: the Creator above Job, wife, comforters;
symbols on the pencil sketch show that Blake saw this vision

57 (*Above*) Frederick Shields: 'The Blakes' Living-room, Fountain Court'; from here, Blake often said, the Thames resembled 'a bar of gold'

58 Pencil, 1825: Linnell aged 33, faintly drawn by Blake at Hampstead

like Italy, respected . . . on account of Art.' Blake will provide his genius: let the government provide the commissions. 'The times require that every one should speak out boldly; England expects that every man should do his duty, in Arts, as well as in Arms, or in the Senate.' Blake's national service would be to paint portable murals in tempera, on a grand scale: 'I could divide Westminster Hall, or the walls of any other great Building, into compartments and ornament them with Frescos, which would be removable at pleasure.' Defiantly, Blake ends his *Descriptive Catalogue*:

If a man is master of his profession, he cannot be ignorant that he is so; and if he is not employed by those who pretend to encourage art, he will employ himself, and laugh in secret at the pretences of the ignorant, while he has every night dropped into his shoe, as soon as he puts it off, and puts out the candle, and gets into bed, a reward for the labours of the day, such as the world cannot give, and patience and time await to give him all that the world can give.

Blake's exhibition may have attracted a few visitors who had heard of his quarrel with Stothard and were curious to see the picture which—according to Blake—had started it. Hardly anybody else came to see this art-show, which occupied several rooms of James's home. On 17 September 1809, *The Examiner* published the exhibition's only known review. In this, Robert Hunt sneered that Blake, 'an unfortunate lunatic, whose personal inoffensiveness secures him from confinement', has published 'a catalogue, or rather a farrago of nonsense, unintelligibleness, and egregious vanity, the wild effusions of a distempered brain'. Hunt quotes Blake derisively and comments on two exhibits. His 'Canterbury Pilgrims' 'is in every respect a striking contrast to the admirable picture of the same subject by Mr Stothard, from which an exquisite print is forthcome from the hand of Schiavonetti'; and ' "The Ancient Britons" . . . is a complete caricature: one of the bards is singing to his harp in the pangs of death; and . . . the colouring of the flesh is exactly like hung beef. . . .'

To this crude attack, Blake reacted by composing caustic verses about 'The Examiner, whose very name is Hunt' and cramming them into his notebook, his depository of personal rhymes. There he wrote bitterly, too, about Flaxman and Stothard:

I found them blind: I taught them how to see;
And now they know neither themselves nor me.

Plaintively, though, Blake questioned whether Nancy Flaxman's friendship need be sacrificed because her husband had—like Stothard, so Blake maintained—copied from him when illustrating Homer and Dante:

How can I help thy Husband's copying Me?
Should that make difference 'twixt me & Thee?

The gratitude which had sweetened Blake's memories of Hayley was eroded, and rhymes about him fester in the notebook with retrospective scorn:

Of H's birth this was the happy lot
His Mother on his Father him begot.

When H—y finds out what you cannot do,
That is the very thing he'll set you to. . . .
And when he could not act upon my wife
Hired a Villain to bereave my Life.

To Fuseli, however, Blake paid tribute in pungently appreciative rhymes in the notebook.

The only Man that e'er I knew
Who did not make me almost spew
Was Fuseli: he was both Turk & Jew—
And so, dear Christian Friends, how do you do?

In the hope of attracting more visitors, Blake's exhibition was kept open beyond 29 September, its scheduled closing date, well into 1810: 'Fit audience find tho' few', Blake had quoted from *Paradise Lost* as the motto on his advertisement. In October 1809, young George Cumberland wrote to his father, who had moved to Bristol, that Blake's *Descriptive Catalogue* 'is a great curiosity. He has given Stothard a complete set down.' Cumberland senior found it 'truly original—part vanity part madness—part very good sense.' Hard pressed by taxes and the cost of living, he could not afford to subscribe for the large engraving of the 'Canterbury Pilgrims', on which Blake was already working. Just over three feet long by one foot high, it was advertised at four guineas.

Blake's prospectus, printed about 1810, describes Chaucer and his pilgrims leaving the Tabard Inn in Southwark. Blake alludes gratefully to the nearby hospital, St Thomas's, 'one of the most amiable features of the Christian Church': the Blakes' surgeon friend, John Birch, provided 'Electrical Magic' there for many years. 'Even at this day,' Blake writes about St Thomas's, 'every friendless wretch who wants the succour of it, is considered as a Pilgrim travelling through this Journey of Life.'

Henry Crabb Robinson, the diarist who recorded conversations with Flaxman, Coleridge, Lamb and Wordsworth, had been intrigued by Malkin's published essay on Blake and wished to write an account of 'this extraordinary genius' for a new German magazine. Crabb Robinson went to the exhibition on 23 April 1810, and later recalled: 'I was deeply interested by the catalogues as well as the pictures. I took four, telling the brother I hoped he would let me come in again. He said: "Oh! as often as you please"—I dare say such a thing had never happened before or did afterwards.' One of those four copies of the catalogue was for the writer Charles Lamb who, according to Crabb Robinson, thought Blake's description of 'The Canterbury Pilgrims' 'the finest criticism he had ever read of Chaucer's poem.' In June, Crabb Robinson took Charles and his sister Mary Lamb to the exhibition. Nearly fourteen years later, in 1824, Lamb in a letter praised Blake's 'marvellous strange pictures, visions of his brain, which he asserts that he has seen. They have great merit. He has *seen* the old Welsh bards on Snowdon . . . and has painted them from memory (I have seen his paintings). . . . His pictures—one in particular, "The Canterbury Pilgrims" (far above Stothard's)—have great merit, but hard, dry, yet with grace.' Lamb went on to refer to 'The Tyger', 'which I have heard recited . . . which is glorious, but alas! I have not the book; for the man is flown, whither I know not—to Hades or a mad house. But I must look on him as one of the most extraordinary persons of the age.' Lamb wrote this three years before Blake died. Robert Southey, who was to become poet laureate in 1813, was also stimulated by Crabb Robinson to visit the exhibition. Years later Southey mentioned Blake as 'that painter of great but insane genius' and called 'The Ancient Britons' 'one of his worst pictures—which is saying much. . . .'

On 7 June 1810 Schiavonetti died of tuberculosis and left his engraving of Stothard's 'Canterbury Pilgrims' unfinished. Blake wrote:

> Thus Poor Schiavonetti died of the Cromek,
> A thing that's tied about the Examiner's neck.

(Before Schiavonetti's plate was finished by Heath, Cromek died of tuberculosis in 1812: for this 'Bob Screwmuch', Blake confessed 'my tears are aqua fortis'—nitric acid.)

In 1810, Blake wrote in his notebook most of his 'Public Address' on art, in which he justifies the linear style of engraving with which he set out in life and which he has resumed. Venom wells up from poisoned friendships with Stothard and Flaxman. Fuseli, however, Blake regards as a fellow victim of public attack.

Blake addresses English engravers:

It is very true, what you have said for these thirty two Years. I am Mad or Else you are so; both of us cannot be in our right senses. Posterity will judge by our Works. Woolett's & Strange's works are . . . Suited to the Purposes of Commerce no doubt, for Commerce Cannot endure Individual Merit; its insatiable Maw must be fed by What all can do Equally well; at least it is so in England, as I have found to my Cost these Forty Years.

England spurns original invention, which cannot

Exist without Execution, Organized & minutely delineated & Articulated, Either by God or Man. I do not mean smooth'd up & Niggled & Poco-Pen'd, and all the beauties pick'd out & blurr'd & blotted, but Drawn with a firm & decided hand at once, like Fuseli & Michael Angelo, Shakespeare & Milton.

Because of the low standard of expensive engraving,

most Englishmen have a Contempt for Art, which is the Greatest Curse that can fall upon a Nation. . . . Let us teach Buonaparte, & whomsoever else it may concern, That it is not Arts that follow & attend upon Empire, but Empire that attends upon & follows The Arts.

Politics Blake now scorns and shuns.

I am really sorry to see my Countrymen trouble themselves about Politics. If Men were Wise, the Most arbitrary Princes could not hurt them. If they are not wise, the Freest Government is compell'd to be a Tyranny. . . . To recover Art has been the business of my life to the Florentine Original & if possible to go beyond that Original; this I thought the only pursuit worthy of a Man. To imitate I abhor. . . . I know my Execution is not like Any Body Else. I do not intend it should be so; none but Blockheads Copy one another.

Public works are what Blake longs to create. 'Painting . . . would make a Noble finish Placed above the Great Public Monuments in Westminster, St Pauls & other Cathedrals.' Blake's boyhood experiences in Westminster Abbey still aroused the fifty-three-year-old artist's ambitions. 'Monuments to the dead, Painted by Historical & Poetical Artists . . . must make England What Italy is, an Envied Storehouse of Intellectual Riches.'

Confident—and justly so—that his engraving of 'The Canterbury Pilgrims' which he published on 8 October 1810 was worthy of him, Blake dared to assert: 'This Print is the Finest that has been done or is likely to be done in England, where drawing, its foundation, is Contemn'd, and absurd Nonsense about dots & Lozenges & Clean Strokes made to occupy the attention to the Neglect of all real Art.' The public ignored Blake's sinewy, live, witty engraving of 'The Canterbury Pilgrims' (44)—which he re-advertised about 1810 at three guineas—but acclaimed the engraving of Stothard's insipid picture (45). The same size and price as Blake's, impressions of Schiavonetti's engraving finished by Heath sold widely, to be framed and hung conspicuously in most houses where the master had a library or any pretensions to a love of art. Stothard gained renown, while Blake, who had hoped to attract a public by his exhibition, remained hidden in obscurity, which shrouded him even more deeply during the next few years.

Blake described in his notebook, as an addition to his catalogue for 1810, one of his paintings—since lost—of 'The Last Judgment'. The engraver, antiquary and writer John Thomas Smith saw this painting. It contained, he wrote, 'upwards of one thousand figures, many of them wonderfully conceived and grandly drawn'. Blake describes the figures, and his comments reveal fascinating glimpses of himself, his vision and thought:

If the Spectator could Enter into these Images in his Imagination, approaching them on the Fiery Chariot of his Contemplative Thought . . . then would he arise from his Grave, then would he meet the Lord in the Air & then he would be happy.

Men are admitted into Heaven not because they have curbed & govern'd their Passions or have No Passions, but because they have Cultivated their Understandings. The Treasures of Heaven are not Negations of Passion, but Realities of Intellect, from which all the Passions Emanate Uncurbed in their Eternal

Glory. The Fool shall not enter into Heaven let him be ever so Holy. . . . Those who are cast out are All Those who, having no Passions of their own because No Intellect, Have spent their lives in Curbing & Governing other People's by the Various arts of Poverty & Cruelty of all kinds. Wo, Wo, Wo to you Hypocrites. . .
The Modern Church Crucifies Christ with the Head Downwards.

Thinking as I do that the Creator of this World is a very Cruel Being, & being a Worshipper of Christ, I cannot help saying: 'the Son, O how unlike the Father!' First God Almighty comes with a Thump on the Head. Then Jesus Christ comes with a balm to heal it.

I assert for My Self that I do not behold the outward Creation & that to me it is hindrance & not Action; it is as the Dirt upon my feet, No part of Me. 'What,' it will be Question'd, 'When the Sun rises, do you not see a round disk of fire somewhat like a Guinea?' O no, no, I see an Innumerable company of the Heavenly host crying 'Holy, Holy, Holy is the Lord God Almighty.' I question not my Corporeal or Vegetative Eye any more than I would Question a Window concerning a Sight. I look thro' it & not with it.

Blake was especially fond of his picture of 'The Last Judgment' and kept it by him until his death. His largest extant painting, 'An Allegory of the Spiritual Condition of Man'—a marvellous pale gold work in tempera—perhaps still resembles in its shimmering effect 'The Last Judgment' as Smith described it: 'The lights of this extraordinary performance have the appearance of silver and gold; but upon Mrs Blake's assuring me that there was no silver used, I found, upon a closer examination, that a blue wash had been passed over those parts of the gilding which receded, and the lights of the forward objects, which were also of gold, were heightened with a warm colour, to give the appearance of the two metals.' Blake wrote in his notebook on 23 May 1810: 'found the Word Golden'; he said of this picture, which hung in his front room: 'I spoiled that—made it darker; it was much finer, but a Frenchwoman here didn't like it.' Blake himself was of the opinion, 'First thoughts are best in art, second thoughts in other matters.'

By 1808 Blake had relief-etched forty-nine plates of *Milton*: he printed three copies and painted them delicately. Some years later he added one more plate to a fourth copy, which he coloured very splendidly and enriched with silver and gold. *Jerusalem*, an epic of a hundred relief-etched plates profusely illustrated with bold, masterly designs (46), continued to occupy him on and off until 1820. He had probably begun to write the poem in about 1804. In the summer of 1807, Cumberland noted: 'Blake has engraved sixty plates of a new prophecy!'—presumably *Jerusalem*. *A Descriptive Catalogue* announced in 1809, when Blake believed that he was about to be recognized: 'Mr. B. has in his hands poems of the highest antiquity. Adam was a Druid, and Noah . . . these things are written in

Eden. The artist is an inhabitant of that happy country; and if every thing goes on as it has begun, the world . . . may expect to be opened again to Heaven, through Eden, as it was in the beginning.' About a year later, while Blake's hopes of fame dwindled, he was revising *Jerusalem* to avenge himself on the vitriolic Hunt brothers through the three-headed giant, Hand, and hoping—as his 'Public Address' shows—to complete *Jerusalem* soon: 'the manner in which I have routed out the nest of villains will be seen in a Poem concerning my Three years' Herculean Labours at Felpham, which I will soon Publish. Secret Calumny & open Professions of Friendship are common enough all the world over, but have never been so good an occasion of Poetic Imagery.' Perhaps, however, Blake lacked resources as well as encouragement to print *Jerusalem* until about 1818.

7

Pilgrimage in Poverty
1809—18

'I laugh at Fortune & Go on & on'

Helping hands were vanishing. Asthma killed Joseph Johnson the publisher in 1809, Ozias Humphry died in 1810. Hayley was no longer in touch with Blake. Some friends, however—perhaps Butts or Malkin—produced a pamphlet in 1811 to arouse interest in Blake's engraving of the Canterbury Pilgrims: but it failed to do so. In keeping with public neglect is George III's reputed remark on being shown some of Blake's drawings: 'Take them away! take them away!'

After 1810, Butts continued to buy from him, but probably less regularly than before. Blake's poverty was noted by young Tommy Butts's friend Kirkup, who emigrated in 1816 but remembered Blake as one of the 'most sincere men I ever knew. . . . There never was an honester man than he, or one who lived in a finer poverty—poor but strictly simple in his habits.' Kirkup wrote that Blake was 'very positive in his opinion, with which I never agreed. His excellent old wife was a sincere believer in all his visions. She told me seriously one day, "I have very little of Mr Blake's company; he is always in Paradise." She prepared his colours, and was as good as a servant.' Because Blake 'could only give his word for the truth of his visions', they seemed incredible to young Kirkup, who as a student saw much of him between 1810 and 1816; 'I thought him mad,' Kirkup wrote in 1870: 'I do not think so now.'

Blake withdrew further from the world that spurned him, but Robert Southey was sufficiently intrigued to seek him out. On 24 July 1811 Crabb Robinson noted in his diary: 'Returned late to C. Lamb's. Found a very large party there—Southey had been with Blake and admired both his designs and his poetic talents, at the same time that he held him for a decided madman. Blake, he says, spoke of his visions with the diffidence that is usual with such people and did not seem to expect that he should be believed. He showed S. a perfectly mad poem called *Jerusalem*—Oxford St is in Jerusalem.'

Blake had evidently not explained to Southey the simple idea from which *Jerusalem*, 'The Emanation of The Giant Albion', evolves. Albion personifies Britain, its history and all its people—past, present and future. Blake developed him from Adam Kadmon, the Universal Man of the Cabbala, who 'anciently contain'd in his mighty limbs all things in Heaven & Earth.' Britons, whose corporate life is summed up in Albion, are his sons and daughters. With imaginative genius, Blake saw Albion's Emanation as Jerusalem, a city attacked, a woman led astray and into captivity by Babylon, and a bride redeemed in 'Great Eternity' where every particular

> Form is the Divine Vision
> And the Light is his Garment. This is Jerusalem in every Man,
> A Tent & Tabernacle of Mutual Forgiveness, Male & Female Clothings.
> And Jerusalem is called Liberty among the Children of Albion.

For most of the epic, however, Albion sleeps and dreams. The vision of liberty is hidden from him by the delusions of war, conquest and corrupt morality in which he reposes. He has rejected Jerusalem's love and forgiveness. To his perverted sight, she seems a foolish sinner. Los, ever-faithful despite his own conflicts with his Spectre and his Emanation (Enitharmon), watches and labours to create true visions for Albion.

Diseased dreams, as corrupt as the visions of a repressive God conceived by warlike Israelites, weave together the biblical fibres of the poem and threads of everyday life surrounding Blake. So, when the daughter of Israel, Dinah, has been brutally hurt, Blake sees 'The Wound . . . in South Molton Street & Stratford place'. The children of Israel are truly the children of Albion. London should be the free holy city, Jerusalem, but she has fallen into the power of jealous Vala and suffered the captivity and corruption of Babylon. Albion's exiled daughters, longing for their lovely land of green mountains, lament on Euphrates:

> I see London, blind & age-bent, begging thro' the Streets
> Of Babylon, led by a child; his tears run down his beard.

Rahab, a name applied to Babylon in The Book of Revelation, is a seductive harlot, one of the two manifestations of the evil Vala: it was Vala's jealousy that caused Albion to reject Jerusalem. With Tirzah, the prudish temptress, Vala's other manifestation, Albion's twelve daughters are identified. They hear Reuben, the average sensual man, and their lament continues:

> The voice of Wandering Reuben echoes from street to street
> In all the Cities of the Nations, Paris, Madrid, Amsterdam.
> The Corner of Broad Street weeps; Poland Street languishes . . .

Albion's twelve beautiful daughters are sadists who use sex and religion to inflict pain: 'If you dare rend their Veil with your Spear, you are healed of Love.' Their names are mostly those of legendary British queens and princesses, such as Cordella, Ragan, Gwinevera and Sabrina. The twelve sons' names derive from Blake's enemies. As already noted, Hand represents the Hunt Brothers and Hyle is Hayley in the Cockney pronunciation, besides being the Greek for 'matter'. Most of the other ten names have been identified with men who participated in Blake's trial. Besides Skofeld and Kox, the oddly spelt list includes, for example, Gwantoke, Peachey and Brertun (magistrates) and Huttn (a lieutenant). Blake links sons and daughters and their districts. For instance, 'Brertun had Yorkshire, Durham, Westmoreland, & his Emanation Is Ragan.' The names of places have more than geographic importance because, as Blake explains,

> all are Men in Eternity, Rivers, Mountains, Cities, Villages,
> All are Human, & when you enter into their Bosoms you walk
> In Heavens & Earths, as in your own Bosom you bear your Heaven
> And Earth & all you behold; tho' it appears Without, it is Within,
> In your Imagination, of which this World of Mortality is but a Shadow.

Blake, believing in the significance of minute particulars and pursuing them in the labyrinth of his mind, is apt to tie many threads of meaning together in knots of baffling obscurity. When his narrative proceeds, however, its main lines are generally clear and his message plain. Divine humanity is everywhere, but man can only see it by imagination. To live fully, he must sacrifice himself and perpetually forgive.

Man's distance from the full life is painfully obvious. In Albion, chastity is called morality. Hidden deceit governs all:

> What seems to Be, Is, To those to whom
> It seems to Be, & is productive of the most dreadful
> Consequences to those to whom it seems to Be, even of
> Torments, Despair, Eternal Death. . . .

The false holiness of Druid law, with its murderous jealousies, is alien to Eden, where the sanctuary is in the camp, in the outline,

> In the Circumference, & every Minute Particular is Holy:
> Embraces are Cominglings from the Head even to the Feet,
> And not a pompous High Priest entering by a Secret Place.

Over west London, despair closes. 'The Shuttles of death sing in the sky . . . weaving black melancholy as a net', and Jerusalem flees 'to Lambeth's mild Vale'. Watch-fiends, who hound out what they call sin to punish it in blood, are not all-powerful, however, even in London.

> There is a Grain of Sand in Lambeth that Satan cannot find,
> Nor can his Watch Fiends find it; 'tis translucent & has many Angles,
> But he who finds it will find Oothoon's palace; for within
> Opening into Beulah, every angle is a lovely heaven.

If man would turn his eyes inward, the world of love and harmony would open its gates.

The difficulty of achieving that vision is shown by the conflicts that Los has to win. He must shatter his Spectre, who refuses to believe without demonstration, and who forms Leviathan and Behemoth, 'the War by Sea enormous & the War By Land astounding'. Los, undaunted and furious, heaves his hammer, swings it and strikes, 'Smiting the Spectre on his Anvil . . . and with many tears labouring'. The Spectre's pyramids become grains of sand, his pillars become 'dust on the fly's wing, & his starry Heavens a moth of gold & silver, mocking his anxious grasp'. Los then sees the amalgamation of Briton, Saxon, Roman and Norman begin in his furnaces. In unity there is hope: although, beneath, in a roaring sea which heaves around the wormy garments of the death-like sleeper 'Albion cold lays on his Rock. . . . The weeds of Death inwrap his hands & feet. . . .' Jerusalem and Vala, now purged of Rahab and Tirzah—whom Chaucer had shown as the Wife of Bath and the Prioress—are reunited to form Albion's complete Emanation. They confess that they have murdered him in dreams of chastity and moral law 'In Stone-henge [the reputed scene of Druid execution] & on London Stone', the datum-point for Roman milestones and the site of Cannon Street.

Albion hears his Emanation and he moves upon the rock. 'The Breath Divine went forth upon the morning hills.' Albion rises. With his burning bow in his hand and his arrows of flaming gold, he compels the four Zoas to their rightful tasks.

> Then Jesus appeared standing by Albion as the Good Shepherd
> By the lost Sheep that he hath found, & Albion knew that it
> Was the Lord, the Universal Humanity; & Albion saw his Form
> A Man, & they conversed as Man with Man in Ages of Eternity.
> And the Divine Appearance was the likeness & similitude of Los.

Albion asks how to destroy his 'Selfhood cruel', the Covering Cherub who covers the mercy seat to prevent man seeing God: 'I know it is my Self, O my Divine Creator & Redeemer.' Jesus replies: 'unless I die thou canst not live' in resurrection 'with me'. This 'Mysterious Offering of Self for Another', under the Covering Cherub's shadow, is friendship and brotherhood. Albion sees Jesus as 'Los my Friend', and Jesus asks: 'Wouldest thou love one who never died For thee, or ever die for one who had not died for thee?' Man and God are love; 'every kindness to another is a little Death In the Divine Image, nor can Man exist but by Brotherhood.' In a fourfold vision of splendour 'The Druid Spectre was Annihilate' and total revelation comes. 'The innumerable Chariots of the Almighty appear'd in Heaven, And Bacon & Newton & Locke, & Milton & Shakspear & Chaucer, A Sun of blood red wrath surrounding heaven, on all sides around . . .'. The fourfold man is released from his 'excrementitious Husk & Covering': his nerves of sensation evaporate, revealing his lineaments,

> Driving outward the Body of Death in an Eternal Death & Resurrection,

Awaking it to Life among the Flowers of Beulah, rejoicing in Unity
In the Four Senses, in the Outline, the Circumference & Form, for ever
In Forgiveness of Sins which is Self Annihilation; it is the Covenant of
Jehovah.

Amidst thunderous majesty and visions in new expanses, Blake witnesses
'All Human Forms identified, even Tree, Metal, Earth & Stone'. They are
'living, going forth & returning wearied', to repose and then awake 'in the
Life of Immortality'. And in the last line of the epic 'I heard the Name of
their Emanations: they are named Jerusalem.'

Blake spells out his message, mostly in prose, in the introductions to
each of the four chapters of *Jerusalem*. He addresses the public (sheep and
goats):

The Spirit of Jesus is continual forgiveness of Sin: he who waits to be righteous
before he enters into the Saviour's kingdom, the Divine Body, will never enter
there. I am perhaps the most sinful of men. I pretend not to holiness: yet I
pretend to love, to see, to converse with daily as man with man, & the more to
have an interest in the Friend of Sinners. Therefore, *dear* Reader, *forgive* what
you do not approve, & *love* me for this energetic exertion of my talent.

Blake considered writing in blank verse, but rejected it as too monotonous
'in the mouth of a true Orator. . . . I therefore have produced a variety in
every line, both of cadences & number of syllables. . . . Poetry Fetter'd
Fetters the Human Race.'

To the Christians, Blake offers the advice:

I give you the end of a golden string,
    Only wind it into a ball,
It will lead you in at Heaven's gate,
    Built in Jerusalem's wall.

He declares:

I know of no other Christianity and of no other Gospel than the liberty both of
body & mind to Exercise the Divine Arts of Imagination, Imagination, the real
& eternal World of which this Vegetable Universe is but a faint shadow, & in
which we shall live in our Eternal or Imaginative Bodies when these Vegetable
Mortal Bodies are no more. The Apostles knew of no other Gospel.

The epic itself incorporates some passages from *Vala* and *Milton*. It is
Blake's fullest, richest and most compelling presentation of his mature
beliefs. The poem's final episodes are overwhelmingly moving. In them,
the voice of the poetic prophet rings with complete authority.

On Sunday morning, 24 May 1812, Crabb Robinson walked across the
fields to Hampstead Heath with Wordsworth, read to him from Blake's
poems, and later noted in his diary that Wordworth 'was pleased with some
of them and considered Blake as having the elements of poetry—a thousand
times more than either Byron or Scott.'

By 1812, Blake had become one of the fourteen members of the Water Colour Society. This year's annual exhibition (their fifth) included, in their rooms in Bond Street, three of Blake's temperas from his one-man show and some detached pages of *Jerusalem*. About this time, his brother James left the old family home. The Golden Square neighbourhood had gone down in the world and was becoming disreputable. James moved his shop to Buckingham Street, Fitzroy Square, near the home of Mr and Mrs Butts. After a while he gave up his hosiery business and, presumably thanks to Butts, became a clerk under him in the office of the Commissary General of Musters. When this office—which had been found inefficient, overstaffed and redundant—was abolished in 1817, James probably received a pension and Butts was able to retire comfortably.

On 3 June 1814 Cumberland visited Cosway at a house in South Molton Street 'facing poor Blake'. After calling on Blake—'still poor still dirty'—Cumberland, who recorded these visits in his notebook, got to his banker at six o'clock for dinner and passed the rest of the evening with Stothard in Newman Street—'still more dirty than Blake yet full of genius'. Blake, continuing to suffer from the painful scars of his break from Stothard, knew that 'It is easier to forgive an Enemy than to forgive a Friend', but wanted to resume their old friendship. He tried, many years later: on their way in to an artists' dinner he went up to Stothard and offered to shake hands. Stothard refused, as he did another time when he was ill and Blake called to see him and to be reconciled.

With Flaxman, however, Blake's friendship, frozen in 1805, had been restored to warmth and life. In 1814 Flaxman recommended Blake as 'the best engraver of outlines', sought work for him, and himself commissioned thirty-seven outline engravings for Hesiod's *Work Days and Theogony* at five guineas a plate. Payment began in 1814. Flaxman had worked on the drawings for at least ten years by the time they were published, engraved by Blake, in 1817. Flaxman was kind, simple and pious. Because he charged reasonable prices, he was not rich in worldly goods. Like the Blakes, the Flaxmans were childless, but they shared their happy home with John's half-sister Maria Ann Flaxman, thirteen years his junior, and with Nancy's sister Maria Denman, twenty-one years John's junior: he adopted her. Not only did Flaxman's practical Christianity and equable temperament endear him to Blake, but learning and ideas attuned the friends to each other. In his lecture on style and sculpture, Flaxman notes that 'the events of Hindu mythology have furnished various extraordinary and poetical compositions more singular and elegant than has been hitherto seen in the published antiquities of Egypt.' His wide-ranging mind met Blake's in remote places.

Because Blake needed more work—however mundane—in order to live, early in 1815 Flaxman put him in touch with Josiah Wedgwood, younger son of the founder of the pottery works. Wedgwood offered Blake the job of drawing and engraving 185 specimens of household ware—such as a soup terrine, cream bowl, fruit basket and butter boat—for a catalogue to be used in the Etruria pottery, but not to be sent out to customers. Wedgwood's London agent provided specimen pieces for Mrs Blake to collect and carry home to South Molton Street, where Blake drew them. By 13 December 1815 he had nearly finished his drawings. Wedgwood then decided how he wanted the articles arranged on each copper plate, and Blake engraved them. For eighteen very clear and elegant engraved plates he was paid £30 in November 1816; but he had possibly received some money for his drawings before then.

At this time of general economic depression after the Napoleonic War, a less basic commission that Blake secured—also thanks to Flaxman—was to engrave seven plates for Abraham Rees's thirty-nine-volume *Cyclopaedia*, which was published in seventy-nine parts from 1802 to 1820. Blake's illustrations were for articles, probably written by Flaxman, on armour, bas-relief, gem-engraving and sculpture. To draw a cast of the Laocoön, Blake went to the Antique School of the Royal Academy, where the Keeper, Fuseli, greeted him with: 'What! you here, *Meesther Blake*? We ought to come and learn of you, not you of us.' This was probably in the spring of 1815. Fuseli's enthusiasm for Greek sculpture had blazed in 1808 when his pupil Benjamin Robert Haydon took him from Somerset House to see the Elgin Marbles in a damp shed in Park Lane. Haydon later wrote: 'Never shall I forget his uncompromising enthusiasm. Thrown off his guard by their beauty, he strode about the collection in his fierce way, saying: "De Greeks were godes! De Greeks were godes!" ' Fuseli, who believed terror to be the chief ingredient of the sublime, wrote that 'Laocoön, with his sons, will always remain a sufficient answer to all that has been retailed in our days on the limits of the art by tame antiquarians from tamer painters.' The Laocoön group held profound significance for Blake. He made another engraving of it some years later and surrounded it with his own aphorisms, a distillation of his profoundest beliefs, many of them at variance with Fuseli's.

Blake was an early riser and an indefatigable worker, amazing in his energy. When a young artist complained of being very ill and asked him what to do, 'Oh!' said Blake, 'I never stop for anything; I work on, whether ill or not.' He and his wife had by now given up their long, refreshing walks into the country south of London. When he lacked commissions, he was always busy with his own creative work. No other absorbing interest, such as the entomology which captivated Fuseli, occupied Blake indoors.

On 20 April 1815 Cumberland's sons, George and Sydney, called at the Blakes' in the evening and found them 'drinking tea, dirtier than ever.' However, George reported to Cumberland, Blake 'received us well and showed his large drawing in watercolours of the Last Judgment. He has been labouring at it till it is nearly as black as your hat—the only lights are those of a *hellish purple*. His time is now entirely taken up with etching and engraving. . . . Blake says he is fearful they will make too great a man of Napoleon and enable him to come to this country—Mrs B. says that if this country does go to war our King ought to lose his head.' Catherine seems to have absorbed her husband's radical opinions. Dressed in common, dirty clothes, and coarsened by the years, she had lost her physical beauty: but her devoted love for Blake still lit her gleaming black eyes and made her other attributes of no significance. Any jealousy of his friends which she may ever have suffered had died away long ago, and any marital discords had been resolved into harmony.

To George, who was thinking of asking Blake's advice about the technique of engraving, Cumberland replied briefly: 'You have a free estimate of Blake—and his devilish works—he is a little cracked, but very honest. As to his wife, she is maddest of the two. He will tell you anything he knows.' Flaxman, however, a far more intimate friend than Cumberland, considered Blake to be sane; and Flaxman had endured for years the violence of Blake's reactions and had put up with what Nancy called his 'odd humours'. When Cary, the translator of Dante and himself periodically mad, dismissed Blake from consideration as a history painter with the remark: 'But Blake is a wild enthusiast, isn't he?' the retort of Flaxman, who drew himself up half-offended, was: 'Some think me an enthusiast.'

It may have been about 1815 that Blake's experiments with tempera began to prove more successful in technique than before: perhaps he was using, instead of glue, a more tractable sticky medium. In 1816, in his charmingly exuberant engraving of 'Mirth and her Companions' from Milton's *L'Allegro*, he relied less on line than on stipple. He also painted six watercolour illustrations for each of the two poems *L'Allegro* and *Il Penseroso*, and he began to engrave the series in that year. He interpreted these poems freely and more personally than Milton's other works, and wrote an explanation of each picture. Characteristically, Blake—at the age of nearly sixty—depicts young Milton's lark as 'an Angel on the Wing', 'Mountains, Clouds, Rivers, Trees appear Humanized on the Sunshine Holiday' and 'The youthful Poet, sleeping on a bank by the Haunted Stream by Sun Set, sees in his dream the more bright Sun of Imagination under the auspices of Shakespeare' and Ben Jonson.

Blake was recognized, in 1816, in *A Biographical Dictionary of the Living Authors of Great Britain and Ireland*, as 'an eccentric but very ingenious artist . . . principally the engraver of his own designs'. Three Lambeth books and *A Descriptive Catalogue* are then listed. John Gibson, a young sculptor, in 1817 brought his designs to Blake, who praised them, showed his own cartoons to Gibson and, Gibson wrote, 'complained sadly of the want of feeling in England for high art, and his wife joined in with him and she was very bitter upon the subject.' At the end of the year, an art critic, William Paulet Carey, digressed from writing about a picture by West to lavish praise on Blake's designs for *The Grave* and to declare: 'Beyond the circle of artists, I anxiously look round for the designer's *patrons*': Cromek bought the work; academicians recommended it, but '*Posterity will inquire the rest.* . . .'

Between 1817 and 1825, Blake painted a series of twelve watercolours of *Paradise Regained*, appropriately less elaborate and detailed than his illustrations of *Paradise Lost*, and less linear in style. He follows Milton in concentrating on Christ, in this rather subdued series in grey wash and muted colours. The idolatrous kingdoms with which Satan tempts Christ are compact, oriental and glowing. Butts did not buy this series, although it would have completed his collection of Blake's Miltonic illustrations: perhaps some lack of sympathy between patron and artist prevented the sale. However, it was for Butts that Blake painted the magnificently conceived series of twenty-one watercolour illustrations for the work on which he had pondered for many years, and of which he had already made some pictures in various media, the Book of Job.

This bold, subtle new series, a worthy culmination of Blake's work for Butts, reveals the artist's faith which had stood the test of his own tribulations. The biblical story of Job does not solve the problem of suffering. Blake's twenty-one pictures do. They portray Job as a complacent materialist, God as divine humanity with poetic vision, and Satan as the embodiment of man's false values. Young Elihu, angry but sympathetic, reveals to suffering Job the true nature of love. Job, seeing his own spiritual self, is transfigured, and Satan is cast out. Creative sight brings to Job revelation and innocence renewed. Blake, in the tradition of Christian artists who had interpreted the story, used detailed, symbolic designs to present this spiritual drama. In some of them he developed visual images from his previous works. For example, the Satanic God in Job's evil dreams is outstretched like Elohim creating Adam, in the colour print designed about twenty-five years earlier. Blake now used colour sparingly, to enhance grey washes sharply lined in Indian ink: the watercolours are monumental and haunting.

8

Patrons of Enlightenment
1818–24

'with such abundant felicity'

Probably early in 1818, Blake was a guest at a dinner given by Lady Caroline Lamb (Byron's former mistress) for 'a strange party of artists and literati, and one or two fine folks', according to the diary of another guest, Lady Charlotte Bury. She sat next to the courtly Sir Thomas Lawrence: commissioned by the Prince Regent, he had painted the chief members of the congress at Aix-la-Chapelle for the Waterloo Gallery at Windsor Castle: but Lady Charlotte was more intrigued by the 'eccentric little artist, by name Blake'. He told her of his visions and designs. He seemed 'full of beautiful imaginations and genius' and, she noted, lacked grace of manner. 'He looks care-worn and subdued; but his countenance radiated as he spoke of his favourite pursuit . . .'. His views she found peculiar and exalted, and she 'could not help contrasting this humble artist with the great and powerful Sir Thomas Lawrence', of whose distinction and fame Blake was 'fully if not more worthy. . . . Every word he uttered spoke the perfect simplicity of his mind, and his total ignorance of all worldly matters. He told me that Lady C— L— had been very kind to him. "Ah!" said he, "there is a deal of kindness in that lady." I agreed with him. . . . Sir T. Lawrence looked at me several times whilst I was talking with Mr B., and I saw his lips curl with a sneer, as if he despised me for conversing with so insignificant a person.' However, Lawrence, the owner of a matchless collection of drawings by old masters including Raphael and Michelangelo, later admired Blake's works enough to buy some of them. Of such prosperous artists as Lawrence, who was elected President of the Royal Academy in 1820, Blake would say: 'They pity me, but 'tis they are the just objects of pity: I possess my visions and peace. They have bartered their birthright for a mess of pottage.'

Unconcerned about money, Blake hated to be reminded of it. When his wife, with barely a coin left for housekeeping, had to tell him 'The money is going, Mr Blake,' he would flare up and shout 'Oh, damn the money! it's always the money!' So, quietly, to remind him to get on with engraving when he was absorbed in his own uncommercial designs, she took to placing on the dinner table whatever was in the house, until the empty plate appeared and he resumed his graver. Poverty and principle had made him abstemious.

The poet Coleridge, who was lent a copy of *Songs of Innocence and of Experience*, at once perceived Blake's quality in the 'poems with very wild and interesting pictures', as he wrote to a friend in February 1818. 'He is a man of genius—and I apprehend, a Swedenborgian—certainly, a mystic *emphatically*. You perhaps smile at *my* calling another poet, a mystic; but verily I am in the very mire of commonplace common sense compared with Mr Blake. . . .' Later in the month Coleridge returned the book with a critical appreciation of the designs, and with symbols to show the degree of pleasure given him by each poem. 'The Divine Image' and 'Night' gave him pleasure in the highest degree: but that pleasure was doubled by the song he most enjoyed, 'The Little Black Boy'. Although Coleridge was very pleased by 'Infant Joy', he objected that 'a babe two days old does not, cannot *smile*. . . .'

Thanks to Crabb Robinson, Hazlitt too had some knowledge of Blake's works. The lecture which Hazlitt gave on Chaucer in May 1818 seems to have been influenced by *A Descriptive Catalogue*. Blake, aged sixty, was beginning to reach an audience.

In the summer of 1818, young George Cumberland took John Linnell, a twenty-six-year-old artist, to call on Blake for the first time. The meeting was providential. Blake and Linnell at once liked each other and soon became friends. Linnell, the son of a carver and picture-framer, was the first of a group of young artists who met Blake, admired and loved him, and with their enthusiastic devotion warmed the rest of his life. He 'soon encountered Blake's peculiarities, and was somewhat taken aback by the boldness of some of his assertions. I never,' Linnell wrote many years later, 'saw anything the least like madness for I never opposed him spitefully, as many did: but being really anxious to fathom, if possible, the amount of truth which might be in his most startling assertions, I generally met with a sufficiently rational explanation in the most really friendly and conciliatory tone.' At the end of 1818, the Linnells moved with their new-born daughter, Hannah, to 6 Cirencester Place, Fitzroy Square: James Blake was living nearby. Linnell and William Blake went regularly to art exhibitions together and sometimes, with their wives, visited each other for the evening. Blake had scarcely enough work to live by, at the prices he could get, so he was glad to help engrave the portrait of Mr Upton, a Baptist preacher, painted by the strongly Nonconformist Linnell. Blake, whose share of the fee of fifty guineas was fifteen, began the process of engraving and Linnell finished it.

John Varley, Linnell's teacher and a successful and prolific watercolour artist, was then living in Great Titchfield Street, not far from Blake: Linnell introduced them to each other, and they began to spend their evenings together (51). Varley, an agnostic, was a firm believer in astrology, palmistry, ghosts and visions. His enthusiasm for horoscopes equalled his passion for watercolours. He cast his own horoscope every morning as soon as he got up, was always prepared to pull his almanacs out of his crammed pockets and foretell the future of friend or pupil and, wrote Linnell, 'readily devoured all the marvellous in Blake's most extravagant utterances.'

Blake's evenings with Varley soon developed into nocturnal séances, during which Blake drew for his credulous friend portrait heads of visionary characters such as Edward I, Wat Tyler, David, Solomon and the Theban poetess Corinna. Varley, who could not see these visitors, according to Linnell 'believed in the reality of Blake's visions more than even Blake himself. . . . It was Varley who excited Blake to see or fancy the portraits of historical personages. . . .' When Varley asked him to draw William Wallace, Blake saw the hero at once: 'There, there, how noble he looks—reach me my things!' Blake drew steadily, then stopped abruptly, saying 'I cannot finish him—Edward I has stepped in between him and me.' 'That's lucky,' said Varley, 'for I want the portrait of Edward too.' Blake took another sheet of paper and began to sketch the King, who vanished and allowed the head of Wallace to be completed. Blake, whom Linnell called 'a hearty laugher at absurdity,' worked very carefully on many of the visionary heads, even if he began them in a spirit of fun. Varley described finding him one evening more than usually excited. 'He told me he had seen a wonderful thing—the ghost of a flea! "And did you make a drawing of him?" I inquired. "No, indeed," said he, "I wish I had, but I shall, if he appears again!" He looked earnestly into a corner of the room, and then said: "Here he is—reach me my things—I shall keep my eye on him. There he comes! his eager tongue whisking out of his mouth, a cup in his hand to hold blood, and covered with a scaly skin of gold and green." As he described him, so he drew him.' A frightening tempera painting of the ghost resulted from this bizarre 'sitting'.

Blake summed up his own religious views in *The Everlasting Gospel*, a fragmentary poem in emphatic, octosyllabic rhymes which he wrote in his notebook, around 1818. What, Blake asks, is the truth about Jesus? 'Was Jesus gentle?' A disobedient child, he became an angry man who subdued nature's 'Serpent Bulk' with wrath and 'nail'd it to the Cross.' 'Was Jesus Humble?' He never asked pardon of his enemies, as the fictitious 'Creeping Jesus' would have done. Jesus, Blake asserts, was humble to God, haughty to man. 'Was Jesus Chaste?' When 'Mary was found in Adulterous bed', Jesus destroyed the law of Moses—commandments not of God but of a jealous angel, the Covering Cherub, the Spectre—and forgave her. Mary, forgiven, explained that because the law had made sex shameful, by rendering 'that a Lawless thing On which the Soul Expands its wing', she had repressed her desires, feigned coldness, destroyed love and committed adultery. Because her deed was secret and selfish, not because it was illegal, Blake regarded it as evil: a blasphemy against love. Jesus forgave it. The Spectre devoured his crucified body. Materialists and law-givers continue to devour dust and clay, the serpent's food. 'Forgiveness of Sins. This alone is the Gospel. . . .'

For the fallen, material world of which sex is a characteristic, Blake did some more work around 1818 on the little book of engravings that he had made in 1793. He showed its deeper meanings, gave it a revised title—*For the Sexes: The Gates of Paradise*—and opened his prologue with the couplet:

Mutual Forgiveness of each Vice,
Such are the Gates of Paradise.

He made his plates fuller and subtler. With augmented captions and 'The Keys of the Gates' (a rhymed commentary) he showed how such images as the veil, Spectre and door of death, which he had developed over the years, now conveyed his maturest thought. The epilogue asserts that Satan, 'The Accuser who is The God of This World', though worshipped as Jesus and Jehovah, is still only 'The lost Traveller's Dream under the Hill': a product of confused, tired minds.

Linnell, devoted to helping Blake, introduced him to artists, connoisseurs and patrons. Dr Robert John Thornton, the Linnell's family physician, published botanical books, wrote about medicine and had produced a school *Virgil*. For the third edition, with 230 illustrations by a variety of artists, he employed Blake not only to draw and engrave a few portrait busts on copper, but also to design and engrave a series of pastoral scenes on wood. These were to illustrate Ambrose Philips's century-old imitation of Virgil's first *Eclogue*, in which the shepherds, Thenot and Colinet, gently converse. Blake had not engraved wood before, but he mastered the medium at once. His superb, tiny wood engravings evoke a complete pastoral world of landscape and people, sky and weather (50). Blake's method was to cut four designs at a time on a single block of wood. Possibly he set no great store by these beautiful illustrations, which did not reveal the main stream of his intellectual vision. Busy with other projects, he made no more wood engravings after these.

To Thornton and his publishers, the unfashionable boldness of Blake's wood engravings looked amateurishly crude. Thornton immediately had three of Blake's designs recut by an anonymous engraver, who degraded them to dullness. Blake's seventeen other blocks would have been similarly maimed if Linnell, James Ward and Lawrence had not met Thornton by chance at the table of the connoisseurs Mr and Mrs Aders—whose hospitality to artists and poets was well known—and spoken admiringly of Blake's Virgil wood engravings. Thornton changed his mind: he printed the seventeen blocks without having them recut. In contrast with the plethora of drab pictures in Thornton's two-volume Virgil, Blake's wood engravings shine magically; yet Thornton nervously added a note to reassure his young readers: 'The illustrations of this English pastoral are by the famous Blake, the illustrator of Young's *Night Thoughts,* and Blair's *Grave*; who designed and engraved them himself. This is mentioned, as they display less of art than genius, and are much admired by some eminent painters'—an apology that echoes the Rev. A. S. Mathew's disparagement of the *Poetical Sketches.* Blake's woodblocks were printed four to a page—his intended arrangement: but all except one of them were brutally trimmed to fit the page, and perhaps it was at that time that they were separated.

In September 1820, the recently founded *London Magazine* printed a rumbustious announcement by T. G. Wainewright (ex-pupil of Fuseli and friend of Lamb) that Dr Tobias Ruddicombe—a pseudonym perhaps referring to Blake's formerly flaming hair—was writing by request for the next issue 'an account of an ancient, newly-discovered, illuminated manuscript, which has to name *Jerusalem, The Emanation of the Giant Albion*!!! . . . The doctor assures me that the redemption of mankind hangs on the universal diffusion of the doctrines broached in this manuscript.' The announced article never appeared, but Blake became quite friendly with Wainewright, who bought some of his works. Later, notorious as a suspect poisoner, Wainewright was deported to Australia for forgery.

Probably about 1820, Blake finished engraving his hundred plates with their majestic, dramatic designs for *Jerusalem,* a book which had taken him at least fourteen years to create. He is known to have printed four copies in black ink (strangely lurid in its effects) and to have made a subtly-coloured version of the first twenty-five plates, but to have produced only one coloured copy of the whole book. On this noble copy, printed in orange, he used a wide range of watercolours, including gold, to convey with brilliance and precision the full intensity of his figures' torment and—near the end of the book—their bliss.

About the same time, he annotated the philosophical miscellany *Siris,* by George Berkeley, who denied the existence of matter. Blake agreed that the soul imparts forms to things, but he added: 'Forms must be apprehended by Sense or the Eye of Imagination. Man is All Imagination. God is Man & exists in us & we in him.' In a single etched sheet *On Homer's Poetry and on Virgil,* Blake declared: 'Rome & Greece swept Art into their maw & destroy'd it; a Warlike State never can produce Art . . . Grecian is Mathematic Form: Gothic is Living Form. . . .' He recorded his creed more pithily in slogans thronging round his engraving of the Laocoön. Blake was then about sixty-three; his dogma included:

If Morality was Christianity, Socrates was the Saviour.

A Poet, a Painter, a Musician, an Architect: the Man Or Woman who is not one of these is not a Christian.

Art can never exist without Naked Beauty displayed.

For every Pleasure Money Is Useless.

Without Unceasing Practise nothing can be done. Practise is Art. If you leave off you are Lost.

Art is the Tree of Life. God is Jesus.

Science is the Tree of Death.

The Whole Business of Man Is The Arts, & All Things Common. No Secresy in Art.

Blake's commercial stipple-engraving of Mrs Harriet Quentin, the Prince Regent's mistress, was published in June 1820. Lawrence, whom Linnell cultivated on Blake's behalf, added to his splendid art collection not only a copy of the proofs of *Job* but also two watercolours by Blake, 'The Wise and Foolish Virgins' (which Lawrence kept on his studio table) and 'Queen Catherine's Dream'. Despite all Linnell's efforts, however, Blake was still very short of lucrative work and very poor. He was even reduced to selling— to Colnaghi—his collection of prints, which he had begun to acquire as a boy. Linnell continued to take him to art exhibitions and to the theatre. In March 1820 at Drury Lane they saw Sheridan's popular tragedy *Pizarro*, followed by *Thérèse, the Orphan of Geneva*, a musical piece. In June they were there again for an opera, *Dirce, or the Fatal Urn*, by various composers, with *The Midnight Hour*, a farce, to follow. Another outing was on Sunday 27 May to Hampstead, a village very popular with young writers at that time. While Blake's contacts with youth were increasing, in 1820 he lost another of his old friends, Nancy Flaxman.

That year the Blakes moved from South Molton Street to 3 Fountain Court, off the Strand near the Savoy. Their landlord, Henry Banes, was married to Mrs Blake's sister, and the Blakes' fellow-lodgers were humble, respectable people. A wainscoted Queen Anne staircase with handsome balustrades, lit by a window above a well-like yard, led up to the Blakes' two-room flat on the first floor. In the front, the reception-room, its panelled walls hung with Blake's works, looked onto Fountain Court where children played. From the smaller room, at the back, it was possible—through a deep gap between gloomy houses—to glimpse the Thames and its muddy banks, with the hills of Surrey and Kent in the distance (57). In this room the Blakes slept, lived, cooked and worked. An old radical acquaintance of Blake, William Frend, was walking in the Strand with his eleven-year-old daughter when, as she recalled years later, they met Blake. He wore a brown coat, and his eyes, she thought, were uncommonly bright. 'He shook hands with my father, and said: "Why don't you come and see me? I live down here"; and he raised his hand and pointed to a street which led to the river. Each said something about visiting the other, and they parted. I asked who that gentleman was, and was told: "He is a strange man; he thinks he sees spirits." '

Blake hoped that his Job watercolours, which Butts generously lent him to show to other possible patrons, would be the source of more work. Only Linnell, however, a practical artist sensitive to Blake's needs, ordered a replica of the set. For two or three days, early in September 1821, Linnell made tracings of the outlines, which Blake later worked on and coloured, giving the replicas individuality. When Blake took the originals back to Butts, he borrowed a watercolour of 'Cain and Abel', also for Linnell to copy. It was perhaps at a dinner party at the Linnells' later this year that a very beautiful little girl from a wealthy home was introduced to Blake, whose clothes, including thick shoes and worsted stockings, were of the simplest. 'He looked at her very kindly for a long while without speaking, and then stroking her head and long ringlets said: "May God make this world to you, my child, as beautiful as it has been to me." She thought it strange at the time . . . that such a poor old man, dressed in such shabby clothes, could imagine the world had ever been so beautiful to him as it must be to her, nursed in all the elegancies and luxury of wealth; but in after years she understood well enough. . . .' (Thomas Woolner told her story in a letter to Dante Gabriel Rossetti, but could not recall the girl's name.)

To further relieve Blake's poverty, Linnell followed his commissioning of a duplicate set of the *Paradise Lost* watercolours, belonging to Butts, by arranging for an application to be made for a grant from the Royal Academy to Blake. The council agreed unanimously, on 28 June 1822, to pay £25 to this 'able designer and engraver labouring under great distress'. Linnell collected the money for Blake, and the quest for patrons continued, although in his own affairs Linnell was an independent, uncompromising young man. Wishing to be elected an Associate of the Royal Academy, in 1821 he had put his name forward as a candidate. He would not, however, play the traditional role of courtier to Royal Academicians and they did not elect him. He ascribed his rejection to the efforts of John Constable and others to thwart him.

In 1821 Blake painted one of his finest tempera paintings, 'The Cave of the Nymphs'. In his preface to *Milton* he had declared that 'all Men ought to contemn' Greek literature; but now in his old age he had become a Platonist in politics, he acknowledged Socrates as a sort of brother and he lovingly painted this picture of a Neoplatonic work by Porphyry, with additions from Homer and Platonic sources. Blake had first read *The Cave of the Nymphs* even before he finished *Thel*. For years he had continued to explore and to recreate in his works, in many symbolic forms, the cycle of the soul's descent into birth, its experience of deadly mortal suffering and its return to life after the body's death. Now he embodied the myth in classical symbols. The picture is scrupulously detailed and brilliantly finished. It shows Odysseus casting back to the sea-goddess Leucothea (or Ino) the girdle which she had lent him. A symbol of bodily life, this dissolves into cloud, above which the sun-god sleeps. Mortal life is, to him, a deathly slumber. Athena, showing the perpetual clock-wise cycle of rebirth and death, points up to the spiritual world and down to the stream of generation. High in the cave, winged nymphs carry urns of honey. The bees that made it are human souls descending. This picture may conceivably have been painted for Cumberland: Linnell's father framed it.

In December 1821 Byron published his sensationally bold drama *Cain: A Mystery*. Parsons preached against it from Kentish Town to Pisa and Blake challenged Byron's pessimism in a terse, seventy-line poetic drama complete with stage-directions, *The Ghost of Abel*: 'A Revelation In the Visions of Jehovah Seen by William Blake'. The prelude, addressed 'To LORD BYRON in the Wilderness' of error, asks 'Can a Poet doubt the Visions of Jehovah?' and concludes 'Imagination is Eternity': although mortal life is unreal, true life is everlasting. When grief-stricken Eve, with Adam, has seen and heard the ghost of Abel, 'the Accuser & Avenger Of Blood', she asks: 'were it not better to believe Vision With all our might & strength, tho' we are fallen & lost?' and Adam concurs. They kneel before Jehovah, who declares 'I have given you a Lamb for an atonement instead Of the Transgressor.' Abel's vengeful Spectre sinks into the grave, from which Satan then arises, armed, to demand human blood on Calvary. Jehovah banishes him to annihilation of self in the Abyss, for only when error is cast out can regeneration begin. Angels sing of Jehovah's forgiveness: peace, brotherhood and love are eternal reality. So the brilliantly condensed drama ends.

This work, dated 1822, is Blake's last in relief-etching. At the end of the two uncoloured plates, he claims to have invented his technique thirty-four years earlier: 'Blake's Original Stereotype was 1788'; so he implies that it pre-dated those experiments in stereotype-engraving which had been referred to in an article in the *Edinburgh Philosophical Journal* in 1820.

Linnell, perceiving that Blake could develop the Job designs to even greater heights, asked him early in the spring of 1820 to engrave a set of twenty plates from them. The engravings would be smaller than the water-colours, so Blake would first have to make another set of drawings, of the right size to work from. According to the contract drawn up on 25 March, Blake was to receive '£5 per plate, or £100 for the set, part before, and the remainder when the plates are finished, as Mr Blake may require it, besides which J. Linnell agrees to give W. Blake £100 more out of the profits of the work as the receipts will admit of it.' Linnell also paid for the copper plates. Not only did he generously bear the whole cost and risk of the venture, but he paid £50 extra in consideration of possible sales. In this way, Blake received weekly payments of £1 0s. 5d. during his three years' work, although sales brought in no profits while he was alive. Perhaps influenced by engravings that he and Linnell had seen at exhibitions and sought out at the British Museum, Blake used his graver with a new freedom.

James Deville, of 17 the Strand, a maker of plaster figures and a keen phrenologist, had not previously taken any life-masks but, according to George Richmond, 'wished to have a cast of Blake's head as representative of the imaginative faculty.' On 1 August 1823 Blake allowed Deville to subject him to the great discomfort of having a life-mask taken: his face smeared with lard and enclosed in drying plaster, Blake could breathe only through straws inserted in his nostrils. Most of Blake's friends liked the mask (52), though Mrs Blake did not. Its features suggest, according to Gilchrist, that Blake's 'head and face were strongly stamped with the power and character of the man. There was great volume of brain in that square, massive head, that piled-up brow, very full and rounded at the temples, where, according to phrenologists, ideality or imagination resides. His eyes were fine . . . prominently set', but they were short-sighted and he occasionally wore glasses. Blake, who wrote: 'I always thought that Jesus Christ was a Snubby or I should not have worship'd him, if I had thought he had been one of those long spindle nosed rascals', himself had a small nose with little, clenched nostrils opened wide. They gave his face, Gilchrist says, 'an expression of fiery energy. . . . His mouth was wide, the lips not full, but tremulous, and expressive' of his great sensibility.

9

Prophet with Disciples
1824–27

'The Real Man The Imagination which Liveth for Ever'

In May 1824 Blake went to the Royal Academy with Samuel Palmer (53), a nineteen-year-old art student virtually untutored, who had been introduced to him by Linnell. The son of a Nonconformist bookseller, Palmer in youth turned to the Anglican High Church. Of his never-to-be-forgotten first interview with Blake, Palmer later remarked: 'the copper of the first plate—"Thus Did Job Continually"—was lying on the table where he had been working at it. How lovely it looked by the lamplight', which was strained through tissue paper to reduce glare. Palmer was enthralled and inspired by the revelations he found in Dürer's works, and in Blake's *Virgil* wood engravings which he called 'visions of little dells, and nooks, and corners of Paradise. . . .' He went on: 'There is in all such a mystic and dreamy glimmer as penetrates and kindles the inmost soul, and gives complete and unreserved delight, unlike the gaudy daylight of this world. They are like all that wonderful artist's works the drawing aside of the fleshly curtain, and the glimpse which all the most holy, studious saints and sages have enjoyed, of the rest which remaineth to the people of God.'

Palmer remembered, from their visit to the Royal Academy in 1824, 'Blake in his plain black suit and *rather* broad-rimmed, but not Quakerish hat, standing so quietly among all the dressed-up, rustling, swelling people, and myself thinking "How little you know *who* is among you!" ' Indoors, Palmer said, Blake was not slovenly, although his clothes were threadbare and his grey trousers had worn black and shiny in front, like a mechanic's. Out of doors he was more particular, but unobtrusively dressed. 'He wore black knee-breeches and buckles, black worsted stockings, shoes which tied. . . . It was something like an old-fashioned tradesman's dress': but he seemed to be 'a gentleman, in a way of his own'.

To Palmer and his young friend and fellow-artist, George Richmond, Blake's home was hallowed ground. The cramped rooms, devoid of squalor despite their air of poverty, glowed with Blake's serene, dignified presence. In the living-room, Richmond watched Blake engrave *Job* at a long engraver's table under the window. He worked facing the light, a pile of portfolios and drawings on his right near the only cupboard; and on his left a pile of books: no bookcase. Palmer wrote that Blake, 'his wife, his rooms, were clean and orderly; everything was in its place. His delightful working corner had its implements ready—tempting to the hand.'

In March 1824 Linnell moved his wife and four children out into the country, to Collins' Farm, Hampstead. From his studio in Cirencester Place he either travelled by coach or sometimes walked, to join the family for a night or a weekend. Blake, a welcome guest who delighted in the children, walked out there from Fountain Court—a distance of five or six miles—quite regularly. Proposing a dinner at Collins' Farm in August, the architect Charles Heathcote Tatham (whom Blake had known in 1799) asked Linnell: 'Can you engage Michelangelo *Blake* to . . . go up with us? Such a party of connoisseurs'—it included Varley and Tatham's nineteen-year-old son Frederick, a future sculptor and painter—'is worthy of Apollo and the Muses.'

Frederick Tatham became one of a group of young men, animated by Palmer and Richmond, who held monthly meetings to discuss poetry and art. Richmond, when he was only sixteen, first met Blake at the elder Tatham's and was allowed to walk home with him, 'feeling as if he were walking with the prophet Isaiah'. Richmond's wonder deepened as he saw more of Blake, whose tolerant kindness to the young was unfailing. 'Never have I known an artist so spiritual, so devoted, so single-minded, or cherishing imagination as he did.' The young men who, with Palmer and Richmond, were drawn to Blake in admiring love and reverence, called themselves 'The Ancients', beings superior to moderns. They spoke of Blake's home as 'The House of the Interpreter', where Blake—like the Interpreter in *The Pilgrim's Progress*—showed excellent things to travellers going to Mount Zion. His conversation was 'nervous and brilliant', Palmer said: 'He was energy itself, and shed around him a kindling influence; an atmosphere of life, full of the ideal.'

In the early 1820s, Blake revised 'Sweeping the Interpreter's Parlour', his early 'woodcut on pewter' inspired by Bunyan, and in 1824 he was working on a series of watercolours of *The Pilgrim's Progress*. He left this series of twenty-eight illustrations unfinished when he died. They are vigorous, appropriate and, though not the finest work of Blake's last years, often beautiful. To Francis Oliver Finch, another of the Ancients, Blake seemed '*a new kind of man*, wholly original, and in all things. Whereas most men are at the pains of softening down their extreme opinions, not to shock those of others, it was the contrary with him.' Blake's sympathetic understanding, however, astonished the young artist Richmond when, sadly bereft of inspiration for a fortnight, he went to Blake for advice and comfort, found the Blakes at tea, told them of his plight and Blake suddenly turned to Mrs Blake and said: 'It is just so with us, is it not, for weeks together, when the visions forsake us? What do we do then, Kate?' 'We kneel down and pray, Mr Blake.' In the young enthusiasts who came to him, Blake stimulated a visionary power of their own which they revealed in their art.

Linnell, a keen reader of a wide range of literature—like Blake, he had never been to school—followed his *Job* commission by asking Blake to make a vast series of watercolour designs for Dante's *Divine Comedy*, a poem then becoming fashionable, and to engrave them. Linnell provided a book of fine Dutch paper and continued to pay a weekly allowance, irrespective of the amount of work Blake did on this new series of 102 pictures. On 9 October 1824, when Blake was almost sixty-seven, Palmer called with Linnell and—as Palmer later wrote—'found him lame in bed, of a scalded foot (or leg). There, not inactive . . . but hard-working on a bed covered with books sat he up like one of the antique patriarchs, or a dying Michelangelo. Thus and there was he making in the leaves of a great book (folio) the sublimest design from his (not superior) Dante. He said he began them with fear and trembling. I said "O! I have enough of fear and trembling." "Then," said he, "you'll do." ' According to Palmer, Blake designed the 102 pictures during a fortnight's illness in bed.

About 1800, Blake had annotated Boyd's translation of Dante's *Inferno* and noted that 'Dante was an Emperor's, a Caesar's Man'. The first accurate, good translation of all three parts of Dante's *Divine Comedy* (*Hell, Purgatory and Paradise*), published in 1814, had been made by Henry Cary, Hayley's old friend, who was probably introduced to Blake by Wainewright in 1825. Fuseli and Flaxman both knew Italian before they created their pictures from Dante. Blake, in his old age, helped by his Latin, taught himself enough Italian in a few weeks to understand the substance of Dante's lines. He appreciated Dante's greatness as a poet but rejected his ideas: 'for Tyrannical Purposes he has made This World the Foundation of All, & the Goddess Nature Memory is his Inspirer & not Imagination the Holy Ghost.' God 'could never have Built Dante's Hell, nor the Hell of the Bible neither, in the way our Parsons explain it.' Consequently, while some of Blake's designs are literal illustrations of *The Divine Comedy* and some parallel Blake's own myths, others show Dante poised on the edge of full insight, but then drawing back into error. Although Blake told Crabb Robinson 'Dante saw devils where I see none—I see only good', Blake concentrated on the least merciful part of Dante's epic, *Hell*, for which he made sixty-nine designs, whereas for *Purgatory* and *Paradise* he made less than half that number. The series of spacious pictures is awe-inspiring. Blake was probably influenced by Flaxman's designs for Dante, published in England in 1807: but Flaxman's cool, neo-classical 'outlines' lack the grandeur and insight shown in Blake's superbly conceived pencil drawings, with their expressive washes of watercolour. Many of the illustrations are unfinished: some are only sketches. The series shows a close and highly imaginative reading of Dante's poem (54).

Palmer, wound up to forget himself by seeing the Dante drawings, showed Blake his own designs and received 'sweet encouragement' which made him work harder and better. The scene later recurred to him 'in a kind of vision', with Blake's 'dwelling (the chariot of the sun) as it were an island in the midst of the sea—such a place for primitive grandeur, whether in the persons of Mr and Mrs Blake, or in the things hanging on the walls.' Even more than the other Ancients, Palmer was affected by Blake and, unlike Richmond, would never argue with him. Before venturing to pull Blake's bell-handle, Palmer would kiss it. Brought up on the Bible, Latin and English literature (he had only spent two terms at school), and living with his father at the bookshop, 10 Broad Street, he became a firm friend of Blake, who often called there on his way from the Strand to Hampstead, so that they could walk together. Their journey ended on an uphill road among trees and fields where Hampstead's new stucco villas and terraces were spreading. The Linnell children would run out of the farm-house—led by Hannah, aged about six—to meet Blake. On cold winter nights, Mrs Linnell would wrap him up in an old shawl before sending him on his way home with a servant, lantern in hand, to light him over the heath to the main road.

The sort of advice Blake gave his young disciples is shown by Palmer, who noted in his sketch-book in 1824 Blake's 'most excellent' remark 'that a tint equivalent to a shadow is made by the outlines of many little forms in one mass, and then how the light shines on an unbroken mass near it, such for instance as flesh, etc.' Blake promised to take Palmer to see Butts' collection: it would have been a revelation, 'but', as Palmer wrote in old age, 'alas! it never came off.' Many aspects of Blake—'a man without a mask', Palmer called him—remained unexplored by the Ancients, but Palmer was to write, in his own last years: 'I remember William Blake, in the quiet consistency of his daily life, as one of the sanest, if not the most thoroughly sane man I have ever known. The flights of his genius were scarcely more marvellous than the ceaseless industry. . . .'

By March 1825 the twenty-two *Job* engravings were nearly finished. Blake and Linnell called on J. Lahee, the plate-printer who was to pull the edition. Although the published plates are dated 8 March 1825, they were not completed and on sale until 1826. Besides minor differences between the watercolours and engravings, there is Blake's major addition of decorative linear borders with biblical texts, not only from Job but from other books of both Testaments (56). The borders, beautiful in themselves, develop the designs that they frame and provide a highly enriching commentary on the work. These borders were an afterthought, designed and engraved on the copper without previous drawing.

On 16 April 1825, Fuseli, mentally alert to the last, died at the age of eighty-four. During most of that summer, Blake was ill with shivering fits, probably caused by gallstones and inflammation of the gall-bladder: 'these attacks,' he wrote, 'are too serious at the time to permit me to be out of Bed, but they go off by rest, which seems to be All that I want.' 'Every death is an improvement of the State of the Departed. I can draw as well a-Bed as Up, & perhaps better; but I cannot Engrave. I am going on with Dante, & please myself.' By Saturday 6 August he was well enough to accompany Linnell to dine with Mr and Mrs Aders. It was at their house that he probably first met Coleridge. Later, Coleridge visited him and together—according to an anonymous witness—they 'seemed like congenial beings of another sphere, breathing for a while on our earth.'

At an uncertain date, Palmer took Blake and perhaps Mrs Blake, with Edward Calvert (a senior Ancient, born in 1799) and Mrs Calvert to visit Palmer's grandfather in unspoilt, rural Kent. They made the twenty-mile journey in a covered stage wagon, drawn by an eight- or ten-horse team, to the quiet old village of Shoreham, where Palmer's grandfather lived in a thatched cottage. Pastoral life inspired Calvert, who found the spirit of Blake's *Virgil* wood engravings 'humble enough and of force enough to move simple souls to tears'. Old Palmer spoke of a local ghost, and Calvert suggested seeking it in Shoreham Castle nearby. With lantern and candles, Blake and Palmer accompanied him to the dark, windy castle. There they heard a ghostly tapping, a grating sound. Calvert was intrigued, Palmer was transfixed, but Blake's reaction is not known. The sound proved to be only the rattling in the wind of a snail shell against glass. The next evening Blake was occupied at the kitchen table, while old Palmer sat and smoked and Calvert, his back to the candles, sat reading. Young Samuel Palmer had left for London about an hour before. Blake put his hand to his forehead and said quietly: 'Palmer is coming; he is walking up the road.' 'Oh, Mr Blake, he's gone to London; we saw him off in the coach.' Then, after a while, Blake persisted: 'He is coming through the wicket—there!'—pointing to the closed door. And Blake was right: a minute later, Samuel Palmer entered. The coach had broken down and he had walked back. Blake's uncanny knowledge seemed clairvoyant.

In 1825 Linnell bought Blake's twelve watercolours of *Paradise Regained* for £10. On Tuesday 11 October Blake wrote from Fountain Court to Mrs Linnell at Hampstead that he had been to see Linnell off in a very comfortable coach to Gloucester.

I accompanied him part of the way on his Journey in the Coach, for we both got in together & with another Passenger enter'd into Conversation, when at length we found that we were all three proceeding on our Journey; but . . . the Coach-man . . . obligingly permitted me to get out, to my great joy; hence I am now enabled to tell you that I hope to see you on Sunday morning as usual, which I could not have done if they had taken me to Gloucester.

On these Sundays, the children at Collins' Farm waited eagerly for Blake to walk into sight over the brow of the hill and greet them with his special signal. Once Blake brought with him a sketchbook of drawings, made when he was about fourteen, from prints. The children found them strange: but one, a detailed drawing of a grasshopper, delighted them. So did Blake's stories and *Songs of Innocence*. His voice tremulous with age, he would sing old ballads, and his own songs to his own melodies.

In contented reverie he would stand at the door of the Linnells' humble, five-roomed home and gaze across the garden to the gorse-clad hill: but he still believed that the air north of London gave him colds in the stomach. When Mrs Linnell, his welcoming hostess, said that Hampstead was a healthy place, he startled her by replying: 'It is a lie! It is no such thing!' Nevertheless, he would sit happily in the arbour at the bottom of the long garden, or walk up and down there at dusk, while the cows munched audibly in the farmyard beyond the hedge. He was very fond of listening to Mrs Linnell sing Scottish songs. He would sit by the piano, tears falling from his eyes, as she sang a Border melody. To simple folk-songs he was very susceptible, but not to more complicated music.

On his visit of Sunday 18 October 1825, he brought the good news that he had taken an advance copy of *Job* to Flaxman who, delighted beyond all expectation, had paid for it. On 10 November Blake wrote to Linnell about the series: 'I have, I believe, done nearly all that we agreed on etc. If you should put on your considering Cap, just as you did last time we met, I have no doubt that the Plates would be all the better for it. I cannot get Well & am now in Bed. . . . I hope a few more days will bring us to a conclusion.'

Temperate in his habits, Blake drank porter regularly in his later years, to soothe himself. He would fetch a pot of it from the corner of the Strand, eat his dinner at one o'clock and sit musing over his pint. Wine, which he seldom drank at home, he liked in draughts from a tumbler: wine-glasses he thought absurd. During the winter of 1825, he and Linnell dined a number of times with Mr and Mrs Aders. Crabb Robinson, a fellow-guest, observed his Socratic countenance, his natural sweetness and gentility, and noted in a diary some of the things he said. 'There is no use in education. I hold it wrong. It is the great sin. It is eating of the tree of the knowledge of good and evil. That was the fault of Plato: he knew of nothing but of the virtues and vices. Everything is good in God's eyes.' 'When Michelangelo or Raphael or Mr Flaxman does any of his fine things he does them in the spirit.' 'I wish to live for art. I want nothing whatever. I am quite happy.' 'Wordsworth is no Christian, but a Platonist' who arrogantly wrote of Jehovah and the angels 'I *pass* them unalarmed.' This impiety had so upset Blake that it brought on a bowel complaint which nearly killed him: 'Does Mr Wordsworth think his mind can *surpass* Jehovah?'—but Blake praised him as the greatest poet of the age. Boehme was 'a divinely inspired man'. Walking home, Crabb Robinson asked Blake about the divinity of Jesus.

'*He is the only God,*' said Blake, but then he added 'And so am I and so are you.'

Crabb Robinson called on Blake a week later, on Saturday 17 December, found him working on Dante and noted 'the squalid air both of the apartment and his dress: but in spite of dirt—I might say, filth—an air of natural gentility is diffused over him; and his wife, notwithstanding the same offensive character of her dress and appearance, has a good expression of countenance. . . .' Years later, Crabb Robinson added to this account of his first visit to 'these worthy people' that Blake's linen was clean, his hand white and Mrs Blake 'with a dark eye had remains of beauty in her youth.' Crabb Robinson called again and read aloud in his 'best style . . . peculiarly well', as he later boasted to Dorothy Wordsworth, her brother's *Ode: Intimations of Immortality from Recollections of Early Childhood*. Blake 'heartily enjoyed' it, especially those parts least intelligible or pleasing to Crabb Robinson, who 'never witnessed greater delight in any listener.' Later Crabb Robinson lent Wordsworth's works to Blake, but the two poets never met.

In 1825 Blake painted his ikon-like 'Black Madonna'. The Virgin and Child in this deeply moving tempera are monumental figures glimmering against a star-studded sky. About this time, he may have painted his large watercolour of 'The Characters of Spenser's *Faerie Queene*', a vigorous procession on horseback which forms a companion picture to 'The Canterbury Pilgrims'. By January 1826 orders for *Job* were beginning to come in, slowly but regularly, with deposits of a pound or a guinea. Freeman, the craftsman employed by Lahee, was making a very fine job of the printing.

On 18 February Crabb Robinson called on Blake and had 'an amusing chat'. Blake recounted what, in vision, Voltaire had told him. 'In what language?' asked Crabb Robinson. 'To my sensations,' Blake explained, 'it was English. It was like the touch of a musical key. He touched it probably French, but to my ear it became English.' Speaking about visionary forms, Blake said of Shakespeare's: 'he is exactly like the old engraving [presumably Droeshout's] which is called a bad one. I think it very good.' Blake spoke of having written 'six or seven epic poems as long as Homer and twenty tragedies as long as *Macbeth*' (works which have not been identified). 'I write,' said he, 'when commanded by the spirits and the moment I have written I see the words fly about the room in all directions. It is then published and the spirits can read. . . . I have been tempted to burn my manuscripts, but my wife won't let me.' He spoke of his horror of money, and impressed Crabb Robinson by his genuine dignity, independence, and scorn of presents.

By the end of March 1826, *Job* was published and Blake's joy must have been great. It was the only book of his own designs and engravings (besides the unfinished *Night Thoughts*) to be published in his lifetime. To Linnell, in grateful friendship, he gave the manuscript of *Vala, or the Four Zoas*.

The President of the Royal Academy, Sir Thomas Lawrence, put a copy of *Job* in the Royal Academy Library and he and various Royal Academicians, some of whom bought copies, sent highest congratulations to Blake.

Blake was ill in March with shivering fits induced by chilly weather. He ended the month in a tottering state. On 12 May, however, Crabb Robinson gave a small party, to which Blake and Flaxman went. Blake was not 'in an *exalted* state', Crabb Robinson noted. 'I doubt whether Flaxman sufficiently tolerates Blake. But Blake appreciates Flaxman as he ought.' Blake relished the lithographs he saw at the party, and stayed till eleven. A week later he was ill again: 'a gnawing Pain in the Stomach . . . a deathly feel all over the limbs', and desperate shivering fits left him too weak to get up.

He longed to be able to visit Hampstead. Linnell suggested taking lodgings for him near Collins' farm, but on 2 July Blake wrote: 'This sudden cold weather has cut up all my hopes by the roots. Every one who knows of our intended flight into your delightful Country concur in saying: "Do not Venture till summer appears again." I also feel Myself weaker than I was aware . . . & also feel the Cold too much to dare venture beyond my present precincts.'

Mrs Linnell gave birth to another fine boy. At once, on 5 July, Blake sent congratulations. He was getting better every hour and believed the paroxysms would 'never more return'. Linnell was to protect his own health from worry about Blake: 'You have a Family,' wrote Blake. 'I have none; there is no comparison between our necessary avocations.' On 14 July Blake made over the copyright of *Job* to him. Another attack of illness brought 'a species of delirium' and 'Pain too much for Thought'. Ease of body followed, but pain of mind began. 'It is about The Name of the Child.' The Linnells wanted this to be William, after Blake: but the name, Blake wrote, 'Certainly ought to be Thomas, after Mrs Linnell's Father. . . . Pray Reconsider it, if it is not too late. It very much troubles Me, as a Crime in which I shall be The Principal.' Yet despite 'this hearty Expostulation' the child was named William. Later in July, when Blake had become well though weak, he developed piles, 'a most sore plague & on a Weak Body truly afflictive'. They abated, and some days later, free from pain and sickness, Blake decided to venture on the journey to Hampstead. 'Our Carriage will be a Cabriolet, for . . . I am still incapable of riding in the Stage . . . being only bones & sinews, All strings & bobbins like a Weaver's Loom.' During this visit, he worked on Dante. Mrs Collins, of the farm, long remembered Blake as 'that most delightful gentleman', and his old friends would call a clump of trees on the edge of the heath 'the Dante wood'.

Possibly in September, Blake visited the Calverts at Brixton. Late at night, after Mrs Calvert had gone to bed, Blake and Calvert were melting some etching-ground on the fire when the pipkin cracked and the chimney was set ablaze. Blake was more worried about Mrs Calvert being alarmed than about the fire. In November a collector, Sir Edward Denny, who had heard of Blake's dangerous illness, wrote to Linnell: 'What shall I say, what *can* I say of *The Book of Job*? I can only say that it is a *great work*: and . . . I do indeed feel its exquisite beauty and marvellous grandeur. . . . It is, I think the most perfect thing I have ever seen from the hands of Mr Blake. . . .'

On 7 December Flaxman died after a few days' illness, at the age of seventy-one: his body was accompanied to burial by the President and Council of the Royal Academy. When Blake heard the news of his old friend's death he smiled and said: 'I thought I should have gone first. I cannot consider death as anything but a removing from one room to another.'

At the end of December, Blake was ill again. He dared not leave his room, let alone venture out to Euston Square to visit Mr and Mrs Aders and to see 'again those Pictures of the Old Masters'—early Italian, German and Flemish—in their remarkable collection. He wrote that he 'must submit to the necessity & be Patient till warm weather Comes.'

On 23 February 1827, as requested by George IV's physician, Linnell sent a copy of *Job* to the King's Library. Linnell was increasingly anxious about Blake's health: he suggested that the Blakes should move to Cirencester Place. Blake, 'getting better every Morning, but slowly' and improving his 'Engravings of Dante more & more', replied:

I have Thought & Thought of the Removal . . . the more I think, the more I feel terror at what I wish'd at first & thought it a thing of benefit & Good hope; you will attribute it to its right Cause—Intellectual Peculiarity, that must be Myself alone shut up in Myself, or Reduced to Nothing. I could tell you of Visions & dreams upon the Subject. I have asked & intreated Divine help, but fear continues upon me, & I must relinquish the step that I had wish'd to take, & still wish, but in vain.

Blake's brother James, whose last years are very obscure, died at the age of seventy-one at Cirencester Place and was buried in Bunhill Fields on 2 March 1827. Blake worked on, and just over a week later he was visited by his old friend the architect Charles Tatham: 'he sat with me above an hour, & look'd over the Dante; he express'd himself very much pleas'd with the designs as well as the Engravings. I am getting on with the Engravings & hope soon to get Proofs of what I am doing.' When cold weather kept Blake indoors, he felt he lost nothing by it. 'Dante goes on the better, which is all I care about.'

To Cumberland, who had been trying unsuccessfully to find a buyer for *Job* in Bristol, Blake wrote on 12 April:

I have been very near the Gates of Death & have returned very weak & an Old Man feeble & tottering, but not in Spirit & Life, not in The Real Man The

Imagination which Liveth for Ever. In that I am stronger & stronger as this
Foolish Body decays. I thank you for the Pains you have taken with Poor Job. I
know too well that a great majority of Englishmen are fond of The Indefinite . . .
[whereas to Blake] a Line is a Line in its Minutest Subdivisions: Strait or
Crooked It is Itself & Not Intermeasurable with or by any Thing Else. Such is
Job, but since the French Revolution Englishmen are all Intermeasurable One
by Another, Certainly a happy state of Agreement to which I for One do not
Agree. God keep me from the Divinity of Yes & No too, The Yea Nay Creeping
Jesus, from supposing Up & Down to be the same Thing. . . .

Blake had no remaining copies of his books in relief-etching for Cumberland to sell.

I cannot Print more Except at a great loss, for at the time I printed those things
I had a whole House to range in: now I am shut up in a Corner therefore am
forced to ask a Price for them that I scarce expect to get from a Stranger. . . .
The Last Work I produced is a Poem Entitled Jerusalem the Emanation of the
Giant Albion, but find that to Print it will Cost my Time the amount of Twenty
Guineas. One I have Finish'd. It contains 100 Plates but it is not likely that I
shall get a Customer for it.

Referring to a message card, printed with Cumberland's name which was
to be surrounded with tiny engraved figures:

The Little Card I will do as soon as Possible but when you Consider that I have
been reduced to a Skeleton from which I am slowly recovering you will I hope
have Patience with me. [Blake was to use his burin for the last time when de-
corating this card for his old friend.]
    Flaxman is Gone & we must All soon follow, every one to his Own Eternal
House, Leaving the Delusive Goddess Nature & her Laws to get into Freedom
from all Law of the Members into The Mind, in which every one is King &
Priest in his own House. God send it so on Earth as it is in Heaven.

In 1827 Thornton extended his varied publications from *Virgil* to a *New
Translation of the Lord's Prayer*. Blake annotated it, beginning: 'I look upon
this as a Most Malignant & Artful attack upon the Kingdom of Jesus By
the Classical Learned', and calling Thornton's 'Tory Translation' a prayer
to 'Our Father Augustus Caesar'. Blake's own religious views he was expressing in illustrations to Genesis, for Linnell. This mystical, unfinished
series shows the Elohim of Genesis as the Trinity and the brand of Cain as
the kiss of forgiveness. Blake also began symbolic illustrations to the Book
of Enoch, an apocalyptic work first translated in 1821.
    On 25 April Blake, 'going on better Every day . . . both in health & in
work', wrote to Linnell: 'I am too much attach'd to Dante to think much
of anything else. . . . I count myself sufficiently Paid If I live as I now do, &
only fear that I may be Unlucky to my friends. . . .' Of the 102 Dante
designs, Blake started to engrave no more than seven. These are among
his largest engravings, and some of the most masterly, but only one, 'The

Whirlwind of Lovers' (55), is nearly complete. These plates, with their linear precision of detail, are a rich development of the powerful designs.

At the end of June, Blake's Sunday journey to Hampstead brought on a relapse, and on 3 July 'I find I am not so well as I thought. I must not go on in a youthful Style; however, I am upon the mending hand to-day, & hope soon to look as I did, for I have been yellow, accompanied by all the old Symptoms.' Blake continued to work in bed to the very end. He spent one of his last shillings on sending out for a pencil. A few days before he died he managed to finish colouring for Frederick Tatham a print of 'Urizen Creating the Universe' (*11*). According to Tatham, Blake then exclaimed: ' "There, I have done all I can; it is the best I have ever finished. I hope Mr Tatham will like it." He threw it suddenly down and said "Kate, you have been a good wife, I will draw your portrait." She sat near his bed and he made a drawing which, though not a likeness, is finely touched and expressed.'

On Friday 10 August Blake was not expected to live. Linnell made a tiny sketch of him lying in bed: his emaciated head, hollow-eyed, in a black skull-cap was sunk in the large pillow. At six o'clock in the evening of Sunday 12 August 1827, in the presence of Mrs Blake and of a humble woman neighbour, he died at the age of sixty-nine years, eight months, 'in a most glorious manner. He said he was going to that country he had all his life wished to see and expressed himself happy, hoping for salvation through Jesus Christ—just before he died his countenance became fair. His eyes brightened and he burst out into singing of the things he saw in heaven. In truth he died like a saint, as a person who was standing by him observed. He is to be buried on Friday at 12 in the morning.' This letter from the eighteen-year-old Richmond to Palmer continues: 'Should you like to go to the funeral—if you should, there will be room in the coach.'

Mrs Blake faced her duties with courage. The simple funeral, arranged by Linnell, was in Bunhill Fields. Calvert, Richmond and Tatham were among the few people there. No stone was placed to mark the grave. Blake left no debts, and Mrs Blake continued to sell his works as a source of income.

About a month after Blake's death, she went to look after Linnell's house in Cirencester Place, but this arrangement seems not to have worked out happily. In 1828 she became housekeeper to the Tathams. She was devoted to this young couple, and probably stayed with them until 1831, when she moved into lodgings at 17 Charlton Street, Fitzroy Square. Some months later, in October 1831, she suffered a short illness: a neglected attack of inflammation of the bowels led to mortification. She composedly sent for her friends, Mr and Mrs Tatham, took leave of Blake's sister Catherine and, according to Gilchrist, calmly and cheerfully spent five of her last hours 'repeating texts of scripture, and calling continually to her William, as if he were only in the next room, to say she was coming to him, and would not be long now.' She died in Mrs Tatham's arms at 7.30 in the morning, on Tuesday 18 October 1831, at the age of sixty-nine. She, too, was buried in Bunhill Fields, where graves of Bunyan, Defoe and Stothard (who died in 1834) are among those that lie between her own grave and that of her husband.

Like Blake, his widow left no will. At her death, her property came into the hands not of Blake's only surviving blood-relation, his sister Catherine, who was the natural heiress and lived on for many years, but of Tatham. There were manuscripts, illuminated books, drawings and copperplates. Tatham printed copies of the illuminated books, but of the copperplates only one fragment now survives; and for thirty years he sold the designs and books for good prices. How many manuscripts Blake left unprinted is not known: we have his remark of 1826 to Crabb Robinson that he had 'written more than Voltaire or Rousseau—six or seven epic poems as long as Homer and twenty tragedies as long as *Macbeth*.' Tatham, misled by puritanical zeal, burnt many of Blake's manuscripts.

The printed word, however, helped to keep Blake's name alive. Despite the obscurity of his life and death, two days after his funeral the *Literary Gazette* published an influential obituary which praised this 'singular and very able man'. Before the end of 1827, four more obituaries appeared. Blake's first biography, in John Thomas Smith's *Nollekens and his Times*, was published in 1828. Two years later, a life of Blake was published in a very successful book, Allan Cunningham's *Lives of the Most Eminent British Painters, Sculptors and Architects*. This helped to foster awareness of Blake until Gilchrist widened appreciation of him with his challenging and important *Life of Blake*, published thirty-two years after Mrs Blake died: never completely reduced to 'a shadow in Oblivion', Blake at last began to emerge from obscurity, and his influence began to spread. Now, a century and a half after his death, his influence continues to burgeon, 'as the seed shoots forth'.

Bibliography

A Summary of Books and Publications Consulted

For readers who want to discover more about Blake, books likely to prove most essential are marked * and books especially recommended for additional reading are marked †.

1. EDITIONS OF BLAKE'S WRITINGS

† *The Complete Writings of William Blake* with Variant Readings, ed. Geoffrey Keynes, London 1969; New York 1966. This, the Oxford Standard Authors edition, gives the standard text with short notes.

* *The Letters of William Blake*, ed. Geoffrey Keynes, London 1968. Short footnotes explain references in the text.

* *The Poems of William Blake*, ed. W. H. Stevenson, text by David V. Erdman, London 1971; New York 1972; in the series of Longman Annotated English Poets. The full explanatory notes are very helpful, concise and—like the very clear text—result from fine scholarship.

† *The Poetry and Prose of William Blake*, ed. David V. Erdman, commentary by Harold Bloom, New York 1970. The commentary is a helpful addition to the scholarly text.

2. FACSIMILES AND REPRODUCTIONS OF BLAKE'S WORKS

*William Blake Trust Facsimiles of the Illuminated Books and other works, with commentaries and bibliographical histories by Geoffrey Keynes, the Trianon Press, Paris. Publication of this series of hand-coloured volumes began in 1951 and it still continues. These superb, costly books, wonderfully like the original works, can be seen in large libraries.

The Blake-Varley Sketchbook of 1819 in the collection of M.D.E. Clayton-Stamm, introduction and notes by Martin Butlin, 2 vols, London 1969.

Drawings of William Blake, Selection, Introduction and Commentary by Sir Geoffrey Keynes, New York 1970.

* *Illustrations of the Book of Job by William Blake*, Introduction by Laurence Binyon and Geoffrey Keynes, New York 1935. Facsimiles of all the drawings, watercolours and engravings show the development of the series in full.

*The Notebook of William Blake: A Photographic and Typographic Facsimile, ed. David V. Erdman with the assistance of Donald K. Moore, Oxford and New York 1973. Reveals Blake at work with pen and pencil.

Vala or The Four Zoas, a facsimile, transcript and study by G. E. Bentley, Jr, Oxford 1963.

†*William Blake's Illustrations to the Bible*, compiled by Geoffrey Keynes with an introduction by George Goyder, London 1957. A comprehensive, fully illustrated survey.

3. REFERENCE BOOKS

†G. E. Bentley, Jr and Martin K. Nurmi, *A Blake Bibliography*, Minneapolis 1964. A full guide to books and articles relevant to Blake, with estimates of their value.

David V. Erdman (ed.), *A Concordance to the Writings of William Blake*, New York 1967.

*S. Foster Damon, *A Blake Dictionary*, Providence 1965; Oxford 1968. An excellent, handy aid to the understanding of Blake.

4. BIOGRAPHIES OF BLAKE

*G. E. Bentley, Jr, *Blake Records*, Oxford and New York 1969. The indispensable basis of biography: a scrupulously edited collection of contemporary references to Blake and of early essays on him. Extremely varied, interesting illustrations.

*Alexander Gilchrist, *Life of William Blake*, second edition 1880, revised with additional notes by Ruthven Todd, London 1945; New York 1969. People who had known Blake supplied some of the material for this first full-length biography of him. It is still vivid and warm.

†Mona Wilson, *The Life of William Blake*, third edition, ed. Geoffrey Keynes, Oxford and New York 1971. An authoritative work first published in 1927, brought up to date by scholarly notes.

†Thomas Wright, *The Life of William Blake*, Olney 1929; New York 1969. Enthusiastic and exciting; illustrations include some intriguing old photographs.

5. SOCIAL, ARTISTIC, LITERARY AND HISTORICAL BACK-GROUND

Jacob Bronowski, *William Blake and the Age of Revolution*, London 1965; New York 1969 (rev. ed. of *William Blake, 1757–1827: A Man Without a Mask*, London 1944).

David V. Erdman, 'Lambeth and Bethlehem in Blake's Jerusalem', *Modern Philology*, XLVIII (1951), 184–192.

M. Dorothy George, *London Life in the Eighteenth Century*, London 1925; New York 1965.

Rev. George Gilfillan (ed.), *The Poetical Works of Beattie, Blaire and Falconer*, Edinburgh 1854.

†Christopher Hibbert, *King Mob*, London 1958. A concise history of the Gordon Riots.

M. G. Jones, *The Charity School Movement*, Cambridge 1938.

James Montgomery, *The Chimney Sweeper's Friend, and Climbing Boy's Album*, London 1824.

Frank A. Mumby, *Publishing and Bookselling: A History from the Earliest Times to the Present Day*, London and New York 1974.

Nikolaus Pevsner (ed.), *London*, London vol. 2, 1969; vol. 1, 1973.

Stuart Piggott, *William Stukeley*, Oxford 1950.

†Marcia R. Pointon, *Milton & English Art*, Manchester and Toronto 1970. A detailed, copiously illustrated study of many illustrators' work: it shows Blake's stature as an interpreter of Milton.

George Rudé, *Hanoverian London 1714–1808*, London and California 1971.

John Thomas Smith, *A Book for a Rainy Day*, London 1845.

A. S. Turberville (ed.), *Johnson's England*, 2 vols, Oxford and New York 1933.

William Whitley, *Artists and their Friends in England: 1700–1799*, 2 vols, London 1928; New York 1969.

6. BIOGRAPHIES, MEMOIRS AND STUDIES OF BLAKE'S CONTEMPORARIES

William E. A. Axon, 'Thomas Taylor the Platonist', *The Library*, 1890 vol. II, 245–300.

G. E. Bentley, Jr, 'A. S. Mathew, Patron of Blake and Flaxman', *Notes and Queries*, CCIII (1958), 168–178.

G. E. Bentley, Jr, 'Thomas Butts, White Collar Maecenas', PMLA, LXXI (1956), 1052–1066.

*Morchard Bishop, *Blake's Hayley*, London 1951; New York 1972. Brings Hayley sympathetically to life and traces his changing relationship with Blake: a fascinating book.

Mrs Bray, *Life of Thomas Stothard*, London 1851.

Adrian Bury, *John Varley of the 'Old Society'*, Leigh-on-Sea 1946.

W. G. Constable, *John Flaxman*, London 1927.

Benjamin Robert Haydon, *Autobiography and Journals*, ed. Tom Taylor, London 1853.

William Hayley, *Memoirs of the Life and Writings of William Hayley Esq.*, 2 vols, London 1823.

R. W. King, *Life of Cary*, London 1925.

John Knowles, *The Life and Writings of Henry Fuseli*, 3 vols, London 1831.

Raymond Lister, *Edward Calvert*, London 1962.

†Raymond Lister, *Samuel Palmer*, London 1974. A helpful presentation of Palmer, Linnell and the Ancients.

Eudo C. Mason, *The Mind of Henry Fuseli*, London 1951.

John Thomas Smith, *Nollekens and his Times*, 2 vols, London 1828.

Alfred T. Story, *The Life of John Linnell*, London 1892.

Stanbury Thompson (ed.), *Journal of John Gabriel Stedman*, London 1962.

Signe Toksvig, *Emanuel Swedenborg, Scientist and Mystic*, London 1949; New York 1972.

†Claire Tomalin, *The Life and Death of Mary Wollstonecraft*, London 1974; New York 1975. Especially relevant in its portrayal of Fuseli and Joseph Johnson.

7. *RELIGION, PHILOSOPHY AND SYMBOLISM*

S. Foster Damon, *William Blake, His Philosophy and Symbols*, New York 1947; London 1969.

George Wingfield Digby, *Symbol and Image in William Blake*, Oxford and New York 1957.

David V. Erdman, 'Blake's Early Swedenborgianism: a Twentieth-Century Legend', *Comparative Literature*, V (1953), 247–257.

*Désirée Hirst, *Hidden Riches*, London 1964. A most enlightening account of Blake's spiritual background and its origins.

A. L. Owen, *The Famous Druids*, Oxford 1962.

†Kathleen Raine, *Blake and Tradition*, 2 vols, Princeton 1968; London 1969. An extremely learned, splendidly illustrated work.

Helen C. White, *The Mysticism of William Blake*, Madison 1927.

8. *STUDIES OF BLAKE*

John Adlard, 'Blake and "Electrical Magic" ', *Neophilologus*, 1969, *53*, 422–423.

John Adlard, *The Sports of Cruelty*, London 1972.

*David V. Erdman, *Blake: Prophet against Empire*, Princeton 1954. An exceptionally thorough, widely-researched account of Blake in his politically turbulent age: a very stimulating book indeed.

Peter F. Fisher, 'Blake's Attacks on the Classical Tradition', *Philological Quarterly*, XL (1961), 1–18.

*Northrop Frye, *Fearful Symmetry*, Princeton 1969. A masterly and exciting study of Blake's poetry and thought.

John E. Grant (ed.), *Discussions of William Blake*, Boston 1961.

Geoffrey Keynes, *Blake Studies*, London 1949.

Ruth Lowery, *Windows of the Morning*, New Haven and London 1940.

Morton D. Paley and Michael Phillips (ed.), *William Blake: Essays in Honour of Sir Geoffrey Keynes*, Oxford and New York 1973.

Alvin H. Rosenfeld (ed.), *William Blake: Essays for S. Foster Damon*, Providence 1969.

Ruthven Todd, *Tracks in the Snow*, London 1946.

W. P. Witcutt, *Blake: a Psychological Study*, London 1946; New York 1974.

9. *BLAKE'S COMPOSITE AND VISUAL ART*

*Anthony Blunt, *The Art of William Blake*, London and Columbia 1959. An admirable introduction to Blake's visual work.

David V. Erdman (ed.), *Blake's Visionary Forms Dramatic*, Princeton 1970.

*David V. Erdman, *The Illuminated Blake*, New York 1974. All Blake's illuminated pages reproduced and analysed in minute detail: a very useful book.

S. W. Hayter, *New Ways of Gravure*, Oxford and New York 1966.

†David Jones, *An Introduction to the Rime of the Ancient Mariner*, London 1972. An expert engraver briefly describes the technique of engraving.

Geoffrey Keynes, *Engravings of William Blake: The Separate Plates*, Dublin 1956.

†Geoffrey Keynes, *William Blake. Poet Printer Prophet*, London 1964. A selection of beautiful colour plates from Blake's Illuminated Books, produced by the Trianon Press, with a short account of Blake's composite art.

†Bo Lindberg, *William Blake's Illustrations to the Book of Job*, Finland 1973. A very wide, thorough study of Blake's treatment of Job.

†Raymond Lister, *Infernal Methods: William Blake's Art Techniques*, London 1975. A comprehensive account of Blake's techniques.

Irene Tayler, *Blake's Illustrations to the Poems of Gray*, Princeton 1971.

†Ruthven Todd, *William Blake: the artist*, London 1971. A small book outlining Blake's working life. Interesting illustrations.

Mary K. Woodworth, 'Blake's Illustrations for Gray's Poems', *Notes and Queries*, CCXV (= New Series, XVII) 1970, 312–313.

†Albert S. Roe, *Blake's Illustrations to the Divine Comedy*, Princeton 1953. An excellent study of the whole series, fully illustrated.

Andrew Wright, *Blake's Job. A Commentary*, Oxford and New York 1972.

John Wright, 'Toward Recovering Blake's Relief-Etching Process', *Blake Newsletter*, 26, New Mexico 1973.

10. *CATALOGUES*

G. E. Bentley, Jr, *The Blake Collection of Mrs. Landon K. Thorne*, New York 1971.

David Bindman, *William Blake. Kunst um 1800*, British Council, Hamburg 1975.

David Bindman (ed.), *William Blake. Catalogue of the Collection in the Fitzwilliam Museum Cambridge*, Cambridge 1970.

Martin Butlin, *William Blake: a complete catalogue of works in the Tate Gallery*, London 1971.

Gert Schiff, trans. Sarah Twohig, *Henry Fuseli. Tate Gallery*, London 1975.

William Wells, *William Blake's 'Heads of the Poets'*, Manchester 1969.

Index

Italicized page numbers indicate quotations; they are followed (in brackets) by page references to the Oxford Standard Authors edition *The Complete Writings of William Blake*, Oxford University Press, 2nd edition, 1966. Illustration numbers are given in bold print; a following **c** indicates colour.